Garden Plant
Survival Manual

Garden Plant
Survival Manual

Ann Bonar

Quantum
Books

A QUANTUM BOOK

This book is produced by
Quantum Publishing Ltd.
6 Blundell Street
London N7 9BH

ISBN 1-86160-670-2

QUMGSM

Printed in Singapore by
Star Standard Industries Pte Ltd.

Contents

Introduction

Today, survival is the name of the game. In gardening what does this involve? Firstly, it means achieving the best possible results with the time and resources available, to create a garden that satisfies your own particular needs. Secondly, it means maintaining your plants in as healthy, decorative and bountiful condition as possible in the face of attack from many sources, from pests and diseases to weeds and bad weather. This gardening survival manual proposes to help you reach this satisfactory state of affairs in a variety of ways, all of them simple and easy.

If your plants are strong and healthy from the outset, half the battle is won; if you supply them with the right growing medium and the right environment, they will continue to thrive. Survival only becomes difficult when they lack sufficient food, water, space, light and air. When plants are weakened in this way, predators and parasites attack, and bad weather deals the finishing blow.

The other half of the battle for survival lies in choice, planning and design: choosing the plants you want, which will grow in the environment created by your garden; planning, to ensure that the garden contains those features and plants that you need; and design, to fit all these elements together in a pleasing pattern that you can maintain without too much effort. In the A-Z section of garden plants (pages 90-183) details are given of the care of each plant relating to its particular needs, together with information on particular pests and diseases and the causes and remedies of ill-health.

Right Azaleas in raised container beds brighten a corner of a city garden. By varying the height of the beds and selecting the plants with care, the problems of gardening on such a small scale have been overcome. Lack of space is not the only problem a city gardener will have to tackle. In urban areas, the soil is often poor, pests are numerous and there may be excessive shade. Taking the existing conditions into account is a vital part of designing a successful garden, appropriate to the setting.

The right environment

Before you set about choosing and acquiring plants, it is important to establish the type of environment your garden provides, particularly in terms of soil and climate. Matching the right plants with the right environment is a large part of garden survival. Heathers, for example, grow on windswept moors and hillsides where there are more rocks than soil, and the soil itself is peaty and acid. Planting heathers in a flowerbed sheltered from wind in a deep, fertile soil will only result in excessively leafy plants, practically without flowers, which will be frequently infected with fungal diseases. Heathers should be planted in a rock garden where the soil is quick-draining and sparse, or in a site open to wind and sky, where the soil is sandy and stony.

Other factors are also important. Is your garden 'warm' or 'cold'? Is the rainfall heavy in your area? How windy is it? How much sunlight does your garden receive? These conditions may also vary considerably within the garden — areas which receive sunlight at different times of the day or not at all, areas which are sheltered from the wind or exposed to the elements. The micro-climate and particular conditions of a specific position are just as important for a plant's welfare as the conditions which pertain to the garden as a whole.

Although this may sound daunting, it is worth carrying out a thorough analysis of the resources in your garden before acquiring new plants. Proper consideration will save you money, time and inconvenience.

Garden planning

Whether you are dealing with a bare area of soil surrounding a new house, or a garden which is already established but new to you, or a garden which has been in your care for some time, you can increase the plants' chances of survival and improve their health if you consider the needs you want the garden to fulfil. In the same way that the rooms of your house should make provision for a wide range of activities and requirements, a garden might need to accommodate not only a range of plants but also provide space for pets, children, crops, recreation and utilities.

If you are a garden enthusiast but have children or pets, do not expect choice plants to survive if you do not provide open space for the children or

A garden should reflect its setting and careful choice of plants is a key consideration. In this sub-tropical garden, cacti and exotic native species are effectively combined with a lawn and less spectacular garden plants *(far left)*. The imposing facade of this American colonial house is perfectly complemented by the formal flowerbeds, neat box hedges and expanse of immaculate turf *(below)*. The classic English country garden is a colourful blend of cottage flowers, herbs and shrubs, informal yet controlled *(left)*.

animals to work off their energy. Shrubs are less vulnerable than herbaceous flowering plants; trees are likely to be climbed or scratched but can stand these attacks when well established — both shrubs and trees will need guards in their early years. Prickly plants will discourage onslaughts. Paths which lead directly to open areas without the possibility of cutting corners over beds or through young hedges are to be preferred.

Areas which are likely to take a lot of traffic, for instance around washing lines, near dustbins, shed, compost heap, frames, garage, drive, carport and so on, obviously need to be surfaced with hard-wearing materials; any grass mixture should be blended accordingly. Plants used to screen utility areas should be both pretty and tough — they are likely to be overlooked and neglected and these areas are likely to be located where draughts, shade, wind and cold are prevalent.

The amount of time you have, or wish, to spend on the garden is an important consideration. Some groups of plants are time-consuming, others cover the ground beautifully year in, year out, without much extra help. If you have little time, but a passion for bedding plants and roses, or a perfect lawn, you are bound to be disappointed unless you restrict the area concerned. Crops, particularly vegetables, are very time-consuming, and beds of herbaceous perennials always need attention. The solution is either to design your garden around plants which do not require a great deal of time spent on their upkeep or to reconcile yourself to spending more time in the garden.

If the overall appearance is your prime consideration, you will have to be more selective in your choice of plants and more careful in positioning so that differences in height, shades of colours, leaf shapes and architectural form are well displayed. If different plants are grouped to create a particular effect, ensure that all require the same conditions for growth and that they grow at roughly the same rate.

Features that provide a design focal point include a pool, herb garden, paved sun-trap, arbour, rock garden or pergola. Making a plan before you start planting will enable you to choose the species and varieties most appropriate for these features. Draw the plan to scale on squared paper to give you an idea of proportions and relative size. If you have any artistic skill at all, try to turn the flat plan

Herbaceous borders should be a blend of perennials with attractive flowers and foliage *(right)*. National garden exhibitions often include show-case gardens, which incorporate the latest accessories *(below)*. Public gardens may also be a source of ideas, such as suitable plants for wooded areas *(centre right)*, or creating an effective pool area *(far right)*.

Right Once you have established what sort of plants and design would suit your garden, try making a more detailed plan. Choosing a wide selection of alpines and border plants must be done carefully, so that the maximum effect of colour can be achieved throughout the year. Plants are not the only feature of the garden, however, trees may also be a focal point. Take care to allow enough space for their branches and choose suitable plants to grow under them. Allow space for an open area of terrace or lawn, so that the garden does not become overcrowded. Other practical areas should be provided for a compost heap, and a vegetable plot if required.

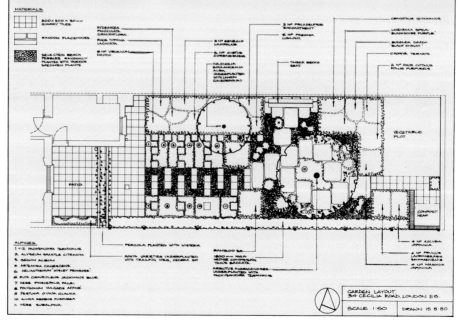

into a three-dimensional sketch, perhaps in colour. This will help you to discover unexpected juxtapositions of colour, and will reveal tall plants that hide window views and footpaths that take the longest way around the garden. These hitches are inimical to your plants' good health and may only be discovered by advanced planning.

Many gardening enthusiasts, however, advocate gardens that 'just grow'; a good argument can be made that the best gardens are loosely planned and do not have a rigid, preconceived structure but accommodate needs and purposes as they arise. The plants that like the conditions will settle down and spread, and those that find them disagreeable will diminish and fade away; survival, if nothing else, is fitness for place.

Choosing plants

Before acquiring or buying new plants for your garden, it makes sense to engage in some research. Visiting gardens and nurseries not only helps you to make up your mind about what you like, it also enables you to assess the type of plants most suitable to your circumstances.

Space is important. If you crowd plants, particularly the large ones like shrubs and trees, they are doomed to dwindling growth, with only a few flowers or fruits and an early death. Visit places where you can see plants actually growing before you start to plant, to get an idea of their size and growth. Local gardens or parks will furnish ideas for plants and for garden design. Neighbourhood nurseries and garden centres often have a display garden showing plants available for sale, and assistants will be able to suggest suitable varieties for your conditions. Gardening society shows and exhibitions are also valuable, not least because they demonstrate a high standard of plant health as well as choice. Specialist societies, in particular, mount exhibits of plants which are seldom seen, but which nonetheless make good garden plants.

If you cannot manage a visit to any of these sources of living plants, it often helps to look at the catalogues of the national nurseries and seedsmen. Many are profusely illustrated in colour and are true to the originals; the shape of the flowers is also shown. Size, time of flowering, other characteristics and cultivation needs will often be given. Browse through specialist gardening magazines and, finally, look at your neighbours' gardens, if only to decide what not to grow!

Take a notebook with you when you go 'plant-hunting', preferably one arranged alphabetically. Whatever else you write, note the botanical name of the plant you like — you may forget it.

Acquiring plants

Plants are available from a wide variety of sources; most places where they can be viewed will also sell them. For common plants the national nurseries and seedsmen, chain stores and garden centres will be adequate, but for rare and unusual plants, and for good ranges of specialist flowers such as chrysanthemums, delphiniums, carnations, lilies or whatever, you will have to apply to specialist societies. Stalls at country fairs and markets or your local garden centre may have an enterprising owner specializing in a group of plants, and there are private seed-lists available which cater solely for the out-of-the-ordinary. Friends' gardens should also be considered as helpful sources of plants, cuttings and seeds.

Wherever you get your plants, make sure that they are as strong, healthy and free of pest and disease as possible. If you are buying container-grown plants from a garden centre, avoid plants which have one or two thick roots protruding from the drainage hole of the container, or which are tightly packed throughout the soil-ball and coil around at the base. Even if they have been fed, their growth will have been restricted by the cramped container conditions. Choose plants

The best source of garden plants are reputable nurseries and garden centres. The dahlia exhibit is a typical nursery display showing the latest varieties *(above)*. Many nurseries have extensive outdoor beds of plants for sale, such as this pansy garden *(below)*. Plants from such places are likely to be healthy and disease-resistant. For specific types of plant, such as alpines, specialist nurseries provide a wide variety from which to choose *(right)*.

whose top growth — leaves and shoots — is well-balanced, evenly growing from around the plant, undamaged and a good positive colour, whether green or variegated. You can buy plants in flower-bud, although it is better to plant them when they are only forming leaves and shoot extensions. It is not advisable, however, to ask a plant which is flowering to establish itself with new roots at the same time. It will do so, but slowly, and the flowers and buds will drop rapidly — it may not even flower the following year. In any case, it will need extra time and attention for either watering, feeding or protection.

Plants whose stems or branches are broken or badly placed, with missing or damaged leaves, and with dangling or fading flowers should be avoided. Also watch out for those infested with pests and disease — greenfly, caterpillars, red spider mites, white patches of mildew, grey mould, brown or black leaf spots — and any plants which are wilting or whose compost is dry. The compost may have

dried out several times already, and the plant can only be weakened as a result.

Plants bought by mail-order should be packed so that they are not damaged in transit, and so that the roots do not dry out — moist peat and polythene sheet help to prevent this. You cannot know in advance whether the nursery will ensure their good survival with good packing, but advance research should establish which are the more careful nurseries. It is particularly important that shrub and tree roots remain moist, especially evergreens.

Many chain stores sell plants, including roses, shrubs and climbers, wrapped in polythene sleeves in winter. Unfortunately, the warmth of the store after a few days encourages these normally dormant plants to break into leaf and start new root growth. Planting them in this state only leads to damage and, if cold and frost follow a few days later, can even mean the end of the plant. Buy plants which are still dormant from these sources, and accustom them gradually over a few days to the colder temperatures of the garden.

Plants acquired from friends may suffer from pests and fungal diseases, but a less apparent affliction is virus infection, sometimes only detectable by the stunting and small size of the plants. It is particularly important to make sure that any plant you obtain from a friend is clean and healthy.

Seeds from seedsmen have to conform to regulations with regard to germination rates and purity. Seeds acquired from friends will not, of course, be guaranteed in this way and you will have to be prepared for the risk of non-germination, or plants which prove to be not all you expected or wanted. If you save your own seeds, keep them in dark, cool (40-45°F/4-7°C), completely airtight conditions. Put some silica gel in the container in advance to absorb moisture, then replace with fresh gel when you put in the seeds.

After all your care and consideration, if your chosen plant eventually does badly in the site where you have placed it, do not hesitate to dig it up and put it somewhere else. Most gardens have no room for sick, lingering plants; and often the disturbance of the move may stimulate the plant into action, regardless of whether the new position is better or not. After replanting, cut off the parts which are dead or dying, protect the plant from wind and cold, and make sure that it is securely supported, if that is necessary. Do not feed it. After heavy rain, carefully make holes in the soil around the plant to aerate the soil.

Care in choosing plants and time spent planning and designing will go a long way to ensuring the survival of your garden. Problems will not only be easier to solve when they occur, but many will also be prevented.

Basic care

The area surrounding most houses is usually covered with many types of plants and vegetation, which will inevitably need some attention. The task of organizing and maintaining this area needs to be approached in a systematic way that will ensure a healthy garden, yet fall within the bounds of the gardener's capabilities.

The gardener's year

The schedule of work in the garden will often depend on weather conditions, particularly in winter if the soil is frozen or too wet or covered in snow. Autumn jobs may spill over into winter, but if they have not been carried out by mid-winter, they may have to wait until spring. Spring gradually becomes very busy; early summer is moderately demanding and late summer is comparatively quiet. However, within the seasons much variation of conditions can occur. In town gardens and, to a lesser extent, suburban gardens, the changes in the weather are mellowed by the surrounding buildings, but in country gardens a day-to-day awareness is as necessary as it is to a farmer. But wherever the garden, it pays to listen to the weather forecasts and to pick your time for doing various jobs. For instance, attempting to cultivate heavy soil that is very wet is damaging and hard work. The same applies when soil is really dry. Wait for a dry period or a drying wind in the first case and some gentle steady rain in the second.

Do not try to plant in autumn or winter when frost or snow are forecast and be very wary of planting during droughts. When spring fever overcomes you, do not rush out into the garden, even if the weather suddenly seems suitable. General seed-sowing time is better left until the weather is more stable and less likely to adversely affect germination. It is advisable not to plant tender species like bedding plants, dahlias and half-hardy annuals outdoors until the warm weather has begun — apart from the risk of night frosts, the soil itself is often still too cold for plants to start well. At the end of the summer, be ready at short notice to take tender plants indoors and to cover up others such as dahlias, which will die given one or two sudden, early frosts. The seasons rarely start at the same time each year, and gardening jobs should be arranged accordingly: when the soil is in the right condition and the plants have reached a stage at which they need the next treatment.

Season	General tasks
Spring	Sowing, propagation, fertilizer-feeding and mulching.
Summer	Planting out, trimming hedges, staking, watering.
Autumn	Deadheading, pruning, digging, laying turfs, storing bulbs and tubers.
Winter	Aeration, protection, winter pruning, digging and manuring.

A well-planned garden is beautiful the year round. If the basic arrangements of beds, borders, lawns, trees and shrubs is pleasing, these elements will remain attractive whatever the season. This public garden, Edinburgh's Royal Botanic Garden, is an excellent example of careful planting. Spring brings delicate shades of pink and green with blossoms and new foliage *(far left)*; summer displays interesting contrasts of texture, all in a lush green *(centre)*. In autumn *(above)* and winter *(left)* the evergreens and evergreys come into their own.

Assessing the soil

No garden has perfect soil and it takes experience to recognize a good type. A good soil needs to be well aerated. This will depend on the type of soil particles present and their quantity. Clay particles are tiny and packed tightly and closely together; grains of sand are comparatively large, loosely combined and spaced further apart. All soils are composed of some particles of each type, but a good one, such as loam, contains all types in the right proportion to ensure the required drainage and aeration.

Another important ingredient is humus, a black, finely divided substance which results from the breakdown of organic matter. Without it, a soil's structure will deteriorate, so that plant roots are unable to breathe, absorb moisture and thereby take in part of their food. Humus is spongy and has the ability to retain the water needed by sandy, stony or gravelly soils, but can also provide the spaces needed for air that are lacking in any of the sticky clays or silty soils.

Any rotting vegetative and animal remains will supply humus. Farm manure is still considered to be the best, provided it is really well rotted, preferably under cover. A good substitute can be made in the garden by collecting together all the debris from ornamentals, crop plants and weeds, piling them into a heap and leaving them to rot. A container will prevent mess and will keep the

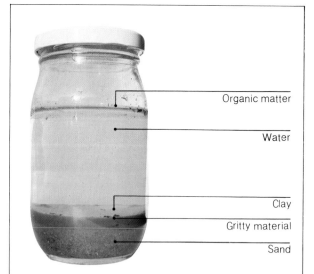

Above Knowing what type of soil you are dealing with is essential to the successful growth of your plants. The best method of testing the soil is to mix some topsoil and water in a jar and leave it to settle overnight. If the level of sand is larger than any other layer, then your soil is sandy. The gritty material indicates the quantity of loam. If this constitutes 40 percent, the soil is considered a good loam. If the layer of clay is equal to the other two layers, the soil is clay-based.

Organic matter

Water

Clay

Gritty material

Sand

Below Compost bins are essential pieces of equipment. Every garden should have one, whether it is bought or homemade. Make sure that homemade ones have holes drilled in the sides to allow air to circulate and aid decomposition. There are a number of different models that may be used: a plastic bin with movable slats (1); a wooden box with drilled holes (2) and an open wire netting type for the preparation of leaf-mould (3). While the compost is rotting it is advisable to cover the heap with plastic sheeting to preserve warmth and moisture. Two compost heaps are preferable, with one in use and one in the rotting process.

material closely packed, thus ensuring that the heap heats up quickly and well. The rotting process will be speedier and, with a good high temperature, weed seeds will be killed together with any pests and diseases, providing the gardener with an excellent supply of garden manure for future feeding and fertilizer dressings.

The decay of compost heap materials is due to the action of bacteria, worms, fungi and insects on them, the bacteria having most effect. For all these to live and multiply they need oxygen, moisture and nutrients. In effect a compost heap is like a bonfire, which burns better with a good draught from below. It should be arranged on a base of crossed sticks, alternating bricks, large stones or blocks of wood, or anything that provides a space beneath the heap for air. To heat up sufficiently, heaps should be at least 4 x 4ft (1.2 x 1.2m). They can be wider, but any higher would be inconvenient. Soft vegetation can be used in layers about 6in (15cm) deep, alternating with a layer of sprinkled lime or proprietary compost-maker. For even better results, a thin layer of rotted animal manure can be added occasionally. Layers of soil are sometimes advocated as well, but so much is added naturally, attached to the plants, that it seems unnecessary to do this.

The material will be ready for use when of a

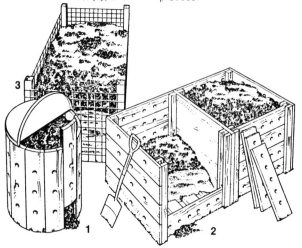

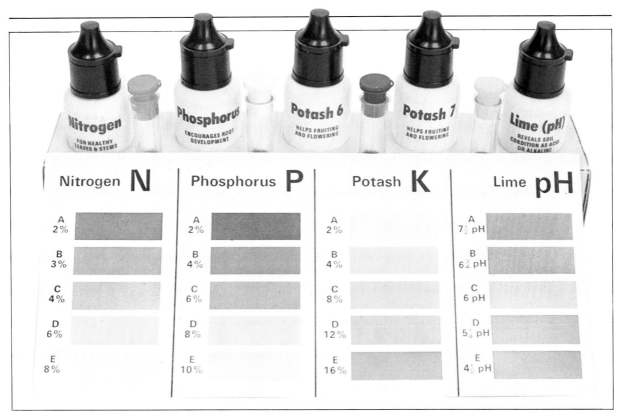

Nitrogen **N**	Phosphorus **P**	Potash **K**	Lime **pH**
A 2%	A 2%	A 2%	A 7½ pH
B 3%	B 4%	B 4%	B 6¾ pH
C 4%	C 6%	C 8%	C 6 pH
D 6%	D 8%	D 12%	D 5¼ pH
E 8%	E 10%	E 16%	E 4½ pH

crumbly, dark brown-black consistency. If it is soil-like, it has been left too long and will have lost much of its goodness; if the shapes of leaves or stems can still be recognized, it has not been left long enough. Time to break down varies between six weeks and several months, depending on the weather, how quickly and how well the heap is built and your own expertise. In winter, it will hardly change and an autumn-built heap will not be ready for use until late spring.

The pH level

Soil is said to be acid or alkaline (limey) and the degree of either is measured by a scale called the pH scale. Figures below 7.0 on this scale indicate acidity, increasing by 10 times for each figure; those above show alkalinity. There are a number of plants which will not grow at all in alkaline soil or which do much better in an acid one. Test kits can be bought at garden shops to determine this aspect of your soil. As the tests are quite simple and quick to do, it is easy to discover the state of various parts of the garden. The kits will also supply a table giving the quantities of lime that need to be added or not, depending on what reaction the soil provides. You may find that different areas of the garden give different results, and, in this case, should be treated accordingly.

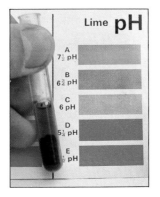

Lime **pH**
A 7½ pH
B 6¾ pH
C 6 pH
D 5¼ pH
E ½ pH

The chemical level of the soil can be measured with a soil-testing kit. This kit contains colour charts and various solutions, which will determine the percentage level of nutrients contained in your soil (above). Take samples of soil from all parts of the garden, leaving them to dry out and removing any foreign bodies. Then crumble the soils with a tool, making sure not to touch the soil with your fingers, as this could affect the results. Quarter fill separate test-tubes with each of the samples (above left). According to the particular substance for which you are testing, add a few drops of the appropriate solution to the soil samples. Wait until the soil has settled, before matching it up with the corresponding colour chart (below left). The result will then determine which fertilizer is necessary to improve the chemical balance.

Garden maintenance

Essential tools

A basic set of the right tools and equipment is important for all garden chores. A digging fork and a sharp knife are vital and a budding knife is useful, especially if roses are increased by budding. A hand-fork, rake, hoe, secateurs, garden string and a watering can are other requirements. For a lawn and hedge, a mower and hand-shears or a powered hedge-cutter will also be required. Hand-mowers are hard work for all except the smallest lawns and a mechanical mower will generally give a better finish. Hand-shears are convenient; buy a good pair which are well balanced, not too heavy, and whose handles are comfortable for your size of hand. They will be useful for cutting any awkward patches of grass and grass edges as well as hedges.

Rakes have a number of uses: raking up leaves, clearing rubbish and dead vegetation from lawns, raking weed out of pools, breaking the soil down for seed beds, levelling gravel paths and drives and general tidying. A digging fork will do much basic cultivation and can double up as a carrier, like a pitch-fork; a hand-fork is useful for all weeding as well as planting small plants such as annuals, bedding plants and young perennials, although a long-handled hoe will do the work more quickly when seedling weeds are the problem. A wheelbarrow is always necessary, and the standard, galvanized, metal kinds with a single rubber tyre and two rear supports are still preferable. They are hard-wearing, long-lasting and balanced so that they can take a large amount of weight. It is also helpful to have some kind of small carrier, such as a bucket, sack or box in which to carry tools or put weeds, plants and pots.

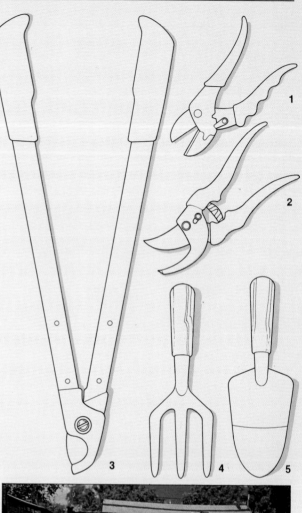

An essential addition to any garden is a wheelbarrow. The various types include the traditional model (1), the ball-wheeled (2) or the two-wheeled trailer (3). The traditional model is generally considered to be the most solid and practical. It is always important to make sure you have sturdy tools for heavy jobs, such as transporting, and also lifting (far right).

Left and **below** Two types of secateurs (1 and 2) and a pair of loppers (3) are a useful addition to any tool collection. A hand-fork (4) and trowel (5) are handy for intricate work, such as sowing or planting. However, a set of larger tools is also necessary. A sturdy garden fork (6) is an essential tool for any garden. It may be used, among other things, to break up soil, remove weeds and aerate lawns. An edge cutter (7) is a particularly useful implement for tidying up ragged lines around lawns and flowerbeds. A spade (8) is virtually synonymous with gardening, and is highly practical for digging and moving soil. The rake (9) will gather up debris and smooth over seed beds. Finally, two types of hoe, Dutch (10) and draw hoes (11), are both worth acquiring as they are excellent as weeding tools.

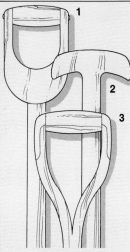

Above Both spades and forks have three basic handle shapes: 'D' (1), 'T' (2) and 'YD' (3). They may also be made or covered in metal, plastic or wood. There is no specific advantage in any of the different materials, but it is always advisable to try out all combinations to find the one most suited to you and your type of garden. The shaft of the tool may also be made in different materials, and again, depending on the work required, choose either a sturdy or light material.

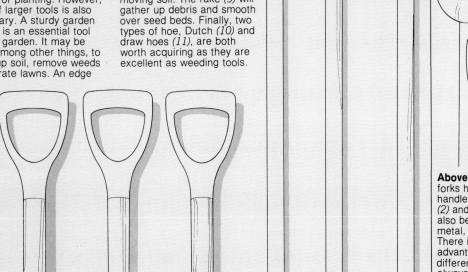

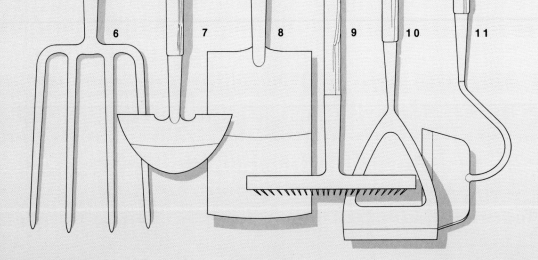

6   7   8   9   10   11

Digging and feeding the soil

Once a garden is established, with its lawn, paving, borders and permanent plantings, digging consists of forking the top few inches of soil between the plants to aerate it, get rid of weeds and work in the remains of garden compost or to work in a fertilizer dressing.

Before planting individual shrubs, roses or trees, and before planting herbaceous borders, deeper cultivation is required. Single digging — digging to a depth which is equal to the length of the fork's prongs (tines), or the length of the spade blade — is sufficient for the smaller plants and where the soil is light. It is at this initial stage that it pays to mix in rotted organic matter at the same time. For deep-rooting and larger plants double digging is preferable. This means penetrating to a depth of two spits (spades) and then forking up the bottom of the hole and mixing bulky organics all through the soil to be returned. It is important to keep the topsoil, the first spadeful, separate and to return it to the top.

Digging helps to air the soil and allows water to soak through it and drain away without becoming stagnant and eventually toxic to plant roots. This, together with the addition of humus, revitalizes the soil's constituents, producing an environment that enables roots to develop fully. Basic, pre-planting digging should be completed a month or so before planting if possible; it should be done in spring for fallowing to allow weed seeds to germinate. Forking is needed in spring and autumn to tidy, break up and weed the soil.

Despite the large number of fertilizers available, it is not as essential for the gardener to use them as it is for the commercial grower or farmer, who is cropping intensively year after year, and needs to reap the biggest possible yield. For the gardener, annual mulching with rotted garden compost or a similar bulky organic in late spring or early autumn is generally all that is needed for medium to heavy soil. Sometimes such soils require a boost feed after wet winters or plants growing in them need bigger rations. Light soil, on the other hand, containing a lot of sand, stones, shingle, shale or grit, needs a second dressing of organic matter in late winter and regular additions of compound fertilizer, one in spring and a second halfway through summer. If a slow-acting organic compound is used, one application in spring will see the plants through the whole growing season.

Aside from dry fertilizers, there are concentrated liquid formulations which need diluting in water; these generally have to be applied frequently while plants are growing, once or even twice a week. Some of these liquid feeds are specially manufactured for application to leaves of plants — these are foliar feeds.

Planting

Planting appears to be a simple proposition, but it is probably responsible for as many sick plants and actual fatalities as all the other garden hazards put together. The most important point to remember is that a plant is a living organism, which breathes, eats and drinks. When it is out of the ground it should be regarded as being in a state of shock and, if it has been dug up rather than grown in a container, it will be seriously injured as well.

Roots are physiologically as well as literally a support system, and damage to them is unavoidable when digging up or transplanting. If possible, however, try to avoid breaking and disturbing the root system when lifting a plant. If tearing does occur, cleanly cut such roots off behind the break. It is also permissible to cut long roots back to a convenient length, since they are mainly present to ensure firm anchorage of the plant and not for sup-

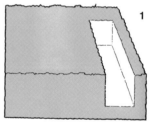

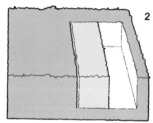

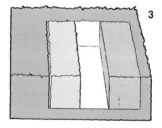

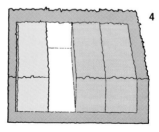

Beds need to be well prepared before planting can occur (above). This involves 'single digging' (left). Divide the area into two strips using garden string. Dig out a rectangular trench at the end of one of the strips — one spade deep and wide (1). Spread manure into the trench. Dig out the next trench (2), tossing the soil into the first trench (3). Do this up the first side and down the other (4), filling the last trench with the soil taken from the first. Double digging means that the trenches are two spades deep.

plying food and drink as the fine fibrous roots are

Keep the roots moist until replanted, particular ly the tiny ones. This cannot be emphasized too strongly; once they become dry, they will not function. It can happen very quickly, so it is a good idea to wrap the roots in polythene sheet as soon as the plant is dug up, and in hot weather to put the plant in the shade if you are not going to replant it immediately.

When planting, it is important to make the hole deep enough. Shallow planting means insecure anchorage and makes it more difficult for the plant to establish. It also bends the roots and often bunches and doubles them up, which effectively strangles them. Roots growing naturally are spread out evenly all through the soil, making the most use of nutrient and moisture content, so it is best to do the same when planting. If you are in doubt about the depth of planting, a good guideline is to ar-

range the plant so that the soil mark on the stem is level with the surface of the soil in its new site.

To give the roots as good a start as possible, use fine, crumbly, moist soil — potting compost is ideal, otherwise the original topsoil broken up — to fill in the hole and cover the roots. Do not use subsoil; if this depth is reached while digging, be careful to line the bottom of the hole with good soil as well. Very wet, sticky soil should be avoided too, and if planting was necessary during dry weather, the soil should be well watered with a spray-like jet.

After planting, tread the soil down around the plant so that it is firmly secured, but without reducing the ground to a concrete-like consistency. Scratch the soil surface a little, so that it is not completely smooth and will allow rain to drain through normally and air to penetrate. This ensures the good health and proper functioning of the roots.

Left A mulch is particularly beneficial to young trees and plants. It consists of either decayed manure, leaf-mould, compost, peat, wet straw or sawdust. A layer of any of these should be placed in a circle around the base of the tree or plant. Make sure that the mulch is kept away from the trunk, otherwise mice will nest there, or the constant moisture will rot the bark. The mulch will conserve the moisture in the soil, supply additional nutrients and suppress weeds. A young shrub often requires this extra attention to encourage growth and young fruit trees, which are just coming into fruit, are particularly grateful for the additional help.

23

Watering

The most elementary and obvious aspect of plant survival is the supply of water. Without it plants wilt, and will die if they are starved for too long. Even if plants are revived with water after a drought there will still be problems, because the mineral nutrients required are absorbed in solution through the roots from the soil moisture. There is also a problem with many vegetables and fruit which do not get enough water in dry weather and, although such crop plants go on living, they could give much higher yields if they were regularly watered.

When the soil becomes baked and dry after weeks without rain and especially in hot, sunny weather, it cracks, and this movement of the soil causes mechanical damage to roots by tearing them. It also exposes them to light and results in even quicker drying out. Shoot growth ceases; leaves dangle limply, turn yellow and fall prematurely; buds drop off without opening.

Watering will be necessary at some time during the dry season; it may be required in cold springs when a harsh wind blows, and also sometimes in autumn, although at this time of the year heavy dews often supply enough moisture to tide the plants over. The method of application and the quantity of water supplied are both important. Turning a hose on with a single jet and leaving it to flood an area is wasteful of water and harmful to the plants. It makes puddles on the soil and pans the surface — makes it smooth and impenetrable, so that the water either stands on top or runs off to the nearest low point, without doing any good to the plants themselves. The plants will only really benefit if the water is applied as a spray, so that it is as much like a shower of rain as possible. There are nozzle attachments for hoses which will do this and many makes of sprinklers are available which can be turned on and left to provide the plants with a constant supply. Watering cans with fine or coarse holed spout attachments are good for individual plants and for seedlings. 'Dribble' hoses can be left on — the water seeps out through holes at intervals along the hose — and are especially good for crop plants grown in rows.

Application is best in the evening or early morning, as the plants take up plenty of water and store it ready for the heat of the day, but in emergencies all-day treatment cannot be avoided, although this does mean that some water evaporates and some is transpired almost as soon as it is absorbed. The amount that should be added is considerable; if enough water is not added at a time, roots are encouraged to develop close to the surface because the water does not penetrate deep down and they then dry out even more quickly. The lowest roots will not get any water at all, and on balance more

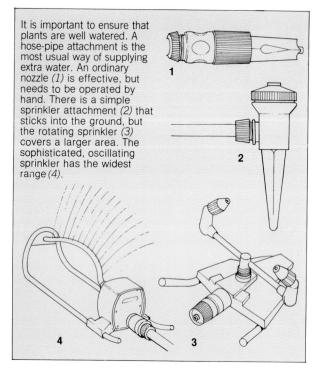

It is important to ensure that plants are well watered. A hose-pipe attachment is the most usual way of supplying extra water. An ordinary nozzle (1) is effective, but needs to be operated by hand. There is a simple sprinkler attachment (2) that sticks into the ground, but the rotating sprinkler (3) covers a larger area. The sophisticated, oscillating sprinkler has the widest range (4).

harm than good is done. It is possible to work out how much water is required by keeping a check on the weekly rainfall: anything less than 1in (2.5cm) in the dry months or ¾in (1.8cm) at the beginning and end of the season will mean that watering is required to make up the difference. One inch of rain is equal to approximately 4½gal/sq yd (20 l/m^2), and by working out how long it takes a hose to deliver 4½ gal (20 l) with a suitable degree of pressure, it can be calculated how long it will take to water a given area.

Weeding

Weeds can be roughly classified into two groups; those that take over by seeding and those that take over vegetatively, by root penetration or runner invasion above ground. Some cheat and do both. Most of those that seed are annuals; that is, they germinate in spring and are dead by autumn. These seeds appear to be small and harmless, but the quantity produced by any one plant is prodigious. Moreover, some plants are ephemerals, completing their life cycle in a few weeks, so that their seeds germinate the same season. In this way several generations may be produced in the space of one season.

The second group are perennials, which live and spread from year to year and are very difficult to eradicate. Those with runners produce plantlets at each leaf joint, which root into the soil below them

Two effective ways of removing weeds are by either using a swan-necked, draw hoe *(above right)* or a hand-trowel *(above)*. The soil surface can be chopped with the draw hoe and the weeds that are loosened may then be scraped away. It is particularly useful for flowerbeds and for covering heavily weed-infested sites. The hand-trowel is invaluable for more specific areas and for removing more deeply penetrating weeds.

and produce runners in their turn. Those with wandering roots are often rhizomatous, that is, the roots are creeping, underground stems which spread all around the parent and develop buds which sprout into aerial shoots. Some of these underground stems go downward to such an extent that their limit has not been determined, but fortunately such weeds are few. One species ensures its survival by developing bulbils, which fall off the parent plant into the soil and remain dormant, sometimes for years, until conditions are suitable for sprouting.

There are two golden rules for all weed control. Firstly, hoe the weeds out or otherwise destroy them while they are seedlings; and secondly, if the weeds are past this stage, kill them before they flower, or at least break off the flowering stems before they can set seed. This means that weeds must be dealt with in spring, as they germinate seeds.

Apart from the weeds already present in the garden, seeds are likely to be blown by the wind or carried by birds. It does not always follow that there will be no more weeds even if spring-germinating seedlings have been prevented from flowering and so it will still be necessary to keep a look-out for weeds all through the growing season. In autumn, a final attempt should be made at weed clearance, in preparation for the winter. If the weeds are not cleared by winter, the weather will

Above Weeds spread by different root systems. Bindweed *(1)* has deeply penetrating, white roots. Any piece that is broken off will root to produce new plants. Goosegrass or cleavers *(2)* is spread by seeds, which stick onto animal coats or other plants. Cinquefoil *(3)* spreads by rooting stems along the soil surface. Couchgrass *(4)* has a strong and extensive root, which needs much work to remove it.

make it increasingly difficult to do so, and weeds left through the winter will have surreptitiously spread tenfold by the spring.

Hoeing, digging and hand-forking are the time-honoured, manual ways of weed control and, with only one or two exceptions, can remove the entire root system. However, it is often the pieces of weed root left in the soil that are the source of new infestations. Chemical control by spraying or with a powder is quicker and easier to do, although it may take several weeks to be fully effective, and it can contaminate the soil for many months. Such materials need to be applied during the growing season. If weeds survive the treatment, they are the sort that need more than one application and this should be noted in the instructions. If there are weeds growing among precious plants, solutions are best painted or sponged onto the top growth of the weeds.

In preference to chemicals, the low-growing weeds can be covered with a mulch, which nourishes the soil at the same time. If this has bad results, it could be because the mulch was not thick enough or did not completely cover the weeds. The object is to prevent any light at all from getting to the leaves and stems so that they cannot carry on photosynthesis or manufacture food for shoot and root increase. Another cultural method is to sow grass seed or turf the infested area. If the weed persists in spite of the frequent mowing required to keep the area as lawn, then mowing is not frequent enough or the grass is weak, probably because of food shortage or soil compaction.

Pruning

If plants are being well cared for, they will continue to grow profusely. This means that for their health and survival, shrubs, climbers and roses must be cut back regularly. Otherwise path access becomes difficult, space in the garden dwindles, the light is cut out and plants become elongated, diseased and unattractive. Basic, control-type cutting back and tying-in will need to be done once a month throughout the summer and into mild autumns, if necessary; in spring some tidying may be necessary after winter damage or where plants grew a little in autumn.

In general, there are three degrees of pruning: severe, moderate and light. Severe or hard-pruning involves removing a large amount of the new growth from all over the plant, or hard-pruning a few shoots in positions where more growth is needed. Hard-pruning will always produce a greater and stronger growth than there was before. Each cut will remove at least three-quarters of the new material. Moderate pruning takes away about half of the new growth from about half the plant. Light cutting may only be a

Pruning encourages compact growth and healthy flowering, which is particularly required on the spiraea *(above)*. The shrub should be cut right down to a few inches from ground level to ensure this vigorous growth and blooming. The right tools are needed to prune all shrubs *(below)*. Pruning saws (*1* and *2*) are useful for cutting back large branches. Any thick shoots should be tackled with long-handled loppers *(3)*, which can be manipulated into almost any awkward spot. The hedge clipping shears *(4)* are an essential tool for pruning bushes. For smaller stems on shrubs and evergreen hedges, use the anvil or parrot-bill secateurs (*5* and *6*).

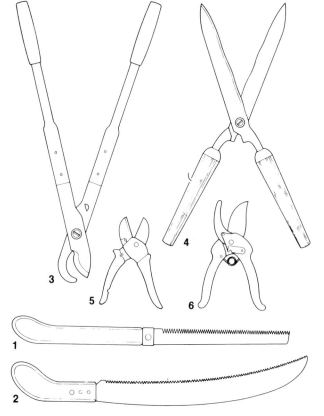

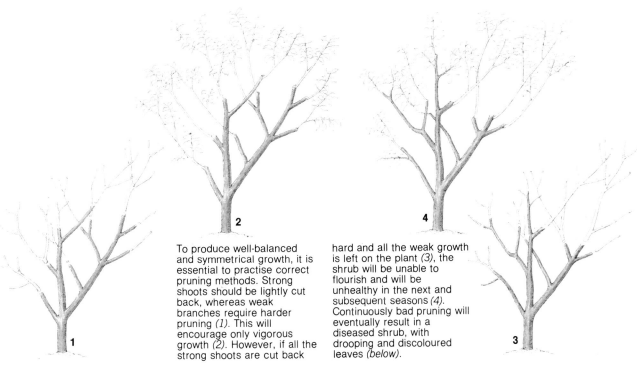

To produce well-balanced and symmetrical growth, it is essential to practise correct pruning methods. Strong shoots should be lightly cut back, whereas weak branches require harder pruning (1). This will encourage only vigorous growth (2). However, if all the strong shoots are cut back hard and all the weak growth is left on the plant (3), the shrub will be unable to flourish and will be unhealthy in the next and subsequent seasons (4). Continuously bad pruning will eventually result in a diseased shrub, with drooping and discoloured leaves (below).

case of tipping, removing the tip of each shoot by 2-3in (5-7cm), or about a quarter of the new growth on about a quarter of the whole plant. In both cases the cutting should be spread evenly over the plant.

Any pruning on flowering shrubs can be done after the flowered growth has been removed and the general clearing out has been completed; some shrubs may not need any pruning at all, particularly the berrying ones. Finally, when cutting, try to keep the plant's natural habit of growth and make cuts so that growth is directed towards producing a well-clothed and shapely bush.

Removing dead growth and fallen leaves
Plants die, branches break off, stems of roses and shrubs die back from the tips and flowers fade in the natural course of events. Left to themselves plants will rapidly become a clutter of dead and living growth. It is advisable to tour the garden every few weeks to remove anything that has died in the interim — dead growth will be brown, brittle and lifeless. This does not take long and is a powerful aid to plant survival. In autumn, leaves will be shed like confetti and dispersed by the wind, so it is worth removing them from the lawn and pool by raking, brushing or using mechanical leaf-sweepers. Leaf mould is a very good source of humus and is what a heap of newly fallen leaves will become in time.

Propagation

Seed

Seed is the obvious and quickest source of new plants, including annuals, biennials, bedding plants, vegetables and herbaceous perennials. However, a good deal of disappointment often follows. A variety of problems can occur right from the start with seeds not germinating at all. The temperature of the soil and air should be 60°F (16°C) or more for germination to occur within about one to two weeks, which is the average time taken for seeds to sprout. Some may take as much as a month, others only two days when the soil is moist and the temperature over 70°F (21°C) during the day. Low night temperatures can slow down or stop germination and cold soil is another factor. Germination is usually quicker outdoors if the soil is basically sandy; heavy soil takes much longer to become warm. In seed trays, the seed can be supplied with a suitable temperature in the greenhouse or home.

Drought, or just lack of moisture, is another enemy. No seed can germinate without water, which means it is necessary to sow in moist soil or compost and to water if there is no rain shortly after sowing. Seeds steadily lose their viability the older they are, and the best results will be obtained with seed sown in the autumn or spring after the summer in which it was set. Some seeds will germinate when two or more years old, but the percentage decreases each year and eventually none will be viable. A soil surface which is too coarse, saturation of the soil or heavy infestation of the soil by pests and fungal diseases can also destroy or discourage growth completely; birds will eat all seed. If a cover which is too heavy is placed on the seed, it will not admit the light or air needed to maintain growth.

Patchy germination may result from the same conditions that produce non-germination, but one of the prime causes is uneven sowing, which leads to weak seedlings and disease infection, mainly damping-off. Another cause is an uneven soil surface, so that seeds get washed into the hollows by watering, leaving the bumps bare.

Seed requirements for successful germination
Sowing time
Spring or autumn after seed has set
Soil and air temperature
60F (16C)
Position
Shallow sowing
Soil
Sand or compost
Well-drained
Moist
Good nutrient content
Water
Plenty of water, especially after sowing
Protection
Glass cover to preserve moisture and warmth
Light
Sunlight necessary for seedlings
Germination time
1-4 weeks

GERMINATION PROBLEMS		
Non-germination	**Patchy germination**	**Slow seedling growth**
Cold	Uneven sowing	Low night temperatures
Draught	Irregular surface of soil or compost	Dry soil
Old seed		Dull light
Badly prepared seed bed or seed tray	Flooding	Naturally slow-growing seed
Attack by pests	Pest or disease infesting the seed	**Yellowing**
Birds	Damping-off disease	Poor root system
Rotting due to fungal disease	Particles of soil or compost not fine enough	Lack of nitrogen
Waterlogging	Old seed	Waterlogging of soil
Sowing too deeply		Cold

Above The lists illustrate the type of conditions that encourage seeds to germinate, and also the reasons for faulty germination. The signs and causes are given to help the gardener indentify seeding problems.

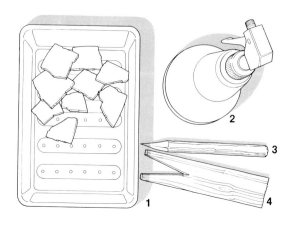

Left When sowing seeds in containers make sure that the bottom of the seed tray is covered with pieces of crock (broken clay pot) with the convex side facing up. This will supply drainage (1). Fill the tray with compost, firming down the surface to make it level. Once the seeds have been sown, cover them with finely sieved compost. When the seedlings appear, use a sprinkler (2) to water them. A dibber (3) and spatula (4) are used for lifting and pricking out seedlings. They may also be used for labelling.

Slow growth generally occurs when it is cold or in temperatures too low for the species. A temperature of 60-65°F (16-18°C) is suitable for the seeds of most of the plants grown outdoors in temperate climates; tender species need warm conditions, 70°F (21°C) for germination. Cold nights need to be taken into account and a useful monitor for these is a maximum and minimum thermometer, which will show the lowest temperature during the night. It can be reset every day. It is surprising how low such a temperature can fall, even in early summer, and may explain why plants are growing slowly. Dry soil contributes to slow or standstill growth and dull, sunless days will also halt all growth.

If seedlings start losing their green colour, they may lack nitrogen, as this is the mineral nutrient associated with leaf and stem development; it is also very soluble and easily washed out of the soil, so that constant watering may completely remove it. If the seedlings prove, on investigation, to have poor root systems, this can account for badly coloured leaves; stunted or brown roots can result from exposure to cold, wet or fungal disease.

Division

Herbaceous perennials are increased by division, which, although simple, can quite often result in failure. For successful division you should ensure that the right parts of the plant are replanted; the old woody centre of herbaceous perennials should not be used, but only the new growth at the edges. Each section should have some roots and one or two dormant buds (eyes) or growing shoots and the plants should be divided at the right time of the year, in early spring. It is important to minimize injury; small plants can be split with a sharp knife, larger ones with two forks back to back driven through the centre, or with a sharp spade.

Separation of the offsets from bulbs is another form of division, and is a quicker way of obtaining flowering plants than can be achieved from seed. Bulb offsets will usually flower in two or three years, sometimes in the year following, whereas seedling bulbs can take five or six years. The best time for separation of spring-flowering bulbs is after the leaves have died down in summer. The largest offsets should be kept for replanting.

Plants grown from tubers or rhizomes can be increased by division, cutting them into sections of rhizome or separate tubers. Each piece should have at least one eye or some shoots, and should be free of decaying material; soft, rotting or discoloured tubers, and cracked and hollow rhizomes are useless. Plant dahlia tubers 3in (7cm) deep in spring, and divide summer-flowering irises immediately after flowering, replanting the rhizomes so that they are only half-buried.

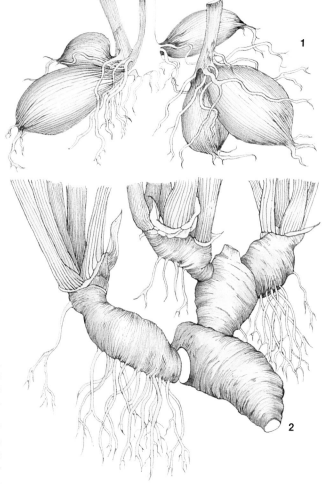

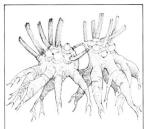

Plants that have a woody crown or clump of shoots just below ground level, or at the surface of the soil, should be divided like the root tubers, through the centre. This crown will be tougher than the normal root tubers and a sharp knife should be used. Make sure that equal amounts of roots and buds are attached to each section.

Division is the usual method of propagation for perennials. The swollen root tubers of plants such as dahlias should be divided with the main stem attached (1). Make the cut up from the bottom of the tuber, ensuring that each half still has a portion of the main stem attached. The underground stems of rhizomatous plants (2) should be split into 3in (7cm) pieces. Only replant the young outer section, making sure each piece has a few strong growths attached. The central part of the rhizome is useless and should be discarded. Small offset cormlets formed at the base of a corm should be removed when the plant is lifted. Keep them in a nursery bed until they have reached the flowering stage.

Cutting

A gardener often feels some years of gardening experience are needed before attempting to increase a stock of plants by taking cuttings. The production of roots from the cut end of a stem seems a miraculous achievement, but it is, in fact, not difficult to induce stems to do this. Cuttings are usually pieces of stem, although cuttings of roots can also be made. There are three different sorts of stem cuttings, which are soft or tip cuttings, semi-hardwood or half-ripe cuttings and hardwood cuttings. All are made out of new stems developed during the season. Soft cuttings are the youngest and shortest, involving only the tip of the stem,

3-4in (7-10cm) long. Half-ripe cuttings can be 2-6in (5-15cm) long, but are always at the stage of turning woody, and hardwood cuttings have, as their name suggests, a hard, mostly brown, outside stem, with a tough shoot. Shrubs are generally increased by cuttings, and so are some herbaceous plants which may be perennial, short-lived or tender.

If rooting does not occur, it may be because the cutting was taken at the wrong time of the year; soft cuttings should be made at any time during the summer, half-ripe ones in mid-summer, and hardwood in the autumn. Failure to root also occurs when shoots older than one year are used to make

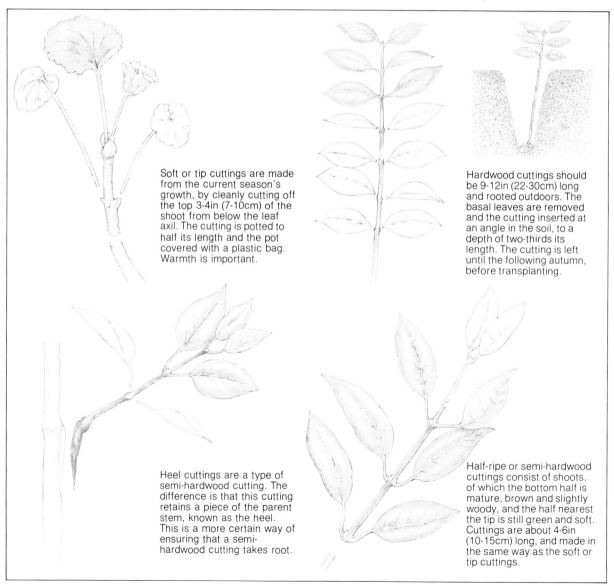

Soft or tip cuttings are made from the current season's growth, by cleanly cutting off the top 3-4in (7-10cm) of the shoot from below the leaf axil. The cutting is potted to half its length and the pot covered with a plastic bag. Warmth is important.

Hardwood cuttings should be 9-12in (22-30cm) long and rooted outdoors. The basal leaves are removed and the cutting inserted at an angle in the soil, to a depth of two-thirds its length. The cutting is left until the following autumn, before transplanting.

Heel cuttings are a type of semi-hardwood cutting. The difference is that this cutting retains a piece of the parent stem, known as the heel. This is a more certain way of ensuring that a semi-hardwood cutting takes root.

Half-ripe or semi-hardwood cuttings consist of shoots, of which the bottom half is mature, brown and slightly woody, and the half nearest the tip is still green and soft. Cuttings are about 4-6in (10-15cm) long, and made in the same way as the soft or tip cuttings.

the cuttings, or the temperature for rooting was too low, or it could be that the cutting formed a callus over the cut end. If the compost is not sterilized, the cutting may become infected with a fungal disease, which would cause it to die, as would dried-out compost or lack of constant humidity in the atmosphere around the cutting.

All stems have the potential to make roots and in rooting a cutting the stem is given the maximum encouragement to do so. The position of the cut is most important; with the majority of cuttings it should be immediately below a leaf joint or dormant bud, cutting the stem straight across and leaving clean, not ragged edges. Soft and half-ripe cuttings are put into pots or boxes, with the protection supplied by a greenhouse, propagator or closed frame. Hardwood cuttings can be put into an open frame or a sheltered border.

Cuttings rooted in containers should be inserted in the compost to half their depth, and any leaves which will be buried should be removed. They should be placed around the side, if a clay pot is used, otherwise anywhere in the pot or tray and inserted firmly and to the full depth of the hole made for them, so that the cut end is not left in mid-air, but is in contact with the compost. Moist compost and a moist atmosphere are essential. This is most important, as the cutting will be giving off water vapour before it has developed roots to take in water from the soil. The pot or tray must be covered with a polythene sheet supported by split canes, or the frame kept closed except for a daily removal of condensation. The cuttings must be kept warm, but shaded from the sun, with an air temperature of at least 65°F (18°C), and if soil warmth can be supplied, rooting is that much more certain and rapid. Soft cuttings should root within 10-14 days, half-ripe kinds may take a few weeks.

Layering

Layering, which is a kind of partial cutting, is a form of increase used mainly for shrubs. The stem is not cut off the plant completely; instead, a slanting cut is made on the underside of a stem directly beneath a leaf joint, part-way up through the stem. Stems treated like this should be within easy reach of the soil, as they are then pegged down into some friable loam or compost, cut side down, with the cut held open by a matchstick. The tip of the stem is left free and trained up against a support. Provided the shoot is a new one produced the season before, it will root at the cut into the soil. The time to do this is spring or early summer and in the autumn the new plantlet can be separated from its parent, but should be left to grow where it is until the following spring, when it can be transplanted to its permanent place. Some shrubs take two years to root. It is important to make sure the soil is always moist around the layer.

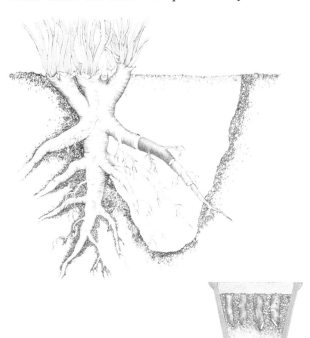

Left Root cuttings are a useful way of increasing herbaceous perennials. Divide thick roots into 3in (7cm) lengths with a slanting cut to distinguish the base. Plant them vertically with the straightened upper end level with the surface. Then cover with a layer of sand. (Thin, fibrous roots are laid horizontally in the soil.) Leave them in a closed frame for the winter.

Above When layering a shoot, choose one close to the soil, making a slanting cut halfway through the underside of a stem, opposite a bud or a leaf-joint on the upper side. Hold the cut open with a small stone, and anchor the layer in some good soil with a hooked wire, so that the cut faces the soil. Bend the tip straight up. As soon as the layer has rooted well, cut off the parent stem.

Care of different plant types

Bulbs

The routine care of bulbs is minimal. Most thrive if planted in a light, sandy or stony soil and a sunny place and continue to flower for many years without any problems. These include tulips, irises, hyacinths, grape hyacinths and narcissi. Some bulbs, mainly daffodils, produce offsets so freely, however, that they become grassy, which means there are a lot of leaves but practically no flowers, because the plants are crowded and are short of food. The remedy is to dig them up after flowering, discard all but the largest, and then replant these in a shallow hole in a sheltered place and leave them to ripen for the summer, letting the leaves die off naturally. Remember to mark the spot and then replant in the early autumn in the normal way, at twice the depth of the bulb. This method of heeling in can also be used when the place where the bulbs have been flowering is wanted for a summer display of bedding plants.

The main point to remember about bulbs is to plant them at the right depth. They are often not put in deeply enough, so a good guide to follow is the one advised for daffodils, making sure that the depth of the soil above the tip of the bulb is at least equal to its length. Planting time is early to mid-autumn for spring-flowering bulbs except tulips, which can be bedded in late autumn; *Iris reticulata* should be planted towards the end of summer for flowering in winter, and summer-flowering bulbs can be put in at the beginning of spring. A few flower in autumn — nerine, crocus, crinum, colchicum — and these will need to be planted in mid-summer.

Bulbs should be planted to a depth equivalent to twice their height and placed in the soil with the point facing upward *(right)*. Spring-flowering bulbs should not be stored until their leaves have died. This often means that they have to finish their growing period in another bed, to make way for other plants, or they can be placed in trays of peat *(below)*. They should be laid out in rows of deep, moist peat.

The crocosmia comes from tropical and southern Africa, and grows from a corm, which produces 3ft (90cm) stems *(right)*. The corms can be left in the ground during winter but in cold areas, liable to frost, they should be lifted and stored. The bluebell is a native of Britain, and grows from a bulb, which has no outer skin *(below)*. This means that storage conditions should not be too damp or too dry, otherwise the bulbs will shrivel and die.

Iberis sempervirens is a heavily flowering, low-growing plant, suitable for rock gardens *(left)*. To encourage this healthy blooming, some cutting back must be carried out. The plants will need attention as soon as the flower heads start to fade *(below)*. At this stage deadheading should also be performed *(bottom)*.

Annuals and biennials

These are short-lived plants, which are grown from seed. Annuals die within a year; biennials do not flower until their second growing season, and then die. Although temporary, they are quick to flower and cover the bare patches until other perennial plants can take over. Good results are due mainly to good seed-bed preparation. This starts a few months before by digging to at least one spade's depth, clearing out weeds, large stones and other rubbish, and then leaving the ground fallow, so that weeds can germinate and be hoed out as they are germinating. This is important; weed seedlings will grow more strongly than the ornamentals and can be difficult to control before the annuals get well established, and without harming the annuals. About a week before sowing, scatter a general compound fertilizer on the soil surface.

On the day chosen for sowing, which should be calm and mild, with rain to come, fork the soil to break up the lumps, firm it by treading evenly and level the surface by raking. At the same time rake out rubbish and break the soil down finely into breadcrumb-like particles. Sow the seeds thinly and evenly in the pattern decided on and rake a light covering of fine soil over them. By mid-spring, the soil should have started to warm up and germination should be within about a fortnight in most cases. However, seeds must have moisture to germinate and as the surface of a seed bed dries out quickly, watering will be necessary if no rain occurs within a day or two of sowing.

If there is a possibility that, in spite of all your care, weed seedlings are likely to appear, there are special weedkillers which can be used on seed beds which will not harm the cultivated seedlings. Non-appearance of seedlings can be due to birds, especially pigeons, taking the seed or sparrows making dust-baths in the seed bed. Seed treated against birds is available or you can put up protection, such as netting, cotton or aluminium foil. Another defence is to cover the bed with a slitted plastic sheet, which allows air and moisture to get to the seedlings and is light enough to rise with the seedlings as they grow, at the same time keeping

33

them warm. This type of sheet needs to be weighted down at the edges with stones.

Once they have begun to grow, annuals should be thinned when small enough to handle, to roughly alternate spacing, and again when they start touching for final spacing. Lack of time or foresight in doing this will mean crowded, weak plants and a dull display — they may even die because of damping-off disease. The taller plants will need staking. If the hardier ones were sown in autumn, make sure they do not become covered in leaves in late autumn, as slugs will eat them, hidden from sight. Sowing in autumn will result in much earlier flowering.

Biennials can be sown where they are going to flower, but the site will remain unattractive for about a year until they bloom, and it is more usual to sow them in a nursery bed, thin them there and then transplant to their flowering place. Early summer is the usual time for sowing biennials and final planting is in autumn.

Linums are prolific bloomers throughout the summer, and brighten up any border *(above)*. *Tagetes patula* (French marigold) was originally a native of Mexico, but may now be seen in many gardens, flowering from the beginning of summer until the first frosts *(left)*. Marigolds are known for their vibrant colours *(below)*.

Above and **right** Salpiglossis, a native of Chile, is an unusual and attractive plant. It may be grown in annual or mixed borders, in a rich soil and sunny position. The annuals need some supporting during their life to ensure healthy, upright growth.

Herbaceous perennials

These flowering plants live from year to year, in some cases for many years. Most species die down to ground level in autumn, though the roots survive the winter in a dormant state, but some are evergreen and even flower in winter, for instance the hellebores. Many of these perennials grow so tall that they can be blown down by wind or become so top-heavy with summer rain that they break; delphiniums, lupins, rudbeckias are a few. To avoid this damage, either obtain plants which grow tall but are sturdy enough to stay upright, or support them.

Delphiniums are a good example of a tall-growing plant, which will need to be staked from an early stage. Use sticks and twine (below) and, as the plants grow taller, add another piece of wire. The adult plants will still need support and several pieces of twine will be required (left). A plastic ring can be used in place of the wire, and adjusted in height as the plant grows taller (bottom).

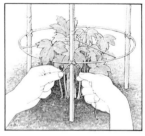

Solidagos are excellent plants for herbaceous borders or rock gardens (above left). Their brilliantly coloured clusters of yellow flowers are also suitable for cutting. Rudbeckias are natives of North America, and are another easily grown herbaceous border plant (left). They thrive in any well-cultivated and well-drained garden soil, and prefer an open, sunny site. Herbaceous perennials require regular deadheading, especially if they are for border decoration.

Perennials are beautiful in flower, but some species will need deadheading through the season as the flower heads droop and die. Deadheading has the advantage, too, of conserving the plant's energy, so that it sometimes goes into a second flowering, or new vegetative growth, instead of fruiting and setting seed. If seed is wanted for increase, deadheading should be ignored.

In autumn the top growth will gradually turn brown and die off. Since this is unsightly, many gardeners prefer to cut it right down to the crown, maintaining that this prevents fungal diseases from overwintering and takes away cover for pests. On the other hand, there are those who prefer to leave the top growth for protection of the crowns through the winter, so that it will rot naturally into the soil and thus maintain soil fertility. If the plants were heavily infested with pests and diseases, it is usually better to remove the dead growth and burn it rather than compost it.

Perennials tend to deteriorate after a few years, but there is no need to discard them completely. It is the central part which flowers badly and grows weak because it is the oldest, so dig the plants up

Many-kinds of poppies are suitable for a rock garden or border. They can be annual, biennial or perennial. Besides the scarlet-flowered original there are now kinds with pink *(top)*, white, orange *(right)* or bicoloured flowers *(above)*. Their petals may be fimbriated or wavy. Lewisias are also suitable plants for rock gardens, needing very sharply drained soil, and will also grow in dry stone walls *(top right)*. Sun is important, and they do best in climates where the winter weather is either always cold or always fairly mild. Alternations of the two lead to injury and death.

early in spring, break off the outside pieces, making sure they have roots attached, and then replant; the old, woody centre should be discarded. Put the sections at the same level in the soil as before and whether you are planting, transplanting or increasing as here, provide a hole which is large enough to spread out the roots in; then crumble the soil back over the roots and firm them down.

A border of herbaceous perennials that is left to itself, will become rather jungly, weedy and flowerless. Borders should be thick and luxuriant, colourful all season and free from weeds. To ensure this healthy state, clear off the rubbish and weeds in autumn, spreading a compound fertilizer dressing on the soil surface around the plants if the soil is light, and fork it in, thus opening up the soil at the same time and helping drainage and aeration. In spring, a further light tidying after winter will be necessary, hoeing to remove any further weeds and, later, staking as required, finishing with mulching.

Cornus alba 'Elegantissima' is grown specifically for its bark and foliage *(right)*. It is best if it is grown as an isolated specimen and not in a group. Pruning is an essential requirement of this species, in particular, otherwise the foliage will look dull and unimpressive *(below)*. The colour of the bark and leaves will be greatly improved if the shrub is cut hard in early spring.

Below *Viburnum opulus* is a native of Europe, including Britain. It is a tall (up to 15ft/4.5m), bushy, deciduous shrub, flowering in late spring/early summer and producing its red berries in autumn. It is an adaptable shrub and able to grow in most reasonable garden soils. No regular pruning is required, although some thinning out may be necessary after flowering.

Shrubs

Most shrubs grow into large plants, several feet high and wide, and go on growing, so that it becomes a problem trying to keep them under control. If they are neglected they will not flower and will grow as uniform masses of greenery, taking up too much room, overhanging the lawn and obstructing the mower. However, with only a little attention during the year, shrubs can be more rewarding than perennials.

Pruning is the main requirement, which means cutting back sensibly, instead of hacking the shoots and branches indiscriminately. Part of the space problem lies in the fact that the size of shrubs when fully grown is not always considered. This is an understandable error because they are so small when planted that all the bare soil around them looks unattractive. However, it is preferable to know in advance exactly what size they will grow to — in a moist and well broken-down, heavy soil, they will grow much larger than expected — plant accordingly and fill in the gaps temporarily with annuals, bedding plants or quick-growing, but short-lived, shrubs like tree lupins.

While young shrubs are growing, pruning will mostly be a matter of encouraging balanced growth and removing the few flowers that appear. Balancing the growth involves cutting off any shoot that is stronger than the rest and cutting off three quarters of short, weak shoots with thin stems. When the plants are adult, any formal cutting that is required can start, although there is no set time in the plant's life for this procedure and it can gradually be blended in with the minimal cutting of the earliest days. In general, flowering

shrubs which bloom in spring and early summer are pruned as soon as flowering has finished; those which flower later in the summer and autumn are dealt with in spring, just as growth is starting, and those which are slow-growing or winter-flowering are dealt with in mid-spring.

The reasons for these different timings are that the earlier flowering kinds produce their blooms on the shoots they grew in the previous summer, so if cut back in summer, all the growth that would flower the following season will have been removed. Those that flower later in the summer do so on the shoots that have grown that year — those which started to elongate in the spring immediately preceding the summer in which they are flowering. If a shrub is cut back early because it is overgrowing the path or blocking the front door, the best of the flowering growth will have been removed and it will no longer be ornamental. Winter bloomers follow the same pattern; the slow-growing kinds hardly need formal pruning — they seem to flower without this help.

Weigela *(below)* needs to have its stems cut back after flowering . *Pieris formosa* 'Forestii' *(far right)* needs to have any faded flower heads removed and straggling shoots cut back. It is important to make the cut at a strong shoot, and to angle the incision *(right)*. Slanting the cut toward the bud *(3)* or cutting too far above *(2)* or too near *(4)* the bud are all incorrect. Make the cut just above, and slanting away from, the shoot *(1)*.

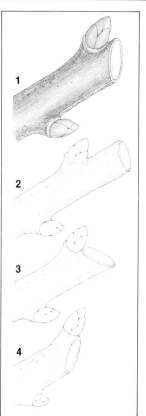

When pruning, cut off the shoots which have flowered, making the cut either just above a good new shoot which is already growing, or just above a bud which has begun to sprout, or at the point of origin of the shoot. Clear out dead growth as well, which will be brown and leafless and may be a whole shoot or branch or only the tip of a shoot; cut away completely the short, thin shoots; remove those which are awkwardly placed and growing into the bush's centre or crossing other, better shoots. All this will help to let sunlight and air into the growth, but if it still seems slightly crowded thin it out a little.

When making the cuts, try to position them just above a bud or shoot at an angle sloping away from the bud. One of the problems with pruning is that cut shoots often die — if dead they turn brown and break easily — from the cut down the stem, because the cut was made in the wrong place or in the wrong way. If the cut is too far away from the sideshoot, leaf-cluster or dormant bud, the snag left can easily be infected; if it is too close, the bud may die or be knocked off and the growth of the adjacent shoot or leaf-cluster may be affected. If cut straight across, it will collect moisture; if cut sloping towards the bud or shoot, rain will be directed

into the bud, and if cut raggedly, it provides even more of an opportunity for fungal rotting.

To help you avoid cutting off flower- or fruit-buds, remember that these are round and fat; vegetative buds, which will only produce a shoot with leaves, are pointed and comparatively long and narrow. There are times when you may have to cut halfway down a flowering or leafy shoot, so you will know from this how much potential flowering growth is being removed. Cutting off part of such growth has the effect of stimulating some of the remaining buds into producing shoots instead of flowers. The reasons for this are complicated, but are connected with the balance of hormones and other biochemicals.

If a shrub is flowering badly, has lots of dead tips to the shoots, grows slowly and always seems to be infested with greenfly, clear out all the extraneous growth, fork the soil around it carefully so as not to disturb or injure roots too much, sprinkle a light dressing of a phosphatic fertilizer onto the surface and water it in and then mulch with rotted compost or manure. The forking, feeding and mulching should be carried out inside a circle at least 2ft (60cm) in diameter around the plant, with the most suitable time being the spring.

Hedges

A common problem with hedges is lack of leaf cover at the base; sometimes they are not very thickly covered higher up, either. Part of the trouble is due to wrong training when the hedge was young, and part is due to poor soil and lack of food. In order to achieve a good thick cover low down, young hedge plants must be treated in autumn or early winter in one of three different ways. Some of the deciduous hedges and some of the evergreens should have their height reduced by a third, cutting to a good dormant bud, immediately after planting and any sideshoots cut back by about half. This is repeated in the second winter. Deciduous hedge plants such as blackthorn, hawthorn, tamarix and the mainly evergreen privet should be cut down very hard to within about 4-6in (10-15cm) of the soil. In the second winter, the new shoots subsequently produced should be reduced by half their length. The third method involves little work; the height of the plants is left alone and the sideshoots are only cut a little if they are straggling. This is repeated in the second winter. If these hedges are planted at the end of winter, they should not be cut then, but left until the next winter, which should be regarded as the first winter from the pruning viewpoint.

In the summer following the second winter, all hedges can be considered as established. The methods of clipping can then be divided into two groups. For the majority of hedges, leave the height alone, do not cut the leaders back, but cut the side growth hard to leave about a quarter of the new season's growth. When the hedge has reached the height required, trim thereafter to keep at that height and do the same with the sides when a suitable width has been reached. This annual clipping is required for the following: beech, cypress, cotoneaster and escallonia, *Euonymus japonicus*, hazel, holly, hornbeam, juniper, laurel, laurustinus, pittosporum, pyracantha, spotted laurel, tamarix and yew. This should be done in summer; sometimes, in mild autumns, a second light trim is needed in mid-autumn. The laurels are best trimmed in early autumn only.

The second group, including blackthorn, hawthorn, *Lonicera nitida* and privet should have their top new growth cut back by about a quarter, until the height required is reached, and sideshoots should always be cut hard as with the first group. This trimming will be needed at least three times during the growing season, as all grow rapidly throughout the summer and sometimes into autumn. Combining this kind of trimming with spring feeding on light soils and dressing with rotted organic matter in autumn each year should ensure that the hedge provides a good cover all year if evergreen and for most of the year otherwise.

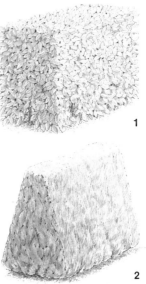

Prunus lusitanica (common laurel), with its glossy, dense foliage, is an example of a hedge that does not require a harsh cut. It is more suited to a light trim, carried out with secateurs, rather than shears, to prevent excess damage to its distinctive leaves. The more formal habit suits coniferous-type shrubs, which look attractive when they are closely clipped *(1)*. It is advisable to shape the hedges so that they are thinner at the top *(2 and 3)* to prevent snow from settling on the top and pressing out the branches.

Established hedges can be badly damaged at the top by the weight of snow, or by wind if the base is bare, and also if they have been clipped so that they are wider at the top than the bottom. The shape of a hedge in silhouette should be completely vertical or slightly tapered toward the top for greater strength and uniformity of appearance, which is so important with formal hedges.

Informal hedges are pruned when mature in the same way that shrubs are, since the object of an informal hedge is to obtain flowers. It should be left to grow virtually unchecked until flowering has finished, and then trimmed. It is worth bearing in mind that, to be effective, informal hedges should be at least 4ft (1.2m) wide.

Trees

There is little general maintenance of trees that needs to be done during the year, but there are some problems that occasionally occur and can kill the tree if not dealt with immediately.

Supporting in the first two or three years prevents wind-rock, in which the constant movement of the base of the trunk gradually produces a hollow in the soil around it. This collects water and

leads to bark rotting and ultimately the death of the tree. Secure staking is essential and can be done with a single post, two similar ones with a cross bar or a single diagonal. For standards and half-standards, the support should extend about halfway up the trunk only. It should be removed in the third year, otherwise the trunk never thickens up as it should and the tree is less strong than it could be. Ties are important; too tight or left too long, they constrict the stem, cut into it and provide entry for disease. Padding made of sacking provides a home for pests and absorbs moisture although there are kinds which are made to avoid these problems.

Like shrubs, trees tend to be planted in places which are too small for them. If this has happened and a tree starts causing problems with shade or space, branches will have to be removed. If this is difficult it is better to obtain professional help, but if the branches are within easy reach and not too large they can be removed safely, by first making an undercut halfway through the branch near its junction with the trunk and a second on top some inches away from the first, until the branch snaps cleanly through. The remaining stump is sawn off

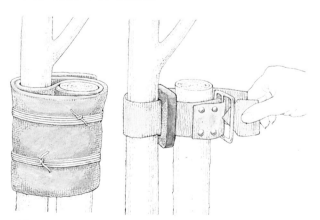

Removal of branches and top growth from trees must be done carefully *(left)*. Dead growth should always be cut away. Make sure that the cut is made level with the healthy trunk or branch *(1 and 2)*. Damaged tips should also be removed, back to a healthy shoot *(3)*. Supports should be tied to the tree or shrub so that they do not cut into the bark. Use padding *(below left)*, but be careful that insects do not hibernate beneath it, or use the special plastic tree-ties that can be loosened as the stem or trunk expands with growth *(below right)*.

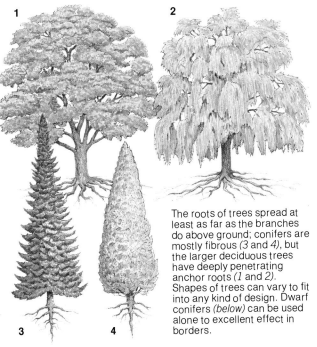

The roots of trees spread at least as far as the branches do above ground; conifers are mostly fibrous (3 and 4), but the larger deciduous trees have deeply penetrating anchor roots (1 and 2). Shapes of trees can vary to fit into any kind of design. Dwarf conifers (below) can be used alone to excellent effect in borders.

so that there is a slight projection from the trunk. The wound will then callus over and heal much more quickly than if left flush with the trunk and a fungicidal paint can be applied.

When planting trees, remember that their roots can spread extensively underground, at least as much as the branches do above ground. House foundations and drains are the main hazards; small trees are unlikely to cause trouble, but trees such as weeping willows and poplars, particularly in clay soil, should be planted well away from the house and drainage system. In any case, they will cut out light from the house.

Some trees are prolific producers of new shoots from trunks and even roots; these are called suckers. Again, poplar is an example and there are others, such as ornamental cherries, lilac and roses. In the lawn these suckers can be mown off, otherwise they must be cut away at the point of origin. It is better if they can be pulled off as this will remove the eye completely, but it can lead to root damage or it may not be practicable. Application of a weedkiller will destroy suckers and is unlikely to harm the tree, but new ones will appear in their place and will also need treatment.

Laburnum flowers in early summer, and L. 'Vossii' makes one of the best small trees for the average garden (above). Its hanging clusters of deep yellow flowers can be as much as 12in (30cm) long, and it has no special growing needs. Rhus typhina (stag's-horn sumach)(left) is usually grown as a shrub, but can become a small tree, and has brilliantly coloured leaves in autumn.

Lawns are a popular and welcome addition to any garden, if the area is large enough to handle one. They offer a feeling of space and provide an excellent foil to borders *(right)*. A smooth, velvet-like turf, however, will not just present itself. It is the result of careful year-round management, which includes feeding, aerating, mowing, watering, top-dressing and raking. A lawn mower is one essential piece of equipment for any lawn. An electric mower *(below)* is a very effective machine and easy to handle anywhere. The lawn must be mown frequently, every five days during the growing season, and the surface should be kept perfectly level.

Lawns

Where a new lawn is to be grown from seed, there are various hazards which endanger its survival, but which are easily avoided. Choose the right time of year; drought and heat or frost and waterlogging will prevent the lawn from establishing itself, and generally spring or early autumn are the best times to sow, when the weather is mild and likely to be moist rather than soaking wet. A badly prepared seed bed will result in thin seedling germination, bare patches, yellowing seedlings and slow growth. It must be evenly firm, of a friable nature and free of weeds and stones. An uneven surface will cause puddles after rain and seeds will be blown by wind or carried by rain into the hollows, which causes thick patches of seedlings to form, interspersed with bare patches on the bumps. Old seed and uneven sowing can produce the same effect and birds can also upset the regularity of the sowing. Even subsoil, brought to the surface in patches, can result in uneven or no germination.

Insufficient fallowing and inadequate advance weed control will produce a flock of seedling weeds along with the grass; besides a thorough preliminary cleaning, a special weedkilling solution can be sprayed onto the soil before sowing, which will kill the weed seedling, but not the grass. There is also a fungal disease, which attacks seedlings of all kinds and can cause a great deal of damage to grass, called damping-off.

Laying a turf lawn is not advisable during a dry period. Dry soil and hot weather makes knitting of the turfs slow and difficult and once they have dried out the grass will be permanently damaged, if not actually dead. The wetter months are preferable, provided snow and frost are not forecast. As with seed, the soil surface must be level and firm and a spirit-level is useful for checking the lines of turfs as they are laid. To get a good close interlocking of the turfs, lay them in staggered rows, like the course in a brick wall, which will avoid four corners meeting and adding to the problems of binding, and lay each turf slightly humped. As soon as each row is completed, gently knock the individual turfs flat. When you lay the next row knock the new row up against the previous one to further ensure successful knitting of the turfs. Finally, work a top-dressing mixture of sand, peat and loam into the cracks, or you can simply use sand only.

Both newly seeded and turfed lawns should be cut lightly when they have begun to grow, at about 1¾-2in (4-5cm) in height. To prevent the seedlings from being torn out of the soil by the mower, it is advisable to roll the new lawn lightly, but make sure the minimum possible rolling is done, to avoid damage to the soil structure.

Once the lawn is established, frequent mowing is necessary to ensure that the finer grasses predominate. Mowing needs to be done every five days in spring and early summer, then every seven until mid-autumn, and from then less often. If left for longer periods than these, the lawn will become more difficult to cut as the coarser grasses overcome the desirable fine ones. A sign of infrequent cutting is ribbing, alternate ridges of short and long grass; this can also be due to cutting when the grass is wet.

There are a number of problems that occur with mowing, which lead to weak grass and weed and moss encroachment. If the grass is not being cut as short as would be expected with the blade setting, and the grass tips are turning brown, then the mower blades need sharpening or resetting or the grass is being cut when it is wet. Some wiry grasses in particular show this tendency.

A trail of bare patches found after mowing along an otherwise grassy covering is probably due to an uneven lawn surface and not from mowing too closely. If this is not put right, weeds will soon cover the patches, but it is easily corrected by cutting an 'H' shape in the turf, lifting and rolling back the flaps and removing the surplus soil. The cut turf, once back in place, will knit together rapidly.

Following the same routes every time the lawn is mowed will eventually produce the condition known as washboarding, in which the soil itself forms regular undulations running across the line of mowing. The same kind of effect occurs when a field is ploughed in the same direction. It is a good idea to occasionally mow in a different direction in

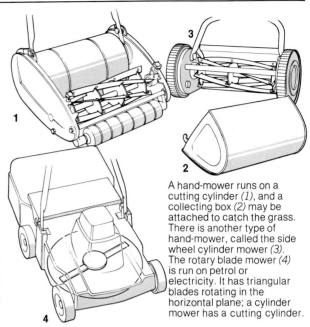

A hand-mower runs on a cutting cylinder (1), and a collecting box (2) may be attached to catch the grass. There is another type of hand-mower, called the side wheel cylinder mower (3). The rotary blade mower (4) is run on petrol or electricity. It has triangular blades rotating in the horizontal plane; a cylinder mower has a cutting cylinder.

any case, as it improves the health of the grass.

Starting in spring, raking will get rid of the leaves, twigs, dead vegetation and worm casts that will have accumulated on the surface during winter. Feeding with a compound fertilizer should follow after the preliminary mowings, preferably applied to moist soil, when rain is due. If weeds are present, a weedkilling solution can be applied a week or two following feeding, or a combined fertilizer/weedkiller can be used if there is not much weed growth. Another spring job is aeration, to get air into the soil and enable surplus water to drain through. Frequent mowing, especially with cylinder mowers, compacts the soil surface to such an extent that it forms an almost impervious layer, making it difficult for the grass's roots to function efficiently. A simple method is to push a garden fork into the soil 4in (10cm) deep, at intervals of a few inches all over the lawn. Autumn is another season when aerating is beneficial and in a drought, if penetration is possible, aeration will often revive the grass almost as well as watering would, although irrigation will still be necessary.

In autumn, spreading a top-dressing mixture of such ingredients as loam, peat and sand will keep the soil structure in good condition. Application is at the rate of about 2lb/sq yd (1kg/m²), put on evenly and worked into the turf at once with a broom or the back of a rake. Finally, raking off any leaves in early winter will avoid yellowing and weakening of the grass and the encouragement of worms. Autumn is also a good time for lawn repairs, such as re-seeding bare patches, removing small bumps and putting damaged edges to rights.

Health and hygiene

Vivid colour and vigorous, lush growth distinguish the healthy garden. Some gardens, however, despite all efforts, just do not flourish. Plants look dusty, tired and colourless; growth is slow and stunted. This type of garden, where cultivation has been attempted but has failed to produce satisfactory results, is often difficult to remedy, as opposed to those cases where the main problem is outright neglect. Locating the underlying cause is the main difficulty. Any number of hazards — from weeds, pests, diseases to nutrient deficiencies and weather damage — can affect a garden's health. While it is possible to treat each of these in a specific way once diagnosed, much can be done to prevent garden ailments in the first place by maintaining a good standard of hygiene so that adverse growing conditions are avoided.

Keeping the garden free from debris does not necessitate destroying the natural habitat of local wildlife. It is possible to retain a nature reserve, long-lasting and self-generating, where natural controls supplement the gardener's vigilance, while at the same time satisfying your basic requirements for beauty and relaxation. Weeds are a major problem. They should be uprooted and placed on the compost heap, not left lying around in containers to encourage plant marauders. Dying or dead growth should be dug out as soon as seen and burnt. Compost heaps should be enclosed in some way, even if only by wire-netting, and lawn sweepings placed on the heap or allowed to rot separately into leaf mould. Every six weeks during the spring and summer cut back new rose, shrub or climbing growth, as well as branches of trees that overhang paths or impinge on smaller plants. In the case of a bad insect infestation, cut off and destroy the whole shoot.

These basic measures will ensure an overall level of hygiene and go far to promote health and vigour in the garden. More specific problems, however, demand specialized attention.

Weeds

Every garden is plagued by weeds and the first step in garden hygiene is to keep this unwanted growth under control. Weeds are most likely to colonize in flowerbeds and borders, rose beds, rock gardens, lawns, drives, paths and paved areas. In general, if the seeding type can be destroyed before they flower, they are easier to keep in hand. Besides hoeing and forking, these seedlings and other small weeds can be sprayed with weedkiller containing paraquat and diquat, which gives quick results and has the advantage that the soil can be planted or seeded within a few days. Paraquat affects plants through their green parts — it has no action on the roots so, provided the solution does not touch the top growth of cultivated plants, they will not be harmed if the solution soaks into the soil. For this reason, it is particularly useful on flowerbeds, borders and rose beds.

For tough weeds, the chemical known as glyphosate is an all-round remedy, although perennial nettles will need about four treatments before they die. This is also a leaf-acting herbicide, sprayed onto the foliage when in full growth. It takes between two and four weeks to have full effect and again must be prevented from contaminating the top growth of a cultivated plant. It is available as a gel with a brush for application, as well as a liquid. Another chemical, which is absorbed through the roots and so must be watered onto the soil, is sodium chlorate, used at strengths varying from 4-16oz/gal (125-500g/l) of water, depending on the strength of weed and degree of infestation. It cannot be used, however, where there are cultivated plants, mainly because it seeps sideways in the soil as well as downward, but it is useful for paths and drives, vacant ground that needs clearing, paving and forecourts. It will remain in the soil for at least six months. Once the weeds have been removed, the ground can be kept clear with simazine, which lasts for about a year, and has the advantage that it stays virtually where it has been applied, in the top few inches of the soil.

Rock gardens are notorious for becoming weed infested. Because the plantings are so concentrated, weeds can become inextricably entangled. Hand-weeding is usually the only satisfactory way; if perennial weeds have become entrenched, you can try painting the leaves with a herbicidal solution, but often weed roots gain such a tenacious hold under the rocks and stones that the only solution is to dismantle the whole rock garden and start again.

Lawns are another special case, where a different collection of weeds emerge. Daisies are notorious, followed closely by plantains and dandelions and many others. There are certain

Weeds spreading by seed	Weeds spreading by underground stems
Annual nettle	Colt's foot
Bittercress	Couchgrass
Chickweed	Ground elder
Dock	Winter heliotrope
Dandelion	Horsetail
Fathen	Sow-thistle
Goosegrass	
Groundsel	
Heart's ease	**Weeds spreading by creeeping roots**
Shepherds purse	Bindweed
Willowherb	Creeping thistle
Weeds spreading by runners	Dead-nettle
	Enchanter's nightshade
Cinquefoil	Perennial nettle
Creeping buttercup	
Speedwell	

Lawns can easily become a mass of weeds *(right)* if the grass is not correctly managed. Use a hormone weedkiller to kill off the weeds and leave the grass intact. Other weedkillers will kill off weeds within 24 hours *(below)*. The area will finally be left completely bare *(bottom)*. Planting can take place at once, provided paraquat was the weedkiller used.

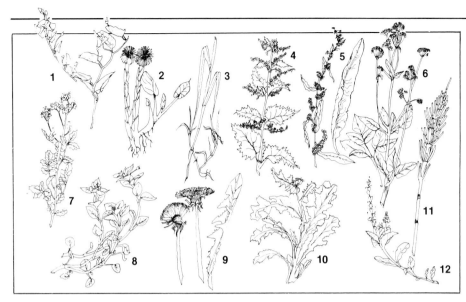

Left Weeds are not advisable in the garden as they tend to smother and impede surrounding growth. The weeds pictured illustrate some of the common ones found in the garden. *(1)* bindweed (*Convolvulus arvensis*); *(2)* colt's foot (*Tussilago farfara*); *(3)* couchgrass (*Agropyron repens*); *(4)* stinging nettle (*Urtica dioica*); *(5)* curled dock (*Rumex crispus*); *(6)* ground elder (*Aegopodium podagraria*); *(7)* large bittercress (*Cardamine amara*); *(8)* chickweed (*Stellaria media*); *(9)* dandelion (*Taraxacum officinale*); *(10)* groundsel (*Senecio vulgaris*); *(11)* marsh horsetail (*Equisetum palustre*); *(12)* speedwell (*Veronica officinalis*).

lawn weeds which grow flat naturally, or have adapted their habit of growth so that they avoid the mower blades. The only overall chemical treatment at present is by the use of the hormone herbicides containing 245-T, 24-D, MCPA, mecoprop, dicamba and others. There is considerable controversy about the possibly harmful effect of these on birds and animal life in general. Current available medical and scientific evidence indicate that they still may continue to be used but further research is recommended.

Weeds spread in lawns where the grass is not being supplied with the conditions it needs for healthy growth — fertile soil containing nutrients, good drainage and the presence of air in the soil. Extremely acid or alkaline soil, shade, close cutting and lack of water are other factors contributing to weak grass. However, some weeds may be tolerated; many provide a green cover and some even flower attractively.

Applying weedkiller

Most weedkillers are dissolved in water and applied as necessary by watering can, sprinkler bar attachment to a can, pressure sprayers or handmisters. These solutions can also be applied with a sponge, rag or brush, or the stem tips can be dipped into the solution. Some are applied dry as powders or granules; one is in gel form. Other remedies include a wax bar impregnated with the lawn weedkillers, and a device which delivers the weedkiller through a nozzle at the end of a stick, piercing the centre of the weed. Some proprietary lawn fertilizers incorporate hormone weedkillers for spreading on the surface of the lawn with wheeled distributors. Whichever implement is employed, it should be cleaned after use.

Pests and diseases

Pests

Although plants can be attacked by a great number of pests of the insect type, there are only a few which are common to all plants and cause widespread damage. If plants are being regularly invaded by heavy infestations of pests, it is almost always a sign that the plants do not have the growing conditions and nutrients that they need. Weak, slow-growing plants succumb more quickly and to a greater degree than constitutionally strong plants, partly because their sap is sweeter, so more attractive to sap-sucking insect pests such as aphids and red spider mites. Maintaining plants in good health through good, fertile soil, and planting them where they receive the best weather and drainage conditions possible is, in effect, a form of preventive medicine.

Slugs *(above)* and snails *(left)* can do a great deal of damage to garden plants by biting large holes in the leaves and stems, and, in bad infestations, they will also attack the flowers. They can eat small plants completely, and will destroy those that are newly planted before they have become established. Even large plants take some time to recover. They are particularly bad in damp situations and in seasons of heavy rainfall. All their feeding is done at night, and many can be caught by hand if they are searched for immediately after dark. Other possible precautions include laying out bait containing methiocarb, which must be shielded from pets and children; saucers of stale beer will also act as traps.

Slugs and snails Damage consists of irregular holes in leaves, stems and flowers near ground level and sometimes higher up the plant. Plants can be stripped of leaves; flowers are not often eaten unless there is an epidemic of these pests and then it is usually snails that destroy them. Feeding takes place at night, especially early on, and during the daytime both slugs and snails retire beneath stones and into cracks. There are some species of slugs which live in the soil and feed on dahlia and other tubers, bulbs and corms. These slugs are small and black, whereas those above the ground are greyish white or brown. Snails and slugs are worst in wet seasons, in shady damp places and badly drained, heavy soil. To control them it is important to keep the garden free of rubbish and ensure a good soil structure. Hand-pick them at night with the help of a torch or trap them in saucers of diluted beer. Encourage hedgehogs, as these creatures feed on slugs, and, if necessary, use proprietary slug-baits containing methiocarb, which should be fully effective.

Greenfly, blackfly, mealy aphids (aphid species) Greenfly infest almost every herbaceous flowering plant, many trees and shrubs, roses and top and soft fruit as well as vegetables. They are the tiny green insects on the underside of leaves, the outside of buds and on and in flowers. Blackfly are also a species of aphid, found on nasturtium, broad bean, cherry and honeysuckle in particular. There are other sorts of aphid, coloured blue, grey or rosy pink, together with woolly aphid (American blight), which protects itself with white wool and is found on the bark of ornamental apple trees and other rose family trees and shrubs. Aphids feed by sucking the sap from plants via long pointed mouthparts. As a result leaves become curled, blistered, puckered and yellowed, buds are small and may die, flower petals become limp and diseased, new young shoots stop growing and plants become sticky with the honeydew excreted by the aphids, on which a fungus called sooty mould will grow. Adult plants are not killed, but can be permanently stunted if attacked annually; small plants and seedlings are liable to die in heavy infestations. Most of the trouble occurs in spring and early summer, and particularly on plants short of water, or on container grown plants short of food, root room and moisture.

There are several methods that may be taken to aid the control of aphids. Make sure water and food shortages are corrected; use finger and thumb to squash the greenfly; cut off any badly infected shoots; spray tar-oil winter wash or bromophos to destroy overwintering eggs on dormant trees or use a specific aphid chemical such as pirimicarb in the growing season.

Woolly aphids appear as tufts of white wool, which act as a protective covering *(above)*. They are often found on the bark of small trees and shrubs and particularly on apples. Aphids also infest the buds of roses *(above left)*, sucking the sap from the plants, so that, eventually, the new shoots are killed off. Leaves are also a favourite target of this pest and especially on the beech. Greenfly shed their white skins, leaving them on the leaves *(below left)*. These aphids mostly feed on the underside of the leaves, excreting large amounts of sticky honeydew as they go. The leaves will gradually curl and become distorted. Aphids generally tend to occur in large numbers and it is best to eradicate them immediately by spraying with pirimicarb. Make sure correct growing conditions are provided, particularly adequate soil moisture, as this is always beneficial in protecting plants from insect infestations.

49

Caterpillars will feed on leaves *(right)*, stems *(above)*, flowers and buds. Those that live in the soil, such as leatherjackets and cutworm larvae, will feed on plant roots. They are the larvae of moths and butterflies, and sometimes also of flies and beetles. Where they occur in large numbers, as is often the case on Solomon's seal, they will strip the leaves down to the centre midrib and the side veins in the space of two weeks. Hand-pick as soon as seen, or spray with insecticide in epidemics.

Caterpillars Caterpillars vary in colour and size, from the very small ¼in (6mm) long, to the giant ones of 5-6in (12-15cm), such as the goat moth variety. They feed on leaves and also stems and flowers, making holes with their biting mouthparts. In bad infestations they can strip a plant completely of its leaves so that only the main veins remain. Solomon's seal *(Polygonatum multiflorum)*, on which sawfly larvae feed, is an example. Trees tend to be the worst infested, along with a few ornamental herbaceous plants and some shrubs, but on the whole caterpillars are not too troublesome. If necessary, spray the infested plants with trichlorphon.

As well as caterpillars which live above ground, there are soil-living species which feed on roots and the crown of the plant at soil level. Slow-moving, generally brownish or white, they are approximately 1in (2.5cm) long when full grown and are extremely damaging. Because they cannot be seen, they can work undisturbed. The first indication of their presence is often the death of a plant. Young or small plants and seedlings are particularly vulnerable, and it is possible to find a dozen leatherjackets feeding on the roots of one small plant. All types of small ornamentals and bulbs can also suffer.

Caterpillars are best dealt with at the egg stage using finger and thumb to crush them; the clusters of round or cylindrical eggs can be found beneath the leaves. Birds are helpful in controlling the eggs, and so are predatory insects. Frequent cultivation of the soil by hoeing or forking exposes eggs to birds and discourages egg-laying. If there is a plague of leatherjackets, cutworms, chafer larvae, swift moth caterpillars or narcissus fly, treat

Capsid buds produce pinprick holes in leaves *(left)* and stems. They also make holes in the tips of shoots, which then become tattered and ragged with severely stunted new growth and flowers that are malformed and fail to open *(below)*.

winter on woody plants, and hatch when the weather becomes warmer; several generations appear in one season and they are particularly bad wherever conditions are hot and dry. Small plants can eventually die; ornamental fruit trees will become unthrifty with successive attacks and fruit will be very poor. The glasshouse species attacks all sorts of greenhouse plants and will continue feeding through winter in heated houses. If no chemical spraying at all is done in the garden, predators and parasites will keep the pests at bay; maintaining moisture levels helps and spraying the top growth daily in hot weather is another deterrent. Derris is the safest chemical, but needs repeated applications to kill the mites hatching from unharmed eggs. If this is not effective, malathion or dimethoate should be tried. Dimethoate is a systemic insecticide which is absorbed into the leaf and persists there, but it is dangerous to bees and not necessarily remedial as some strains of mite are now resistant.

the soil the following year with trichlorphon at the time suggested by the makers, usually before sowing or planting. Plants already infected are usually past saving, but any larvae on the roots or in the bulb or tuber should be destroyed.

Capsids These insects, which include the tarnished plant bug, cause tiny holes in the young leaves at the tip of a new shoot. The tip itself is likely to be twisted, curving over or dangling, and attacked flower-buds unfold to produce a one-sided flower. Leaves become ragged and tattered and shoot stems cease to grow. Fuchsia, hydrangea, dahlia and chrysanthemum are some of the plants most likely to be infested, but damage can occur on other plants, from spring to mid-summer. Capsids are green, comparatively large insects about ¼in (6mm) long, very quick-moving and rarely seen, as they disappear when disturbed. Control is difficult, but there are predators; malathion or fenitrothion are the best sprays; the ground around the plant should also be treated.

Red spider mites Neither true insects nor true spiders, these tiny pests are only just visible with the eye alone, and a magnifying glass is necessary for confirmation. They are sap-sucking insects, which feed on leaves making them speckled yellowish, greyish or bronze and generally turning a sickly shade of green. Leaves become dry and brittle, then wither and fall much too soon. In bad attacks, the mites produce webbing on the leaves and leaf stems and can be found on the underside of leaves in all stages from egg, to pale yellow when young, to pink or red adult mites with white skins which they cast as they moult. Eggs over-

Red spider mites are tiny pests, which can be pale pink, straw-coloured or red. They live on the undersurface of leaves, where they feed on the plant's sap. Leaves become a speckled yellow, lose their green colour and wither, falling prematurely *(below)*. In bad attacks, webbing will be produced beneath the leaves *(left)*. Hot, dry conditions encourage them, and several sprays may be required for control.

Leafhoppers are tiny, pale green insects usually found on the undersurface of leaves *(right)*, and their feeding results in a characteristic light green stippling of the upper leaf surface *(far right)*. Although they do not actually kill the plants, they will weaken them and cause poor new growth. This, in turn, opens up the way for other problems, such as fungal infection. If the damage is not extensive, control is not necessary. Otherwise use bioresmethrin or a soap and water solution.

Leafhoppers These are small, light green insects related to aphids and similar in appearance but their colour is much paler. When disturbed they move in the way their name suggests, unlike aphids which walk about the leaf or stem. They are found on the underside of foliage and feed on the plant's sap which produces a stippling effect of white speckles on the upper side of the leaf. They can be a serious problem on small container plants and will also feed on roses, rhododendrons, beech and various other ornamentals. Control is not always necessary, but if they become too numerous on roses, rhododendrons and container plants, use bioresmethrin or a soap-and-water solution.

Ants Ants can be alarming when they produce mounds of soil in flowerbeds and when the swarms of flying adults appear. In many cases the first sign of their presence is a wilting group of plants or a brown patch on the lawn. This is not because they feed on the plant roots, but because their tunnelling encourages quick drainage and dries out the soil or leaves plant roots dangling in mid-air in the tunnels, without access to water. Ants are also found high up on the stems of plants already infested with greenfly. In this case it is not the plants but the greenfly which are the target, since the ants feed on the honeydew excreted by the greenfly. In order to obtain this they will protect the greenfly from predators, to ensure their survival and increase. Spraying the mounds and nests with a solution of trichlorphon is the most effective treatment. Otherwise use sugar as a bait, permeated with the solution.

Woodlice Sometimes called pillbugs or slaters, these insects will also feed on roots, mainly of seedlings or container-grown plants when they live beneath the container and feed through the drainage holes. They will eat holes in leaves near to the soil during the night and hide, like slugs, in daytime in cracks in walls or under stones. Rotting vegetation will attract them, and badly made compost heaps can be infested with them. However, they do not cause much trouble except in enclosed, shady gardens that are little disturbed and cultivated; garden hygiene greatly helps to keep them under control. Chemical spraying is not necessary if they are purged as soon as they have been seen.

Millipedes These are black, shiny creatures, which coil up into a circle when they are disturbed. Damage to plants is below ground as they feed on roots and other underground parts. Small plants and seedlings are most vulnerable, but they will also enlarge other damage made by slugs or caterpillars or rotting caused by fungi.

Earwigs Earwigs are notorious for feeding on dahlia petals, but they will also nibble other ornamental plants. Holes in leaves are often ascribed to slugs or caterpillars and ragged flower petals to caterpillars, capsids or chafer beetles, but in summer it is much more likely to be earwigs that cause the damage. Chrysanthemums, clematis, pansies and delphiniums are among the other plants that can be heavily infested. Start looking for damage from early summer right through the season; look for the creatures at night, when they feed. In daytime they will hide and advantage can be taken of this by supplying them with hiding places such as pots filled with straw or newspaper, hung upside down on the top of stakes, and then destroying them daily. If numbers continue to rise, spray or dust with trichlorphon. The removal of garden rubbish and practising garden hygiene will be especially useful in discouraging them. Earwigs are also quite useful, however, as they feed on aphids, among other insects, providing natural control and a certain degree of competition.

Thrips These appear during thundery, summer weather in great numbers. They are minute black insects about ⅛in (3mm) long, and the damage they cause consists of silvery white patches and mottling of flowers such as sweetpeas or gladioli. If young plants are infested, damage can be quite serious as the silvered leaves fall early. Like red spider mites, the thrip thrives in hot, dry conditions; epidemics can be prevented by keeping the roots and top growth of plants supplied with water by overhead spraying. Control can be obtained with resmethrin, which is available as a mixture with pyrethrum.

Leaf miners If you discover leaves with white, wavy lines winding about on the surface, or leaves with small, irregular, beige-coloured blisters, the damage is being caused by leaf miners. Some are of no concern, but they can increase rapidly and a leaf can be completely covered by the tunnels or blisters, with the result that it dies and falls early. The least that a bad infestation can do is to weaken and slow down a plant's growth so early control is always advisable. Complete removal and burning of damaged leaves as soon as they are seen should be all that is necessary then, otherwise trichlorphon will be needed. Some plants that can be badly affected are cineraria, chrysanthemum and lilac; holly will need dimethoate for control, as the leaves are so leathery.

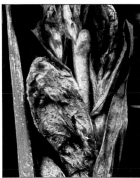

Many insects are damaging to plants. Earwigs will chew the petals of many flowers, especially border plants, including coneflowers *(above)*. Thrips can be a bad pest of gladioli *(right)*, feeding on the flowers and causing silvery patches. This is disfiguring and will gradually weaken the plant. Leaf miners produce these pale brown, wavy lines on holly leaves *(below)*, as well as blotches and blisters, inside which the minute maggots live and feed.

Mealy bugs Insect pests which feed by sucking the sap from plants, mealy bugs have a protective covering of white fluff, and the first sign of their presence is usually such a patch, formed by a colony of bugs. In cool, temperate climates they are found on greenhouse plants and house plants; elsewhere they are an outdoor pest, widespread on a great variety of plants, particularly cacti, bulbs (in the neck between the scales), palms, ferns, vines and begonias. In warmth, they will breed all year round and considerably weaken plants by their feeding, as well as fouling them with honeydew and sooty mould. Control under cover is possible with predators, otherwise hand-pick them where possible, cut off completely any

Mealy bugs suck the sap from leaves and stems *(left)*, and will seriously weaken the plant *(below left)*. Dimethoate should be sprayed.

Whitefly look exactly like minute, white moths, living on the undersurface of leaves, where they lay eggs *(below)*. These hatch into tiny, round, transparent nymphs (larvae), which then feed and moult, growing larger each time until they become the adult fly.

badly infested plant part and brush the remaining bugs with surgical or methylated spirit. In obstinate infestations, spray with the systemic insecticide dimethoate, but follow the manufacturer's directions as some plants are damaged by this chemical.

Wireworms These pests live in the soil, and should be a prime suspect if you discover plants collapsing and dying for no apparent reason. All sorts of ornamentals are potential victims and gladioli, dahlias, chrysanthemums and primulas are a few of the most likely. The damaged part will be the root, tuber, corm and any part on which the wireworm feeds. Infestations of larvae are worst in the soil under undisturbed grassland and in neglected gardens, causing most trouble in spring and autumn. They have a much longer life in this larval stage than most insects, up to five years before they change into the adult brown click beetle. The yellow shiny wireworm is 1in (2.5cm) long when full grown, slow-moving and segmented. Neat, round holes bored into root vegetables, potato tubers and bulbs, as though made with a knitting needle, are the characteristic symptom of their feeding. Control will be helped by digging in autumn to expose the wireworms to birds and frost; traps of old carrots or potatoes make good bait. Hand-pick while forking, before planting or sowing; apply bromophos in heavy infestations — this is a persistent soil insecticide which is harmful to wildlife and livestock, and at least seven days should be allowed to elapse between application and harvesting edible plants.

Eelworms These microscopic pests, also known as nematodes, cannot be seen without considerable magnification. Symptoms of their presence are many and varied, but not obvious until the infestation is well advanced and the plant dying. Leaves become twisted, distorted, discoloured or bumpy and bulbs have dark rings of tissue internally, which swell, split, and crack. Phlox, chrysanthemums, ornamental bulbs, some herbaceous perennials, ferns and scabious are some of the most vulnerable ornamentals likely to be attacked — but the eelworm has a universal, worldwide distribution, and can be the cause of death of many soft-tissued plants and some woody ones. It feeds on the sap of plants, whether root, stem or leaf, and can thus spread viral diseases. It needs water to live actively, but can survive dry conditions in a dormant state for many years.

Unfortunately there are no chemical controls available to gardeners and hot water treatments, which will be effective without killing the plants, are difficult to carry out in home conditions. In general, if plants are suspected of being eelworm-infested, they should be dug up completely and burnt and the site left unplanted with the same species for three years. Although it might sound as though most garden plants are riddled with eelworms, in practice, it is rare for one to be seriously affected. Mixtures of plants, rotation, fallowing and normal garden hygiene including weed eradication, help to keep their numbers down, as do predators. If damage does occur, it is usually because the plant is already in trouble with the wrong growing conditions.

Weevils These are tiny brown, black or clay-coloured, beetle-like creatures, between ¼-⅜in (6-9mm) long. Damage is characteristically in the form of semi-circular holes cut out of the edges of leaves near to soil level; this results from the night feeding of the adult weevils, which live in the soil. Attacks by the white, grub-like larvae are much more serious as their presence is not suspected until the plant dies. Larvae of the vine and clay-coloured weevils eat the roots of many plants, in particular causing much damage to primulas, polyanthus, camellia, rhododendron, azalea, clematis and vine. Container plants of all kinds are also vulnerable.

Control is difficult, but keeping the garden clear of rubbish and removing the grubs by hand when you discover them will help. Dust or water the soil with malathion or lindane, also the lower foliage and stems, but follow manufacturer's instructions carefully with regard to the use of the latter on edible plants.

Scale insects These are not obvious insect pests, but the first signs of their presence may be honeydew and sooty mould. If no greenfly or mealy bugs are apparent, look for the scales on the underside of leaves, on the stems of leaves and shoots and on bark. Scales generally line themselves down the main veins, but they will also be found on the remainder of the leaf. They will be round, oval or mussel-shaped, raised blobs, brown or white in colour; the young are much smaller, translucent green-white on the leaves, pale brown on bark. The hard, brown coating is a protective covering for the insect which lives and feeds beneath it, remaining in the same place all its life. When eggs hatch, the young move out to their own feeding ground. Both indoor and outdoor species occur and can be a serious problem particularly on citrus trees. On indoor plants, they can be removed by hand, wiping off with a sponge and then spraying with bioresmethrin, which will kill the young, small specimens. Outdoors tar-oil winter wash can be brushed or sprayed onto woody plants which are completely dormant, but follow maker's instructions.

Scale insects *(below)* are often found on the bark of woody plants, and also on the leaves, usually clustered along the central vein on the underside *(left)*. They feed in the usual way by sucking the sap, and remain in one place until they die. They should be scraped off with the fingernail, gently, to avoid harming the plant. In bad attacks, spray the plant with malathion, several times until the infestation is controlled.

Below Eelworms live in the soil and migrate to plants where they feed. They produce brown areas on leaves, and may cause withering.

Rust disease is often found on the leaves of ornamental plants, including mahonia *(far left)*. Red-brown spots appear on the underside of the leaf and powdery spots of yellow show on the upper surface. Slugs and snails can also cause a good deal of damage to leaves, particularly verbascum leaves *(top left)*, which are large and juicy. Much of the feeding occurs from late summer through autumn, and is generally concentrated around the lower leaves *(bottom left)*, which tends to slow down growth in the early stages. Violas are another victim of leaf damage. They can be badly infected by this fungal disease, powdery mildew *(right)*, which causes white, powdery patches on the surface of the leaves and also on the stems, and even the flowers and buds become discoloured. Dry soil and plants sited too close together encourage it. Pick off leaves at the first signs of an outbreak, and spray immediately with a suitable fungicide.

Chemical remedies

The choice of proprietary products available to control insect pests is so enormous that it is difficult to know which to use and which is the most effective for a particular purpose. One that is safe and universally effective is bioresmethrin. Permethrin and resmethrin are similar — the former persists for three weeks. All will deal with greenfly, blackfly and other aphids, small caterpillars, whitefly adults, leafhopper, thrips, beetles and ants.

Pirimicarb will only kill greenfly or blackfly and is harmless to bees; follow the manufacturer's directions as to prohibited plants. Derris (containing rotenone) is very safe to use; it will deal with whitefly adults, thrips, caterpillars, wasps, raspberry and flea beetles, red spider mites and aphids. It is very poisonous to bees and fish. Provided it is fresh, it is effective, and rotenone content should be 0.5%. Malathion is a phosphorus insecticide, one of the derivatives from the nerve gases of the First World War. It is useful in that it will control many insect pests — aphids, thrips, leafhoppers and suckers, and has some control of whitefly young, red spider mite adults, leaf miners, scale insects, mealy bugs, woolly aphids and some maggots and grubs — but it has been used so extensively, and where other phosphorus-containing insecticides have been previously ap-

plied, that many insects have developed resistant strains. It will also kill predators, parasites and pollinating insects, is toxic to birds and fish and is not advised for use where the operator has already done much work with other phosphorus products. There are various plants on which it should not be used as it will damage them.

Where pests are particularly obstinate, dimethoate (phosphorus-containing) can be tried, a partial systemic which is absorbed through the leaves of plants and persists for at least a week. It should eradicate leaf miners, scale insects, mealy bugs and red spider mites, provided they are not a resistant strain. It is poisonous to fish, birds and mammals, and some plants are also vulnerable. For soil-inhabiting pests, trichlorphon (phosphorus-containing) is reasonably effective, and only dangerous to fish; it is not persistent, and there is no risk of taint. There are no restrictions on plants. HCH, which used to be called BHC, is a wide-spectrum insecticide, likely to cause taint in edible crops, and is dangerous to fish, bees and livestock, damaging to some plants and persistent, particularly in the soil. It can also accumulate in the body. Chemicals for slugs and snails include metaldehyde, available as a solid and a liquid, and which has an anesthetic effect, and methiocarb, which is more effective. Both, however, are harmful to pets and other mammals and birds.

Fungal diseases

Insect pests are an obvious enemy, easily seen and fairly easily dealt with, but ill-health in the plant caused by fungi is a different problem, in that many of the symptoms can be missed altogether. They may be blamed on the weather or soil, or thought to precede or follow pest damage. Many of the discoloured spots or blotches on leaves, especially the dark-coloured ones, are due to invasion by a fungus; most of the rots on roots, bulbs and fruit are fungal in origin, and cracked or splitting bark on shrubs and trees often occurs because a fungus enters through a tiny injury, perhaps caused by bird pecking or pest nibbling. Fortunately, there are not nearly as many common fungal diseases as there are pests.

Powdery mildew This infects a great many herbaceous and woody plants, especially towards the end of summer. If the leaves of plants gradually become covered in white patches on the surface, spreading to the stems and buds, the plants have this disease. Those with their roots in dry soil, whose top growth is subjected to heavy dew when the weather is warm to hot, are likely to be worst infected, particularly plants in enclosed situations, growing up walls and in crowded conditions. Although this disease primarily infects the external tissues of the plant on which it lives and feeds,

it can nevertheless weaken plants seriously. Remember that it is plants that are already weak that are most likely to be invaded, and invaded seriously.

Growth slows down, flower-buds do not open and the flowers themselves are discoloured and pale; berries are coated with white and fall early; shoot tips die back. Prevention is possible in this case by avoiding planting too close; by thinning the plants themselves of surplus stems, which especially applies to Michaelmas daisies, and by ensuring a flow of air around the plants — supports for climbing plants should be held away from the vertical surface, so that air can circulate behind the stems. Soils should be mulched when moist or watered when dry. Badly infected plant parts are best cut off completely, making the cut well back into the healthy growth, and then destroyed. The rest of the plant can be thoroughly sprayed, using a fungicide such as benomyl or thiophanate-methyl, which are both systemic; or dinocap; or dusted with sulphur. If plants are regularly mildew-infected every year, consider moving them to a different part of the garden, discarding them and substituting resistant varieties of the same genus, or planting new genera altogether. The alternative is to start spraying in spring and continue throughout the growing season. Some of the modern roses have to be treated like this.

Grey mould (Botrytis cinerea) This is the disease often known as *botrytis* and it is ubiquitous to a degree, as practically any plant can be infected through a previously made injury. It looks just as it sounds — grey fur appears in spots and patches on leaves and stems, which turn yellow or brown beneath the fur. The infected parts rot and gradually the whole plant will be destroyed. Flowers can also be invaded — on chrysanthemums the disease is known as petal blight — and die even before the buds open. Leaves close to the soil are especially vulnerable and you will find that it causes most damage in cool, wet summers or in greenhouses where the temperature is too low and ventilation sluggish. Tender plants in particular will suffer from the disease when there is not enough warmth.

Cultural remedies are not very easy, as there is little that can be done about cool, wet summers, but controlling slugs and snails helps, as well as keeping the garden clear of any piles of vegetation. Fortunately, trouble generally occurs with container-grown plants and in the greenhouse, where it is unlikely that superfluous vegetation will build up. In both cases, adequate air circulation can be arranged and, if necessary, extra heat in the greenhouse. Where the disease gets out of hand and cutting out of infected parts is not sufficient to control it, a systemic fungicide, such as benomyl, can be thoroughly sprayed onto the plants and should prove fully effective.

Canker is a fungal disease, which infects the bark of apple trees *(above)*, whether ornamental or edible, causing the bark to crack and flake off, exposing the heartwood, and destroying the layer of tissue that regenerates and produces new plant cells. It is also often seen on roses *(right)*, most frequently near the soil and can gain entry through an injury made to the stem while cultivating.

Canker This is a generic term which covers various fungal or sometimes physiological or bacterial conditions, but which all produce the same symptoms of cracking and splitting of the bark on shoots, branches and trunks of woody plants. Bad attacks will result in the bark fragmenting and detaching from the plant, and if this encircles the affected part, the shoot or branch will die back to the site of infection. If the bark falls away, the vessels just beneath the bark, which carry food around the plant, will then be destroyed. The green tissue immediately below the bark, the cambium, will also be killed, so that no new bark can form. Most canker trouble occurs where plants are growing in badly drained soil and humid climates or on shoots and smaller branches.

If shoots or branches are dead, they should be cut well back into the healthy material. Cankered parts on otherwise living shoots should be pruned away with a sharp knife, painting the resultant wound with a suitable grafting wax or other sealing compound. Any material removed should be destroyed and piles of wood in the garden, including fallen trees, should be avoided or dealt with, if present. Try to improve the soil structure and thus the general health of the plant, at the same time thinning out crowded growth, and spacing plants further apart. Trouble of this kind is most likely to be found on roses and ornamental cherries and apples.

Honey fungus (Armillaria mellea) Trees and shrubs are the plants most commonly attacked by this fungus, which is fatal. If you see a cluster of toadstools with pale yellow caps at the foot of a tree trunk or the base of a hedge plant in autumn, you will know that this disease is present. It is a common cause of death for privet hedges, where one plant will die, then those on either side of it and so on, until the entire hedge is killed. The bark at the base of the stems becomes loose and can be pulled away easily; underneath, the wood will smell of mushrooms and have a network of white threads on the surface and if the soil is dug away from the crown, long, black strands will sometimes be found, the fungal equivalent of stems, which spread through the soil and infect other plants. Infection can also spread via roots and spores from the toadstools. The wood and roots of infected plants become soft and brown, later fibrous and light-coloured.

This disease, because it is soil-borne, is very difficult to cure. Infected plants, together with all the roots, are best dug up and destroyed as, even if some cure can be effected, they are likely to remain weak. It is better not to replant in the same soil, nor to put in any woody species for at least a year, longer if possible. There are some species

Grey mould (*Botrytis cinerea*) on chrysanthemums can infect leaves, stems and buds. It will also make the petals on open blooms turn brown, wither and fall, and will quickly and easily ruin the whole bloom *(left)*. Grey mould is a universal fungal disease affecting practically any plant, especially those with soft tissues and during cold, damp weather. Primulas *(below)* are particularly prone to the disease, and affected buds become discoloured and may not open. Keep plants in well-ventilated gardens or greenhouses, do not overcrowd the plants, remove dead plant material and keep the plants well-watered. Spray with benomyl.

which can be planted — clematis, hawthorn, holly, mahonia and tamarisk — without too much risk of reinfection, but the chance is always there, and removal of the soil in the area well beyond the limits of the roots is advisable, if replanting is to succeed. Alternatively, the soil can be treated with formaldehyde solution or a proprietary fungicide specifically formulated for the disease, derived from tar-oils.

Sooty mould This fungus is most often seen on plants grown under cover, nevertheless it does sometimes occur on outdoor plants heavily infested with a sucking insect pest such as greenfly or scale insects. They secrete large quantities of sticky honeydew which falls onto the surfaces of leaves below, hardens and provides a suitable base for the fungi known as sooty moulds. Black patches appear on leaves and, together with the honeydew, build up relatively thick layers which prevent the leaves from carrying on photosynthesis. This is especially troublesome in dry, hot weather when no rain washes the deposits off the leaves. Early leaf drop occurs and plants are weakened — lime trees, bay, camellia, willow and roses are notable victims. The moulds themselves

do not feed on plants. Prevention is the best remedy here, by controlling the pests before the deposits appear to provide a base for the sooty moulds. Wiping or sponging the leaves in the absence of rain is effective if practicable.

Rust This is an aptly named fungal disease found on the undersurface of leaves in summer, and consisting of a mass of small, raised, rust-brown spots. Many kinds of ornamental plants can be infected, as well as garden weeds, each having its own specific strain. Yellow or yellow-green spots show on the corresponding areas of the upper surface and sometimes the typical rust colour is replaced by dark brown or beige. Flowers can also be infected, becoming distorted or discoloured and eventually dropping off. On some plant species and in some seasons the disease is serious, resulting in early leaf fall and stunting, but weakening of the host without actually killing it is the usual effect.

The disease can be avoided altogether by planting rust-resistant varieties of antirrhinum, hollyhock and carnation, and there are some modern hybrid roses which are less susceptible. Removal and destruction of infected leaves and

Right Seedlings can suffer from a soil-borne fungal disease called damping-off. This disease will infect the roots and stems at soil level, so that they turn black and collapse, and remain lying on the soil surface. The problem is most often encountered in container-sowing, or when a lawn is grown from seed. It is best to use sterilized sowing compost, and to make sure that any lawn seed bed is thoroughly prepared, and is equipped with good soil drainage. It is advisable to take measures to prevent further outbreaks by watering the affected area with Cheshunt compound.

shoots as soon as possible helps to control it, and destruction of infected plants at the end of the growing season will cut down the spread of the following year's infection. The fungicidal chemical mancozeb will aid control, as will fungicides containing copper.

Damping-off Primarily a fungal disease of seedlings, damping-off causes patches of seedlings to collapse and die for no obvious reason. The disease is present in the soil and infects seedlings through the roots and the stems at soil level, which may, in some cases, be discoloured dark brown or black. Remedies are to use sterilized soil or compost, not to sow thickly, but thinly and evenly, not to water heavily and, if the disease does occur, to remove infected seedlings and water the remainder with Cheshunt compound. Water from clean containers and make sure that seed trays or pots are thoroughly cleaned and preferably sterilized before re-sowing.

Chemical remedies

Fungicides were originally mainly based on copper and sulphur, which protect plants, but at present there are two systemic chemicals which will eradicate as well as protect and remain effective for up to a month. One is benomyl, the other thiophanate-methyl, and both will deal with mildew, grey mould and many other fungal diseases but, as with insects, resistant strains have appeared. Moreover, benomyl has been found harmful to earthworms. Grey mould in particular has become tolerant, so alternating sprays should be used, and another called dichlofluanid in-

troduced into the range. This also is systemic, but is based on sulphur.

Rust diseases can be difficult to treat, but mancozeb is useful and, if it can be obtained, oxycarboxin, although it is usually only supplied in large packs for commercial use. Bordeaux mixture contains copper and has some effect on rusts; it is also used for protection against some bacterial diseases. Cheshunt compound is another copper-containing fungicide, mainly watered onto soil for damping-off and associated root-infecting diseases of seedlings and small plants. A new chemical which has recently become available and produces excellent results in rust control is propiconazole. As well as being a strong eradicant, it has a protective action and is a systemic fungicide. Its effect on mildew and rose black spot is also excellent and regular use on roses with drooping flower stems improves this condition.

Pest and disease control without chemicals

Much can be done to prevent the appearance of pests and diseases without resorting to chemical sprays. Predators and parasites of both fungi and insects provide natural checks and balances. If the garden is left unsprayed, these populations will adjust to a level that the plants can cope with, provided the plants have the right conditions for healthy growth throughout the growing season. Garden hygiene is also important, especially the removal of weeds, which are centres of infection for fungi and supply cover for insects.

Where population explosions occur, suitable predators or parasites can be introduced, which are obtainable from companies that breed and supply them expressly for this purpose. Red spider mites, whitefly, caterpillars and woolly aphids are among the insect pests treated in this way.

Pest and disease control can also be improved by careful selection of plants. Look for resistant strains — annuals bred to be immune to fungus diseases, roses which are resistant to mildew or black spot, and the herbaceous perennials which are least likely to get mildew. Concentrate on plants which remain healthy in most seasons — for instance, those with aromatic leaves are generally strong and the old shrub roses are hardly ever afflicted with black spot or mildew. If plants become sick year after year, remove them, obtain different varieties or species and plant in a different site. In any case, it often pays to dig plants up and put them in a slightly different place every few years as it rejuvenates them and restores their flowering performance. Cut off any badly damaged or infested shoot, leaf, flower or bulb, or dig up the entire plant and burn; do not encourage further trouble by leaving it on the compost heap.

Not all plants are full of pests and it is worth investigating which ones are trouble-free. Pelargonium, the greenhouse geranium *(above left)*, is a half-hardy flowering plant from South Africa. It is an eye-catching plant, whose flowers are usually various shades of red or pink, but it is not nearly as easy to grow as other geraniums. It is prone to attacks by several insects and liable to disease. Nepeta *(left)*, on the other hand, is a particularly trouble-free plant. It is also an attractive plant with its grey leaves and spikes of blue flowers, and will sometimes even flower twice in the season. As well as buying pest-free plants, you will find that insects will often control their own levels in the garden. For instance, the larva and adult ladybird will prey on the greenfly *(below)*.

Bacterial diseases

Fortunately there are few of these, as control is best effected at present by antibiotics, which are not permitted for plant bacterial diseases in some countries.

Soft rot This rotting disease is the most common trouble of this nature, which reduces the infected part, whether root or tuber, to a soft, ultimately liquid, foul-smelling mass. Soft rot is most often found on stored root vegetables and on the bulbs and corms of ornamentals. Sometimes infected plants can be saved by cutting out the diseased part, leaving only healthy tissue, and treating the wound with a copper-containing fungicide. Otherwise the plant will have to be destroyed, as will any tissue that has been cut out. The disease enters through an injury, so control of other pests and diseases helps, as well as ensuring good drainage, addition of moderate amounts of compost or farm manure and storing only undamaged bulbs, tubers or roots.

Fireblight This is another serious bacterial disease, most often seen infecting shrubs and trees of the rose family, such as the rowan, crab apple, cotoneaster, hawthorn and pyracantha, but not roses themselves. Infected plants first show the

Leaf spots of various kinds due to fungal diseases, often occur on plants, including rudbeckias *(above)*. However, the majority do not do any great damage, and often all that is needed is to pick off the affected leaves and burn them. Sometimes a copper-containing spray helps as a protectant. Bacterial canker is a serious disease of ornamental cherries *(right)*, which shows as splitting and decaying of the bark on branches, stems and trunk.

symptoms in late spring. These include brown and black withered leaves at the tips of new shoots, spreading down the shoot, and dead, brown blossoms. The disease is readily spread by rain running down the stems, by bees working the blossom and by pruning. It can kill a small tree within one season. In Britain, if it is suspected that any tree or shrub has the disease, by law the Ministry of Agriculture must be notified, who will then give advice on treatment, which may consist of taking up the plant and burning it.

Bacterial canker Ornamental cherries are susceptible to this disease. The first symptom to be noticed is usually yellowing of the leaves in spring on one shoot or branch, then stunted development of the new shoots, followed by death. But, preceding the leaf discolouration will be cankering of the bark where the bacteria have invaded it and, from these cankered areas, blobs of amber-coloured gum will ooze and run together to form an appreciable quantity, gradually turning brown. This initial invasion happens in autumn or early winter; later in spring or summer a secondary invasion of the leaves can occur in which small, brown, circular spots appear and drop out of the leaves as though holes had been cut out. This stage gives the disease the name of 'shothole'.

Fortunately ornamental cherries are not so frequently or so seriously affected by this kind of canker as edible cherries and plums. Control is difficult and, once branches are infected, there is little hope of saving a tree. The shothole stage can be treated by spraying trees with Bordeaux mixture in spring and is worth trying on ornamental cherries; otherwise, sprays should be applied in late summer or early autumn to protect the tree from bark infection through injuries after picking and leaf fall. Cankers on branches or shoots should be removed and destroyed; dead shoots or branches should also be removed and the wounds treated with a sealing compound.

Viral diseases

These diseases can be the most serious of all. Signs of infection are usually irregular white or yellow variegation such as mottling, mosaic or rings on normally plain green leaves, often combined with dwarfing of the entire plant. They can also result in leaves that are curled, crinkled and distorted, as well as producing discoloured and malformed flowers and causing early leaf fall.

Once a plant is infected, there is no chemical treatment that will destroy the virus without also destroying the plant and most viruses result in the plant being severely stunted and unable to flower or produce fruit. Some plants are merely 'carriers', but can be more dangerous as they do not show

These healthy leaves at the top of this camellia indicate that the viral disease was distributed by eelworms through the soil and has infected the lower part first.

The disease infects the cells of the plant and travels through the stem to reach all parts.

The yellow and white mottling on these lower leaves is a characteristic sign that a viral disease is present. It can be attractive and will often not be harmful to the plant.

symptoms, although plants next to them or nearby which are susceptible can be badly infected. Some plants seem to be able to go on growing just showing signs of infection. One example is 'broken' tulips whose ground colour is broken up with white flecking and blotching, and another is *Abutilon megapotamicum* 'Variegatum', whose leaves display irregular yellow markings.

Viruses are distributed from plant to plant by insects, mainly by greenfly, as they suck the sap from an infected plant and then feed in the same way on a healthy one. Thrips, whitefly, red spider mite and some beetles are among other insects causing the same trouble, and eelworms are the carriers in the soil. Some control over viruses can be obtained by keeping these pests at bay. Heat treatment of plants will clear the disease in some cases, but needs apparatus not readily available to gardeners. Where plants are obviously badly affected, they should be dug up and burnt and the site should not be replanted with new stock if the disease was due to soil eelworms. Weeds can be infected, which is another reason for their control.

Viral diseases have not been named in the same way that plants, fungi and insects have and mostly take the name of the host plant, together with the symptom description, for example, tomato mosaic, chrysanthemum green flower or carnation ringspot virus. But generally the host name is that of the plant on which the virus was first discovered; many viruses will affect a variety of plants.

Nutrient deficiencies

In the average garden, plants do not suffer a great deal from shortages of mineral elements. Such elements are essential to plant health and growth and are absorbed from the soil along with the soil moisture, in which they are dissolved. In commercial cropping where land is used intensively and only one type of plant may be grown, a particular element can easily become depleted, and symptoms of its deficiency will then show in the aerial growth of the plants.

Garden soils support an extremely varied collection of plants, all differing slightly in their food requirements; their roots penetrate to different levels and thus tap varied sources of minerals. It is unlikely that deficiencies will be troublesome, although a few do occur in specific plants, and in particular soil types. The symptoms for a missing element can differ from species to species, and are easily mistaken for signs of virus infection or physiological disorders, such as waterlogging or salt-laden winds.

One deficiency which is common, however, is that of iron. Known as lime-induced chlorosis, this shows up as yellow to bleached leaves, starting at the tip of new shoots and gradually extending down the stem. Plants growing in chalky soils with a pH of 8.0 or more are likely to show these symptoms, which result in stunting and slow growth, together with general weakening. There are a large group of plants that will die if grown in such soils, as they need an acid soil with a pH of 6.5 or less — these are plants of the heather family, including heathers, rhododendrons, azaleas and others that are not ericaceous, such as magnolia, camellia and witch hazel. In markedly alkaline soil, roses, polyanthus, apples and strawberries are among plants which will show this iron deficiency, although it is quite probable that only one or two shoots or branches will be affected.

Alteration of soils to increase acidity is difficult and slow. The addition of organic matter annually and use of acidic fertilizers helps, or sites can be dug out and filled with suitable soil or compost, although, in time, alkaline water will seep in from the sides. An alternative is to water plants annually with sequestrene, a chemical compound which supplies the necessary iron in a form which the plants can absorb — lime-hating plants are unable to extract the iron from alkaline soils. Rather than forcing the plant to grow in alien conditions, it is more satisfactory to concentrate on plants which do not object to alkalinity. There are plenty of these and many which actively need an alkaline-based soil.

Other mineral elements, occasionally in short supply for one group of plants, include potassium, magnesium and manganese. Nitrogen, which is chiefly responsible for the production of green

Bright yellow and cream-coloured leaves are a sign of lime-induced chlorosis. It appears at the tips of shoots on an otherwise healthy plant, and gradually works its way down the stem. The cause is generally due to an iron deficiency (right). This problem is brought on by planting in a soil that is too chalky for the plant. Magnolia (left), in particular, likes a well-balanced soil. The remedy is either to move the plant to a neutral to acid soil, or to water with sequestrated iron.

colouring and general growth of stem and leaf, and whose lack shows in pale green or yellow shoots and leaves, will sometimes be deficient after heavy rain, since it is very soluble and quickly washed out of the soil. However, nitrogen deficiency is often associated with a general lack of plant foods, as can occur in sandy, shingly, stony or gravelly soil, and the remedy for these soils is plenty of rotted organic matter and proprietary compound fertilizers, the latter applied until the soil is suitably fertile. For nitrogen shortage alone, a 'straight' fertilizer such as sulphate of ammonia, hoof and horn or nitro-chalk can be used, although it is not advisable to put nitro-chalk on alkaline soil.

A lack of potassium (potash) manifests itself generally in brown leaf edges, leaves which curl up and in, poor flowering both in quantity and quality, and slow, rather stunted growth. This deficiency is seldom seen on ornamental plants in private gardens, although gooseberries are prone to it; if deficiency is suspected, treat with ashes from wood fires, provided they have been kept protected from rain. The application rate is about 4oz/sq yd (125g/m^2).

Magnesium deficiency can show as yellowing between the veins of leaves, manganese deficiency as yellow speckling and dotting, but both are difficult to differentiate from insect attack or viral disease. In any case, other symptoms can occur and diagnosis is thus sufficiently complicated to warrant calling in a professional if the problem does not clear up after a period of regular feeding and manuring and all other possible causes have been eliminated.

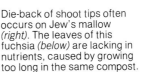

The quickest way of getting mineral nutrients to plants is by spraying the leaves with fertilizers in liquid form, diluted with water as directed by the manufacturer. The leaves absorb the solution rapidly, and the benefit is visible after a day or two. Fertilizer solutions can be applied to the soil for root absorption in the normal way and then need to be used frequently, about once a week. Powder or granular fertilizers are sprinkled onto the soil near the plants and watered or hoed in. The plant will be harmed if a dry fertilizer is applied in a tight circle around it, as the concentrated substance burns the roots when it reaches them — the same occurs if plants are put in directly on top of fertilizer. Fertilizer should always be applied all over the soil for some distance around the plant, so that it permeates to all the roots; the fibrous roots and root tips are some distance from the main stems.

Compound fertilizers largely contain the three most important mineral nutrients: nitrogen (N), phosphorus (P), and potassium (K), phosphorus being associated with root activity, and particularly necessary to seedlings. The amounts of each present in the fertilizer are expressed as percentages, which are shown on the container, following the symbol of each nutrient and vary depending on maker and purpose. For instance, flower fertilizers will have a higher percentage of potassium and general use compounds will have equal amounts. Application rates will be supplied by the manufacturer. Time to apply is usually spring; some plants need a summer application as well, or vice versa; for instance roses need a second application in early summer, camellias in midsummer instead of spring.

Die-back of shoot tips often occurs on Jew's mallow *(right)*. The leaves of this fuchsia *(below)* are lacking in nutrients, caused by growing too long in the same compost.

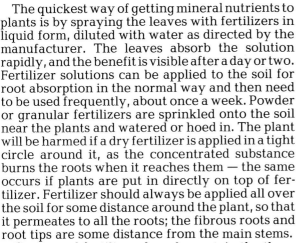

Weather damage

Wind and gales

Herbaceous plants can be broken down and blown over by strong winds: to prevent this, stake them securely when young. If a branch breaks off a tree, trim the wound left on the tree and treat it with fungicidal healing compound. Trees damaged by lightning should also be treated in this way. When a tree has actually been blown down, saw up as much as possible, take out the stump or, if not possible, saw it off cleanly at the top, seal the wound and use the stump as a support for climbers. If the stump is too short for climbers, peel off all bark and when it is finally dead, clear it away. There is no remedy for leaves torn off by summer gales, but it is advisable to grow a screen or hedge or put up some form of barrier against prevailing wind. Nor is there a remedy for the harm caused to leaves — brown and tattered edges — by a summer gale carrying salt spray. Barriers should be put up to prevent the prevailing wind bending trees and tall shrubs over in one direction. Wind-rock of inadequately supported, young trees will cause a hollow to form in the soil around the trunk, which will fill up with rainwater and rot the bark at the trunk base. Supports should immediately be renewed and strengthened, the hollow filled in and the wound painted with sealing compound.

Rain

Rain breaks flower spikes and beats down flowering stems, if these have not been securely staked when young. After prolonged wet periods or in very heavy soils, the leaves of shrubs, roses and trees will turn yellow near the base and be followed by the death of the whole plant. The soil will be waterlogged and there may also be soil-borne fungal diseases present, such as *Phytophthera cin-*

Wind can cause much damage, from blowing off leaves and twigs to uprooting large trees or breaking off branches *(above)*. Heavy rain will make the soil waterlogged, which can damage plants irretrievably by suffocating their roots. It can also beat down tall plants, such as perennials, and damage flowers and unopened buds, such as these roses *(below)*, causing spotting of the petals.

namomi, which will be able to get a firm grip on an already weakened plant. Remove the dead plants and improve the drainage as well as raising the height of the bed. Plant herbaceous plants on the site or build a rock garden with a pool.

Frost

Leaves and stems of tender plants, such as dahlias and nasturtiums, become blackened with frost; the tips of shoots on tender shrubs, such as rock rose (*cistus*), ceanothus and escallonia turn brown and the rest of the shoot dies progressively down the stem; small tender plants, such as bedding plants, are killed completely and the young leaves of roses shrivel and pucker and the shoot tips die. Prevent all this damage by covering the plants concerned with sacking where possible, scattered straw or polythene sheet or sacks — even netting affords some safeguard; remove the plants to the safety of a heated greenhouse, conservatory or home and do not plant outdoors too soon. If plants actually have ice on them, spray with cold water and leave them to thaw, out of the sun's rays. Rhododendron leaves will hang down in persistent

Frost damage on rhododendrons *(left)* can take the form of browning of the buds, thus killing them and destroying any future flowering display. It can also cause browning of the petals, and prolonged cold will cause the leaves to hang down, although they should not be damaged. Brown buds can also occur as a result of infection by a fungal disease, but you will recognize the difference as such buds will have black bristles all over them. There are various methods of protecting plants from the cold *(above)*: keep them in a closed frame over winter, opening it occasionally for ventilation in daytime; shield them from wind and frost with sacking, or a plastic sheet attached to posts so that the plant is still open to light and air; finally, wrap them up completely with a protective covering where winters are very severe, or the plant especially tender.

frost, but this is their method of protection and they are seldom damaged. Observe the parts of the garden where frost persists in winter and avoid planting anything but the most hardy plants there. Cold air will collect at the lowest point and build up, especially if there is a fence or wall preventing its onward flow. Gaps near the bottom of such barriers will allow the air to escape.

Snow and hail

If snow arrives before the ground becomes really frozen, it will act as a protective blanket, so that any frost that follows will be much less damaging. Snow is more likely to cause problems because of its weight, which will break down evergreen shrubs and trees. It also drifts on the ground, covering herbaceous plants and low growing shrubs, but damage here is less likely and less great. Knock snow off trees and shrubs if possible, but leave the smaller plants covered for protection. Lawns may have patches of pale yellow grass after heavy snow has been lying for a long time before melting; this is a fungal disease sometimes called snow mould (fusarium patch) which can kill the grass. Melting snow can lead to floods.

Hail tears leaves and flowers to shreds and makes pits in the skin of ornamental berries and fruits. Hail storms are sudden and violent, so ad-

vance protection is usually not possible, but fortunately they are infrequent.

Drought and heat
Leaves and flowers, particularly of herbaceous plants, wilt and hang down when waterless and will die in prolonged drought; many plants run to seed; new growth slows down and stops; lawn grass goes limp and discolours to a pale brown. The remedy is to water before signs of distress occur, as afterward is too late and can lead to further problems. If high temperatures are combined with drought, damage will be intensified and occur sooner.

If snow falls before the ground is frosted, it will act as a protective blanket, and any frost that comes after it will do much less damage (far left). However, heavy falls will break branches off trees and shrubs and flatten herbaceous plants (top). Excessive heat can also be a hazard. Light brown to beige-coloured patches will occur on young camellia leaves if they are grown in very sunny places (left). Prolonged hot weather will shrink, crack and split soil (above) so that roots may be damaged by tearing.

Bird and animal damage

Birds

Leaves, flowers and buds are likely to be pecked; soft fruit and berries on ornamentals may be attacked and, if left unprotected, seeds will be eaten and seed beds used as dust baths by sparrows. Starlings may attack lawns, but they are generally searching for and eating leatherjackets and do not feed on the grass.

To prevent further damage, netting can be spread temporarily over plants to protect buds. Repellant sprays or dusts can be applied, which last about six weeks and are unpleasant-tasting to birds, although harmless. These are not suitable for edible crops, however. Scarers, including strips of aluminium foil, scarecrows, balloons and windmills on stakes, have some temporary effect, but need to be changed or moved every few days. Another deterrent which works is the old-fashioned remedy of attaching black cotton or twine to canes or stakes above the plants.

Animal pests

Rodents, rabbits, hares, squirrels and wild deer will either gnaw or strip off bark and will also attack bulbs, leaves, shoots and flowers from shrubs and trees. Fruit, berries and seeds also need to be protected. Tunnelling moles seriously disrupt lawns and cultivated ground, causing rows of seeds or lawn edges to collapse. Cats and dogs will also dig up soil; bitches' urine can cause yellow patches on lawns. Various remedies can be tried for each problem.

Rodents Mouse-traps are an obvious possibility. Sweetpea seeds will need to be sown in trays or pots, and then planted outside as soon as they can be handled after germination. Protect bulbs in store by keeping them in tightly shut containers, preferably not made of wood; keep bases of tree trunks and shrubs clear of compost, leaf mould, straw, dead grass or any material suitable for nesting material; treat tulips with seed dressing.

Rabbits, hares and squirrels Supply wire-netting tree guards for tree trunks and the base of shrubs, to a height of 3-4ft (90-120cm); use wire-netting around beds and borders buried at least 12in (30cm) deep, and extending 3ft (90cm) high, and examine these frequently to ensure that there are no enlargements of the mesh to allow entry; use proprietary animal repellant sprays containing thiram, quassia or anthroquinone on ornamentals and crops where specified by the manufacturers; store bulbs and treat seeds in the same way as for mice protection.

Wild deer Protect tree trunks and shrub stems with individual wire-netting guards; put up sheep net-

ting fences to a height of 6ft (1.8m) so that the deer cannot jump over, and erect gates if necessary.

Moles A large part of a mole's diet consists of worms, which are more common in damp soil; much mole trouble is found near streams, marshy ground, natural ponds and lakes, but any fertile soil is likely to contain a good many worms. Soil which is friable and easily dug is also likely to be mole-infested. Anything with a strong smell, such as naphthalene, creosote or garlic, can act as a repellant; holly leaves, rose or bramble stems or other prickly plants placed in the tunnels are also effective. Traps can be set in the main tunnels or gas cartridges used to poison the animals. However, once moles have taken up residence, it is difficult to get rid of them permanently.

Cats and dogs Use animal repellant sprays and dusts as directed by the manufacturers; protect seed beds and borders with netting or prickly stemmed prunings; water grass and other areas copiously immediately after urination by bitches to minimize damage. Protect the bark of trees and shrubs with wire-netting guards.

Seeds and seedlings are frequently attacked by birds and rabbits, with birds scratching them up as they make dust baths, or actually eating the seeds, and rabbits eating the seedlings as they appear. Protection with wire-netting is effective and simple, and easy to put in place and remove *(far left)*. Squirrels will attack trees, gnawing the bark in small patches *(above)*, especially when winters are hard and prolonged, the grey squirrel can be very destructive in this way. Squirrels will also eat hazelnuts and walnuts and dig up bulbs, such as tulips and lilies. Wire-netting placed around tree trunks, and prickly material around bulbs, will help to deter these pests. Crocus bulbs are particularly popular with squirrels, and their flowers *(bottom left)* are attractive to sparrows. Damage by deer can often be quite serious. They will strip the bark off trees in winter *(top left)*, feeding at dawn and dusk, and in spring will feed on young shoots and leaves of shrubs as well as trees. Prevention can only adequately be affected with fences at least 6ft (1.8m) tall, using large mesh-netting, such as sheep-netting.

Problems with lawns

Brown patches

A wide variety of problems afflict lawns; luckily, only a few are likely to affect one lawn at a time. The most common symptom of trouble is brown, discoloured patches, spoiling the surface and appearance of the turf. There is no one cause or remedy for these ugly patches; the season in which they occur and the shape and colouration of the damaged areas are factors which will help to determine the cause of the problem. Causes include bird, pest and animal damage, scorching by fertilizer or petrol from a mower, problems with soil structure and balance, drought or excessive quantities of water and fungal disease.

The table outlines the times of year in which problems occur and gives causes and solutions.

Worms and worm casts

Worms can be troublesome in wet seasons and in permanently damp soils; their casts make mowing difficult and gradually ruin the soil structure, as well as infesting the turf. Worms do help with soil aeration, but there are generally so many of them that they tend to outweigh the good they do. Both brushing off the casts before mowing and improving drainage will help. Derris watered into the soil will kill worms, but it is extremely poisonous to fish and an alternative to use if there are streams or ponds nearby, is potassium permanganate, in the ratio ½oz to 1gal/sq yd (15g to 4.5 l/m²) of water. Worms thrive in alkaline soil, so it is advisable to use acidic fertilizers as a means of discouraging them.

BROWN PATCHES IN SPRING	BROWN PATCHES IN SUMMER	BROWN PATCHES IN AUTUMN
Light brown, irregularly shaped brown patches: resulting from leatherjackets eating the grass roots. Starlings piercing the lawn with their beaks is another indication. Water the area heavily and cover with sacking overnight. Collect up the grubs that appear on the surface and kill them. Dusting with HCH will kill off the remainder. *Small, medium brown patches*: caused by mowing with a power mower or one that has just been cleaned or oiled. Grass is likely to die, so area should be re-seeded and some of the soil replaced. Fill up with petrol and oil the mower away from the lawn. *Dark brown, almost black patches, following fertilizer application*: fertilizer scorch due to applications that are irregular and too heavy. Watering helps to disperse excess fertilizer. Fertilizer should be applied evenly, at the rate directed by the manufacturer, and watered in if advised. *Pale, yellowish brown patches, randomly distributed*: signifies localized compaction due to changes in soil type. Spike the areas concerned, repeating in autumn and after prolonged heavy rain. For long-term remedy, try to improve soil structure by top-dressing, regular spiking and, in bad cases, tile-drainage. *Small, deep brown, circular patches*: signifies dead grass due to bitch urine. Water copiously immediately.	*Pale, yellowish brown, circular patches, becoming large and pink-tinted*: caused by tiny red needles ¼in (6mm) long, attached to blades of grass, and known as red thread disease (*Corticium*). It does not kill the roots, but will kill the grass blades. Often seen if a lawn is grown on sandy soil, and in late summer. Feed and water the grass, and treat the disease with thiophanate-methyl or benomyl. *Pale brown patches*: occurs especially where the lawn is growing on sandy soil, eventually turning the entire lawn brown. Due to drought if hot, dry weather is occurring. Preceded by limp, dull green grass. Spike if the soil is penetrable, and water with spray lines or sprinkler. *Brown patches after mowing*: due to grass with long, creeping stems, which radiate from a central point, known as creeping bent (*Agrostis stolonifera*). This grass only has green blades at the tips of the stems. Appears and dominates where good lawn grasses have become weak. Rake up before mowing, and repeat at right angles; cut out worst patches with a sharp knife and re-seed. Feed, spike and keep the lawn well watered in dry weather. *Yellowish brown patches or lines; especially in dry weather*: due to bricks, stones or wood buried beneath lawn, or on old flowerbeds which have been turfed over. Remove rubbish and spike along lines, following with top-dressing mixture.	*Medium brown to rust coloured patches, spreading to 12in (30cm) wide*: due to infection by a fungal disease called fusarium patch. White fluff appears at the edge of the patches when dews are heavy or after wet weather, and they may be present after heavy snow has melted. Grass will die, so should be treated as soon as the patches are noticed after mowing, with thiophanate-methyl or benomyl. *Large, circular, brown patches, 1-3ft (30-90cm) wide, surrounded by a ring of dark green grass, containing toadstools*: due to fairy ring, where the threads of the fungus live in the soil and die there as soon as they have used up all the nutrients. They form a waxlike covering, which waterproofs the soil and kills the grass. The toadstools and threads at the edge of the ring extend the affected area continuously. Control is difficult. Try to dig out the turf and soil well below the area invaded by the white threads, and beyond the diameter of the ring. Replace with fresh soil and re-seed. The contaminated soil should be entirely removed from the garden. *Small yellowish brown to yellow patches*: due to infection by dollar spot disease (*sclerotina*) in lawns with a lot of red fescue (*Festuca rubra rubra*) and especially in mild, damp weather. Treat with thiophanate-methyl or benomyl and feed the grass with high-potash compound fertilizer or high-nitrogen in spring.

There are a number of reasons why moss may appear prolifically on lawns *(far left)*. It generally indicates weak grass, and damp conditions will encourage the moss to spread. Fairy rings *(left* and *below)* consist of rings of toadstools, which are the fruiting bodies of various fungi living in the soil. They do not always cause trouble. However, there is one type that is harmful, because the fungal threads in the soil, which are covered in wax, effectively waterproof the soil so that it becomes dry and kills the grass inside the ring.

Burrowing bees

Although not directly damaging to grass, these solitary bees dig out a hole up to 12in (30cm) deep, leaving the soil in a mound outside on the grass. At the bottom they make a nest. They are active in spring and pollinate fruit trees; after this no fresh burrows are made. The mounds can easily be swept away, without using chemical controls.

Moss

It is impossible to find a lawn that is moss-free. This growth will slowly increase while the grass is virtually dormant and the soil and atmosphere permanently moist and can eventually get out of hand. It may be because the soil is heavy, inadequately drained and aerated, or because of grass starvation, mainly a fault of light soil, but also possible in other soil types. Moss can also spread in extremely acid soil or on shady lawns or where grass is cut too close. It will also increase in autumn after a dry summer, if the lawn has not been watered.

Moss which is established can be eradicated with a moss-killing chemical called dichlorophen. There is also a product available containing this and other ingredients, which keeps the moss at bay for the rest of the growing season as well as feeding the grass. Another moss-killer is lawn-sand. Dead moss can be raked out, but trying to remove living moss by raking will only cause more trouble in the long run by spreading living moss plants and moss spores.

For long-term control, the aeration of the lawn should be put right, nutrient supplied, acidity corrected by liming over two or three years, shade resistant grasses sown, the height of cut increased — ½in (1.2cm) is about right — and water supplied during drought. Shade is the most difficult to adjust; the grass still tends to die and you may have to resign yourself to moss in these areas, or pave or put plants there.

Dog lichen

Lawns on sandy soils are frequently overrun by this growth, which produces patches of leathery, flat tissue, rounded and with a ragged edge, growing from a central point. Colour is black-grey on the upper side, and white-grey on the lower. The grass dies beneath the patches, and the lichen is slippery when wet. The whole lawn will need a good deal of invigorating by feeding, spiking, top-dressing and weed control. Any lichen actually present should be treated with dichlorophen.

Algae

Green, jelly-like patches or black slime coating the grass are sometimes found on lawns which are very wet — beneath the drip line of trees, for instance, or on newly seeded lawns where the soil structure is not as good as it might be. If they keep returning after removal, dichlorophen or lawn-sand, as for dog lichen, will be temporarily effective, but soil-drainage correction is important for permanent prevention.

Areas and treatments

Site problems, of one kind or another, are evident in every garden. Areas where, for whatever reason, plants are difficult to grow, can rapidly develop into eyesores, harbouring pests and weeds which may threaten the rest of the garden. Careful selection of plants can go a long way toward overcoming the problems presented by awkward locations. Many plants are specifically adapted to conditions that are generally inhospitable; others can be used to disguise unattractive features or brighten a dull corner.

From the gardener's point of view, the amount of time and effort that can be spared for working in the garden are just as important determining factors. Here, again, selecting the right plants and careful design consideration can help to create a garden which is labour-saving as well as attractive.

Difficult conditions

Shade

Most ornamental garden plants are grown for their flowers, and many of these need actual sunlight, not just daylight. But a surprising number will either flower in shade or need shade in order to flower. Shade varies in degree, too; it can be light or dappled, where light filters through small trees, shrubs or fencing; or it can be deep and permanent. The soil in shady areas is often responsible for lack of growth. It can either be wet and badly areated or dry, because tree roots suck up the moisture or the canopy is too heavy to allow rain to penetrate. The soil must be carefully examined first, then suitable material added to supply humus and grit for drainage, or nutrients if it is sandy. Digging alone will improve matters in most cases; if tree roots are an obstruction use a hand-fork and deal with a pocket of soil at a time.

Above and **left** Foxgloves are easily grown plants, and are naturally found in areas of light woodland, where there is some shade during the day. They self-seed, and there are many hybrids in various shades of pink, purple, cream and yellow.

Plants suitable for growing in shady conditions	
Ajuga reptans	Hedera spp
Aquilegia	Helleborus
Japanese anemone	Heuchera
Bergenia	Hosta
Cyclamen	Lilium
Dicentra spectabilis	Lysimachia
Digitalis	Narcissus
Deutzia	Primula
Endymion	Polygonatum
Camellia	Rhododendron
Ferns	Vinca

Lysimachia punctata also enjoys shade as well as moisture, and can be situated in borders or by water *(far left)*. *Lysimachia nummularia (centre top left)* is a particularly useful species as it will also thrive in dry sites. The hosta is another ideal plant for the shady spots *(centre bottom left* and *below left)*. They are noted for their mass of attractive foliage as well as their tubular flowers

Damp or wet soil

Bog or water-loving plants require this type of soil, but excess moisture will have to be removed if other plants are expected to grow. One method of improving conditions is to dig down to a depth of one or two spits and mix grit into all levels of the soil; or to dig a trench 12-18in (30-45cm) deep and either half fill it with brushwood, replacing the topsoil, or quarter fill it with rubble, quarter with brushwood and the remaining half with topsoil. Use tile-drains, if all else fails. Imported soil can be used to build raised beds or, if there is a sunny place, a rock garden could be built.

Plants suitable for growing in damp or wet soil	
Alnus	Lysimachia
Japanese anemone	Mimulus
Astilbe	Primula
Caltha	Polyanthus
Hemerocallis	Pulmonaria
Hosta	Rodgersia
Iris	Salix

Left *Rodgersia pinnata* 'Superba' is a useful plant as it may be grown satisfactorily in any damp site, such as by a stream or pool. Large bronze-purple leaves and pink flowers are produced in mid-summer and the genus was originally a native of China and Japan.

If you are faced with a damp patch of garden, marsh marigolds are the ideal plants to grow. *Caltha palustris* is able to thrive in water, 6in (15cm) deep, and flowers profusely in shades of golden-yellow in mid-spring *(above)*. *Primula denticulata*, or the drumstick primula, is another border plant, which thrives in damp, waterlogged conditions *(left)*. It flowers throughout the spring in purplish colours. The monkey flower also grows naturally in boggy conditions. *Mimulus luteus* is a useful species as it grows as a mat-like cover, producing attractive yellow flowers, often with red markings *(below left)*.

Dry soil

Dry patches can occur anywhere in the garden: in open, sunny positions, under trees and especially at the foot of walls facing the sun. To moisten the soil, work in organic material in early spring and again in early summer, which will act as a sponge and help retain the water. This should be followed by a heavy mulch of the same material, which must be placed on moist soil to trap the moisture and keep in the soil warmth. If no vegetative mulch is possible, stones used as a continuous covering will keep the soil moist; so will black polythene sheet, straw or sawdust. Supply nutrients little and often, and make watering these areas a priority in drought; keep a good stock of watering equipment handy, and arrange for at least one standpoint in the garden.

Potentilla fruticosa 'Katherine Dykes' grows to a height of 4ft (1.2m) and requires a dry, sunny position *(left)*. *Achillea filipendulina* is a suitable plant for rock gardens *(below)*.

Plants suitable for growing in dry soil		
Achillea	Genista	Potentilla
Alyssum	Geranium	Sedum spp
Allium spp	Helianthemum	Sempervivum
Artemisia	Iberis	Salvia
Campanula	Phlomis	Tulipa
Cistus	Santolina	Verbascum
Cytisus	Lavandula	Veronica
Eschscholzia		

Sedums are ideal wall plants, with their unusually shaped leaves and flowers *(above)*. They flourish in dry conditions and can survive well in prolonged droughts. Another such plant is the rosette-shaped houseleek (Sempervivum) *(left)*. The curved leaves are often purple-tipped.

Right Alliums are easy to grow, and are often found growing wild in temperate regions. They are bulbous plants, preferring a sandy soil and sunny position. Some have a distinctive onion smell.

Acid soil

Fortunately the majority of plants will thrive in any soil regardless of its pH level, but there is a small group which can only be grown easily in acid soil. It is possible, however, to grow any of these in a lime-containing soil, if the soil is suitably prepared. Either dig out a pit and fill it with specially mixed compost whose reaction is acid, or water plants annually with sequestered (chelated) iron, magnesium and manganese, formulated in one product. Otherwise, the pH level of the soil can be gradually altered with rotted organic matter, acidic fertilizers, and flowers of sulphur, but this is a slow method and, in the case of the sulphur, fraught with danger, as the chemical balance of the soil can be detrimentally altered.

The majority of calcifuges (lime-hating) plants are shrubby; virtually all conifers grow much better in acid conditions. However, some plants are border-line calcifuges, such as camellia, enkianthus, fothergilla, magnolia and mahonia, and, although they will grow in neutral soils, they will do better if helped with leaf mould or a similar material. Hydrangeas will need acid or alkaline soil depending on the flower colour.

Rhododendrons *(above)* will not grow well in alkaline soil and will even struggle in a neutral one. An acid-reacting soil is essential, preferably containing leaf-mould, to produce a longer-living and more floriferous shrub. *Pieris formosa* 'Forestii' *(left)* is another acid-loving plant. Its young leaves are coloured brilliant red, providing contrast with its sprays of white lily-of-the-vally-type flowers. In suitable conditions it will grow to at least 15ft (4.5m).

Plants suitable for growing in acid soil	
Calluna	Lupinus
Camellia	Lithospermum
Chimonanthus	Lilium
Daboecia	Magnolia
Erica	Mahonia
Ferns	Pieris
Fothergilla	Rhododendron
Gentiana	Vaccinium
Hamamelis	

Wind

Wind can be a serious problem, and gardens that are exposed need to have screening and protecting plants put in as a major priority, otherwise nothing will grow satisfactorily. The problem is doubled in coastal gardens where salt is carried on the wind, but fortunately there are barrier plants which do not burn brown in a salty gale. Shrubs and trees which will provide good dense screens are advisable.

Plants suitable for growing as windbreaks	
Aucuba japonica	Ilex
Arundinaria japonica	*Ligustrum ovalifolium*
Berberis darwinii	*Lonicera nitida*
Berberis stenophylla	*Picea omorika*
Chamaecyparis	*Pinus mugo*
Corylus avellana	*Pinus nigra*
Crataegus oxyacantha	*Prunus laurocerasus*
Cupressocyparis leylandii	*Prunus spinosa*
Deutzia escallonia	Pyracantha
Euonymus japonicus	Tamarix
Fagus sylvatica	*Ulex europaeus*
Hippophae rhamnoides	Viburnum

The Lawson cypress *(above)* will grow into a good windbreak, given time. It is advisable, however, to shield it from prevailing winds just after planting, for about three years until it has established. It is a quick-growing shrub and can be obtained with foliage in various colours. Beech hedges make a good, formal, dense barrier *(far left)*, useful for privacy and as a windbreak, and although they are deciduous shrubs, they retain their green-coloured leaves in winter, when they change to russet-brown. In very exposed positions, they should be shielded for their first two years. Berberis *(left and below)* is a prolific flowering shrub, with berries and prickly, sometimes evergreen leaves. It is an excellent informal hedge.

Problem areas

Plants suitable for growing in odd corners	
Agapanthus	Lathyrus
Alchemilla mollis	Lavandula
Alstroemeria	Lilium
Calendula	Nasturtium
Campanula	Rosa spp
Elaeagnus maculata	Vaccinium
Erica	*Verbascum bombyciferum*
Helleborus	Yucca
Hosta	

Nasturtiums *(far left)* will quickly fill an odd corner with their bright-coloured blooms and continue to flower all summer with very little attention. *Campanula cochlearifolia (left)* is another easily grown plant, fitting into any spare corner, and flowering profusely in summer. It is a low-growing perennial, spreading by creeping underground stems. One of the most attractive of the campanulas, *C. carpatica (below)*, is distinguished by its large, bell-shaped flowers.

Odd corners

However carefully designed a garden is, however good the general health of all the other plants in the garden, there are always places that do not fit into the scheme, or where plants obstinately refuse to grow. Large, outstanding, eye-catching plants are useful for filling out these awkwardly shaped or solitary patches. However, not all plants will be immediately suitable and it will be necessary to analyze any such site problems. Temperature, exposure to draughts or strong winds, bad ventilation or shade can all create problem areas. The soil is another obvious suspect: very acid, very alkaline, starved of food, always dry or permanently waterlogged and sour. There may be rotting wood, bricks, tins, stones, or pollution such as oil or creosote underneath the top few spadefuls of soil, or perhaps the soil is only a few inches deep on top of solid clay or chalk subsoil, or there may be slates or a drain-pipe.

If it is a question of aspect and plants are not growing, then it is a case of choosing plants to fit the micro-climate; if it is the soil, then replace it completely if possible, otherwise improve it. Plants are always riddled with pests or diseases when they are struggling, and better growing conditions for the plants will automatically reduce their enemies to negligible numbers. If all else fails, try carpeting plants or pave the whole area and grow plants in containers.

Long narrow passages

The corridors found between houses or sheds and fences are nearly always shady and draughty, and the soil, if there is a bed, is often a haunt of cats. Tough plants are needed, upright rather than bushy in habit, and decorative without flowers. There is usually only room to make use of one wall or fence, and any herbaceous plants should ideally be tall or ground-hugging and slug-resistant.

Rose of Sharon (*Hypericum calycinum*) is a wiry stemmed, tough-rooted perennial with evergreen leaves (*below* and *bottom*). It is a good plant for growing on banks. Bear's breeches (*Acanthus mollis*) is an attractive herbaceous perennial (*right*), with a tall, spire-like flower stem, useful for long, upright spaces.

Plants suitable for growing in long, narrow passages	
Acanthus mollis	Heuchera
Japanese anemone	Hypericum calycinum
Chaenomeles	Jasminum nudiflorum
Convallaria majalis	Lonicera periclymenum
Doronicum	Lysimachia punctata
Ferns	Montbretia
Forsythia suspensa sieboldii	Pyracantha 'Watereri'
Garrya elliptica	Saxifraga x urbium
Hedera	Verbascum

Blank vertical surfaces

Brick walls, continuous wooden fencing and house and garage walls all look bleak and forbidding, particularly in winter, in even the most attractive and well-designed of gardens. Living cover for these surfaces is easier on the eye and provides a link between architecture and garden. It also provides more scope for planting choice. If concrete, paving or brick covers the soil at the foot of these vertical surfaces, tubs and large troughs containing good potting compost will enable surprisingly large, wall and climbing plants to be grown.

Plants suitable for growing against blank, vertical spaces	
Actinidia kolomikta	Lathyrus odoratus
Campsis 'Madame Galen'	Lonicera periclymenum
Ceanothus 'Gloire de Versailles'	Parthenocissus quinquefolia
Clematis	Parthenocissus henryana
Eccremocarpus scaber	Passiflora caerulea
Hedera	Pyracantha 'Watereri'
Humulus lupulus 'Aureus'	Rosa
Jasminum nudiflorum	Solanum jasminoides
Jasminum officinale	Vitis coignetiae

Parthenocissus henryana (*right*) is a form of Virginia creeper, but with dark green leaves marked with silver and pink. It is particularly effective if it is planted against a sheltered wall. It is a deciduous shrub and climbs by sticky tendrils. The ivies (*below*) are extremely useful shrubs. They not only make excellent ground-cover, but also successfully clothe vertical surfaces, as well as sloping sites. Plain, green-leaved kinds can be mixed with the variegated-leaved types to create a patchwork effect.

Steep slopes or banks

The problem here is threefold: which species to grow on such a site, how to make it ornamental and how to retain the soil. Furthermore, since the angle is difficult to stand on, the plants should not need much care and attention. A laborious and expensive alternative to plants is to terrace the site and build retaining walls, but this may not be practicable. Trailing or creeping plants are good; there are some tough, low-growing species, too, which need little care and will bind the soil.

Plants suitable for growing on steep banks	
Ajuga reptans	Hedera
Bergenia	Helianthemum
Calluna vulgaris	Hypericum calycinum
Campanula portenschlagiana	Juniperus horizontalis
Campanula poscharskyana	Lamiastrum galeobdolon
Cerastium tomentosum	Lamium maculatum
Cotoneaster dammeri	Lonicera japonica halliana
Cotoneaster horizontalis	Saxifraga x urbium
Cytisus x kewensis	Sedum spurium
Erica	Thymus serpyllum
Fragaria indica	Vinca major
Genista lydia	Vinca minor
Hebe pinguifolia	Viola odorata

Cerastium tomentosum (*below left*) will help to hold crumbling banks together, and provide an attractive silvery effect all year. However, it is inclined to spread, so should be sited with care. The periwinkle (*above left*) will grow in sun or shade, although preferring sun. Its stems root as they grow along the ground, and it provides good, labour-free cover on any sloping site. Deadnettles (*above*) also cover the ground well and need no attention.

Neglected gardens

Gardens which have not been looked after for several months or years, for whatever reason, turn into a daunting jungle of growth. Coherent planning can seem impossible when the whole garden needs attention at once. However, it is possible to tame it and bring it into some sort of order fairly quickly if you are organized.

Start by clearing a path into the middle of the site, or to any convenient point, and make a site for a bonfire. Then decide on a place for a compost

Neglected gardens *(above)*, will have lawns like hayfields, and herbaceous borders reduced to a tangle of weeds and shrubs. This sight may look daunting at first, but can be satisfactorily retrieved if it is dealt with systematically. Cutting down overgrown grass, and getting rid of weeds and leaves will help to discover the basic design of a neglected garden. Raking up the debris at the start *(right)* will reveal the original lawns and beds and also provide compost material.

heap. Using the path as a focal point, go through the garden marking clearly and distinctively the plants that seem worth keeping. At the same time look for the outlines of lawns, beds and borders. Cut the lawn short with a billhook or rotary mower and clear the beds section by section, working from the house outwards. This can be done by cutting back the shrubs and trees first and piling them into a barrow. Any unwanted plants, weeds, brambles, seedling trees and saplings must be removed with a fork, mattock, secateurs or loppers and destroyed. If patches of troublesome weeds (colt's-foot, ground-elder) infest the ground, remove the top growth and come back to them later.

Once this has been done, tidy and clear out retained plants by removing dead and broken leaves, stems and branches, faded flowers, broken rotting material and decaying tubers, bulbs and berries. If the lawn is beyond redemption, kill it with paraquat/diquat and start again, but do not try to do this early on, as it will become a quagmire or crack in drought, if not dealt with immediately. New plantings should not be attempted in the first year as the cleared ground needs to be left fallow.

Lack of time

For those who garden against the clock or lack enthusiasm, a garden which looks after itself is the ideal. Unfortunately, many gardens are designed in such a way that they require constant attention in order to keep them decorative and under control. There are ways, however, of overcoming this incessant labour problem.

First do without a lawn, if at all possible, and replace it with flowerbeds or paving. But if a lawn is essential, keep it small or grow alternatives to grass such as chamomile, creeping thyme *(Thymus serpyllum)* or pennyroyal *(Mentha pulegium)*.

Flowerbeds should be completely filled with plants, so that there is no room for weeds to grow. It also helps to use perennial plants, which do not need constant planting, sowing, thinning and weeding; and to avoid bedding plants, which need greenhouse protection when young, and planting out in great numbers to produce a satisfactory show. Do not grow large-flowered (hybrid tea) or cluster-flowered (floribunda) roses as they need successive pruning, feeding, digging, weeding, spraying, deadheading and mulching, but concentrate on old-fashioned shrub roses instead. Honeysuckle, climbing roses, ivy and jasmine are good climbers because they can be virtually left to their own devices. It is useful to grow as many bulbs as possible, except tulips and gladioli, which are dug up after flowering and replanted.

Grow herbaceous perennials which do not need staking and plant shrubs, which cover a lot of ground per shrub and only really need pruning. If you have to dig a plant up and get rid of it, replant at once with another plant, otherwise weeds will take its place. Do not have a rock garden but aim to grow plants which are happy in your soil and climate; apart from other considerations this will eliminate a good deal of spraying for pests and disease. Make sure there is sufficient space for plants to grow to their natural size. If it is necessary to plant hedges, use informal, flowering ones which only need pruning.

Left and **above left** These two gardens illustrate what is possible for the gardener who is short of time, short of labour, or even short of interest. A completely paved area is suitable for a small town garden, with one small flowerbed and containers to provide colour *(above left)*. There is no grass to mow, and the containers only need attention in spring, with titivating at other times. The small flower border can be planted with herbaceous perennials, rather than bedding plants or annuals, both of which can be bought rather than grown from seed. The larger paved area has been treated according to its bigger size *(left)*. Spaces have been left in the paving for planting evergreens, which supply green in winter, or flowering plants, which can also be permanent.

Greenhouses

The size of a greenhouse is very important as, the smaller it is, the more difficult it is to control the temperature. It will change very rapidly from very hot to very cold, so that 10x8ft (3x2.4m) should be the minimum size. Ventilators are a vital part, especially in the roof where there should be at least two, one on each side of the ridge. They are also important beneath the staging.

It is advisable to look for greenhouses with the minimum amount of framework which will admit as much light as possible. Aluminium alloy structures are good because they let in maximum light, but need little upkeep. (The inside of any greenhouse, however, will need disinfecting at least once a year, including the staging and all the equipment.) Horticultural glass should be of the grade weighing 24oz/sq ft (750g/30cm²) without bubbles, and shatterproof glazing made of polycarbonate sheet is obtainable. Remember that houses glazed to ground level let in more light, but let out more heat than those with half walls. If plants are to be grown in the soil, they will need the greater degree of light. Shading will be necessary in summer to prevent the temperature in the greenhouse from rising too high. Look for greenhouses with a doorway wide enough to take a wheelbarrow, and tall enough for your own height, for example, 2½x6ft (75x180cm). In some models sliding doors tend to fill up with soil in the slot at ground level. If the pitch of the roof is greater than 30°, it is likely to collapse under the weight of a heavy snowfall.

Run the greenhouse from north to south to give all the plants equal light, especially if it is going to be used in winter for crops. Align it east-west to grow a mixture of plants, some of which prefer cooler and less well-lit conditions. Position it away from anything which may cast shade onto it, particularly trees which will shed leaves in autumn, although if it is reasonably adjacent to the home it will be easier to deal with watering, heating and electricity. Make sure it is on a dry site. A concrete path in the centre cuts down mess and is easy to keep clean and work on, but slabs of paving can be substituted which can be removed or, less conveniently, duckboards can be used. Staging should be of a height convenient for working on, and can be of wood and wooden slats, or metal with removable, metal trays, or a mixture of the two.

Florist's chrysanthemums may be early or late flowering, depending on their natural flowering time. They are classified according to their flower shapes. Those with five or six rows of petals around a central eye are the single-flowered type (above). Celosia is another greenhouse plant, which is only suitable for outdoor planting in summer bedding. C. argentea 'Cristata' (cockscomb) is an attractive dwarf plant with an unusual crested flower head (right).

Greenhouses come in four basic designs (left): the round or hexagonal shape (1); the lean-to variety (2); the sloping-sided or Dutch type (3) and finally, (right) the vertical-sided greenhouse. The hexagonal greenhouse is useful for displaying ornamental plants, but is not the most practical type. The lean-to structure is generally more heat-retaining than other models, especially if it is situated against a wall facing the sun. On all greenhouses it is important to note that the roof must be sloping at such an angle that no debris is able to collect on top. This would prevent sufficient light from entering the house. The sloping-sided, or Dutch, greenhouse is a useful design, as it allows the maximum amount of light to enter. The slanting sides capture and transmit sunlight, although if they are erected at too great an angle, the space inside will be affected. Glass walls right down to the ground also means that additional light is admitted. This makes most use of the space available as plants may also be grown under the staging. The vertical-sided greenhouse is generally the most popular and versatile structure, and is suitable for most plants.

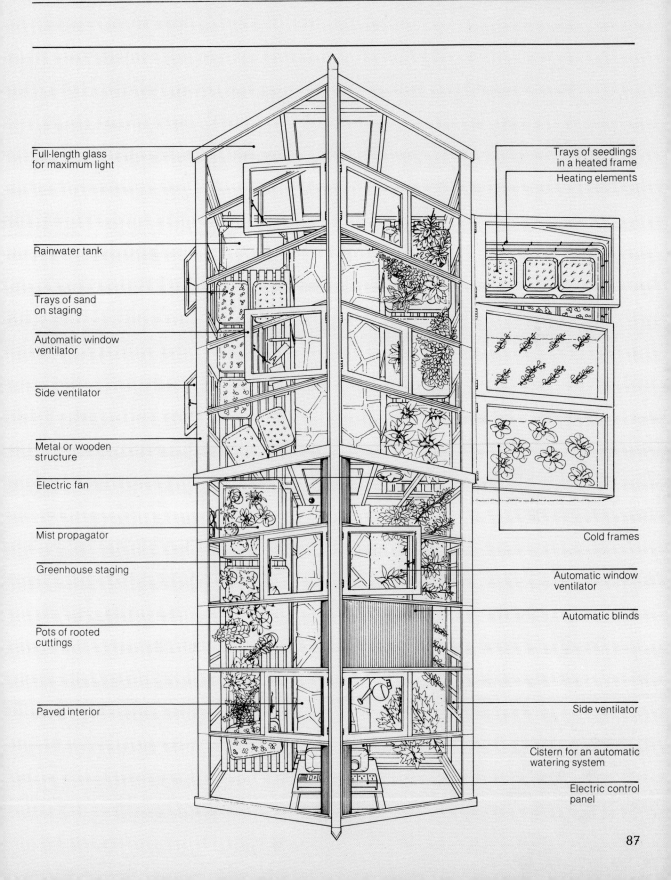

Full-length glass
for maximum light

Rainwater tank

Trays of sand
on staging

Automatic window
ventilator

Side ventilator

Metal or wooden
structure

Electric fan

Mist propagator

Greenhouse staging

Pots of rooted
cuttings

Paved interior

Trays of seedlings
in a heated frame

Heating elements

Cold frames

Automatic window
ventilator

Automatic blinds

Side ventilator

Cistern for an automatic
watering system

Electric control
panel

Gardening for the disabled

A disability usually means that heavy garden work involving carrying, prolonged deep digging, sawing and mowing is out of the question. However, designing the garden and choosing plants can be done and most people with a disablement can also do work such as hand-forking, sowing seeds, taking cuttings, deadheading and titivating, pruning, picking, hoeing and a little light forking and container-growing, provided plastic pots and soilless compost are used.

It helps to put in raised beds up to waist height. These make working with the plants easier — annuals, alpines, many perennials, bulbs or bedding plants, vegetables and fruit such as strawberries and melons can be planted in this way.

Paths should be of firm material such as concrete or paving if gardening is done from a wheelchair, and have slopes and ramps rather than steps, with sufficient width allowed in all cases for a wheelchair. The right tools are a great asset, too, as they can do much of the work that hands cannot do or that is prohibited by stiff backs and knees. Some manufacturers now provide specially adapted tools for digging and hoeing without bending, for extending to parts of a bed that are difficult to reach, for picking up or holding and for carrying. There are also gadgets for helping anyone without sight to sow seed in rows or prick out at even spacings, to measure pesticides and fertilizers, and to weigh out specified quantities. Anyone without sight will want plants with aromatic odours, so herbs are a good idea as their chief quality lies in the leaf aroma, and not in their appearance.

1 Angelica
2 Fennel
3 Meadowsweet
4 Marjoram
5 Thyme
6 Mint
7 Woodruff

Careful planning needs to go into designing a garden for the disabled *(below)*. Lawns should be avoided, as, besides needing heavy manual work, they are not easy to manoeuvre on if gardening is done from a wheelchair. Open areas should be covered with paving stones. Flowerbeds should be raised up to a height of 1-1½ft (30-45cm) for easier access. Ramps are more practical than steps if different ground levels are present. Careful choice of plants is another consideration. Aromatic herbs are often popular for their practical use and also for their scent *(below left)*.

Aromatic plants		
Basil	Geranium	Marjoram
Chives	Hyacinth	Rose
Chrysanthemum	Lemon balm	Rosemary
Curry plant	Lilac	Savory
Fennel	Lily	Tarragon

Geraniums *(left)* are often a popular plant because they will grow in a great variety of places, from rock gardens to borders and groundcover. *Philadelphus* 'Avalanche' *(above)* is an extremely attractive plant, and is also easy to grow. One of its chief qualities, however, is its pungent aroma of orange blossom. The table *(above)* lists some of the other plants and herbs that are particularly fragrant.

Garden plants A-Z

Whichever plant you choose to grow in your garden, it is important to provide the right conditions and care. The needs of different plants vary, and so do the pests and diseases to which they are susceptible. Plant by plant, this alphabetical section provides all the information necessary for successful gardening, from special growing requirements to individual problems and solutions.

Common name(s)

Plant type

Family

Genus

Background information on the plant, its origins, flowering times, colours and popular species and varieties

Pests and diseases likely to affect the plant — advice is given on how to treat the problem where the infection is specific to the plant; treatment for common problems is outlined in the section in Chapter 2 (pages 48-71)

Illustrations of popular plant species and varieties, or common symptoms of pests and diseases and the effects of improper care

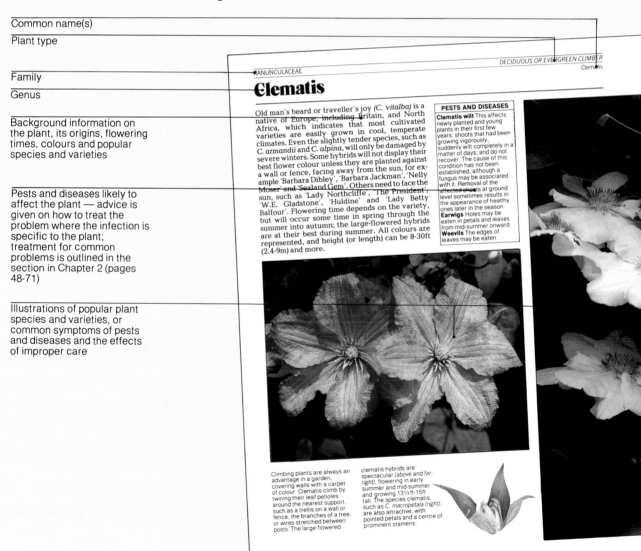

DECIDUOUS OR EVERGREEN CLIMBER
Clematis

RANUNCULACEAE

Clematis

Old man's beard or traveller's joy *(C. vitalba)* is a native of Europe, including Britain, and North Africa, which indicates that most cultivated varieties are easily grown in cool, temperate climates. Even the slightly tender species, such as *C. armandii* and *C. alpina*, will only be damaged by severe winters. Some hybrids will not display their best flower colour unless they are planted against a wall or fence, facing away from the sun, for example 'Barbara Dibley', 'Barbara Jackman', 'Nelly Moser' and 'Sealand Gem'. Others need to face the sun, such as 'Lady Northcliffe', 'The President', 'W.E. Gladstone', 'Huldine' and 'Lady Betty Balfour'. Flowering time depends on the variety, but will occur some time in spring through the summer into autumn; the large-flowered hybrids are at their best during summer. All colours are represented, and height (or length) can be 8-30ft (2.4-9m) and more.

PESTS AND DISEASES

Clematis wilt This affects newly planted and young plants in their first few years; shoots that had been growing vigorously, suddenly wilt completely in a matter of days, and do not recover. The cause of this condition has not been established, although a fungus may be associated with it. Removal of the affected shoots at ground level sometimes results in the appearance of healthy ones later in the season.
Earwigs Holes may be eaten in petals and leaves from mid-summer onward.
Weevils The edges of leaves may be eaten.

Climbing plants are always an advantage in a garden, covering walls with a carpet of colour. Clematis climb by twining their leaf petioles around the nearest support, such as a trellis on a wall or fence, the branches of a tree, or wires stretched between posts. The large-flowered clematis hybrids are spectacular *(above and far-right)*, flowering in early summer and mid-summer and growing 13½ft-15ft tall. The species clematis, such as *C. macropetala (right)*, are also attractive, with pointed petals and a centre of prominent stamens.

110

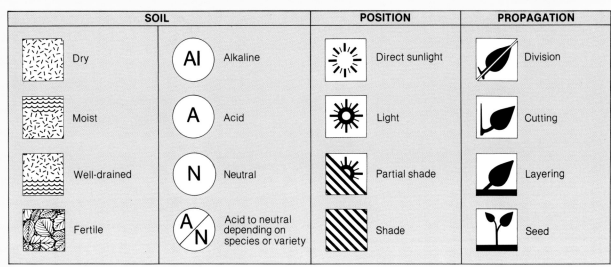

SOIL				POSITION		PROPAGATION	
	Dry	Al	Alkaline		Direct sunlight		Division
	Moist	A	Acid		Light		Cutting
	Well-drained	N	Neutral		Partial shade		Layering
	Fertile	A/N	Acid to neutral depending on species or variety		Shade		Seed

Green indicates correct condition(s) or type of care.

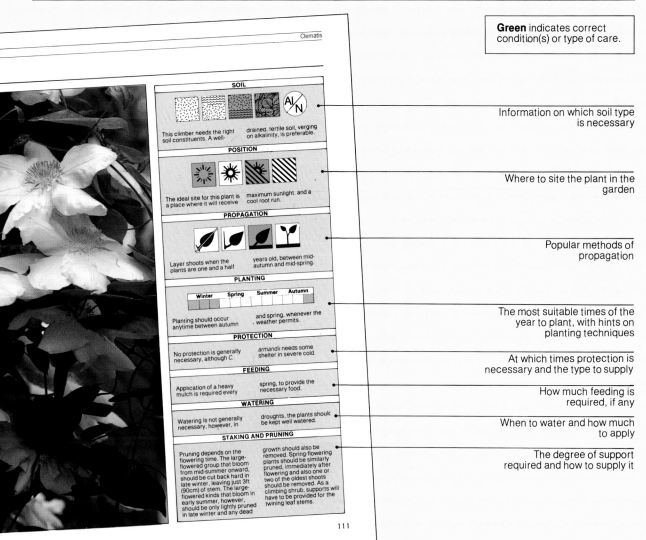

Clematis

SOIL

This climber needs the right soil constituents. A well- drained, fertile soil, verging on alkalinity, is preferable.

Information on which soil type is necessary

POSITION

The ideal site for this plant is a place where it will receive maximum sunlight, and a cool root run.

Where to site the plant in the garden

PROPAGATION

Layer shoots when the plants are one and a half years old, between mid-autumn and mid-spring.

Popular methods of propagation

PLANTING

Winter	Spring	Summer	Autumn

Planting should occur anytime between autumn and spring, whenever the weather permits.

The most suitable times of the year to plant, with hints on planting techniques

PROTECTION

No protection is generally necessary, although C. armandii needs some shelter in severe cold.

At which times protection is necessary and the type to supply

FEEDING

Application of a heavy mulch is required every spring, to provide the necessary food.

How much feeding is required, if any

WATERING

Watering is not generally necessary, however, in droughts, the plants should be kept well watered.

When to water and how much to apply

STAKING AND PRUNING

Pruning depends on the flowering time. The large-flowered group that bloom from mid-summer onward, should be cut back hard in late winter, leaving just 3ft (90cm) of stem. The large-flowered kinds that bloom in early summer, however, should be only lightly pruned in late winter and any dead growth should also be removed. Spring-flowering plants should be similarly pruned, immediately after flowering and also one or two of the oldest shoots should be removed. As a climbing shrub, supports will have to be provided for the twining leaf stems.

The degree of support required and how to supply it

111

91

Agapanthus

These plants are natives of South Africa where they flourish in the warm climate. Their inability to survive cold was a major problem when attempts were made to cultivate them in cooler climates. However, a race called the Headbourne hybrids has overcome this, provided they are planted in a sunny place with shelter from cold winds.

The plants produce clusters of beautiful, mid- or sky-blue, bell-like flowers in summer on stems 2ft (60cm) high, which emerge from a bunch of strap-shaped leaves of the same length.

Below The blue lily of the Nile, agapanthus, is one of the most ornamental of perennials to be grown in recent years, and the Headbourne hybrids are hardy in all except the most severe cold, provided some protection is given in winter.

PESTS AND DISEASES
Agapanthus do not suffer from many pests or diseases. **Mealy bugs** may be found. **Leaf-tip die-back** may also afflict this plant. It should be treated with a copper spray.

Right Agapanthus provide a lovely splash of blue when other flowers are beginning to fade. Each head of flowers contains at least 20 individual florets and is about 3-4in (7-10cm) wide. The flowers last about a month.

SOIL

Any fertile soil that is well drained will provide a suitable base for these plants. The soil should previously be treated with leaf-mould.

POSITION

The African lily needs to be situated in direct sunlight, and in a spot that is sheltered from the wind.

PROPAGATION

Division and replanting in late spring, or sowing seed, are the best methods of propagation for these plants.

PLANTING

Winter	Spring	Summer	Autumn

Plant in spring, taking care of the fleshy, but brittle roots. These can be easily bruised and broken, causing the death of the plant. The roots must be spread out carefully, and soil crumbled over them to fill in the hole. Do not bury the crown and make sure the join between the leaves and roots is level with the soil surface.

PROTECTION
Protection against the cold is essential, especially during the first winter. Heavy mulching is advisable, or a plastic sheet covering.

FEEDING
A leaf-mould mulch, applied in mid-summer, will do much to encourage vigorous and healthy growth.

WATERING
Watering the young plants is important, and also whenever prolonged periods of drought occur.

STAKING AND PRUNING
Provided the plants are situated in a sheltered position, they should not require any staking. There is no need to prune either.

Althaea

Hollyhocks derive their common name from *halig*, 'holy' and *hoc*, a 'mallow'. These are both Anglo-saxon words — mallows are members of the same plant family — and hollyhocks are said to have been brought back from the Holy Land by the Crusaders in the Middle Ages. Like so many plants that have been grown for centuries, the hollyhock had many medicinal applications, one of which was to coagulate blood.

It is another much-loved, cottage garden plant, often seen growing close to the walls of the cottage itself, where it towers up to between 6-8ft (1.8-2.4m) tall. *A. rosea* is originally a native of China, but now also grows wild in Asia, including the Middle East, and in Europe and North America. Although hardy, this plant is nevertheless cursed when elderly by a propensity to the fungal disease,

rust. This infection can be so serious that plants are defoliated by the height of summer and sometimes killed. This is the reason why they became unpopular as a florist's flower and a garden plant, but it is now possible to obtain seed which will produce plants that are more or less immune. If the disease does appear, plants can be sprayed with the fungicide propiconazole.

Hollyhocks have large, heart-shaped leaves with rounded lobes, and single, saucer-like flowers in long spikes, which are typically pink, but sometimes white. Modern hybrids have double flowers looking like crêpe-paper rosettes in colours such as rose, salmon, yellow, crimson, lavender and white, with a height of 2½ft (75cm), 5ft (1.5m) or 8ft (2.4m). Flowering time occurs during the summer.

PESTS AND DISEASES

Red spider mites This can be a serious pest in hot summers.
Leafhoppers These insects may infest the leaves, but are unlikely to be really troublesome.

Hollyhocks are among the most traditional of cottage garden flowers; grown against sunny walls, they live for many years *(left* and *above)*. Pink, white, purple and crimson varieties have been bred from the original *A. rosea*; there are also double-flowered forms with rosette-like blooms in a colour range which also includes yellow and cream.

SOIL

A deep, fertile soil is important, and it will benefit the plant greatly if the soil is supplemented with plenty of organic matter.

POSITION

These plants like to be situated in the sun, although they will grow in a slightly shaded area.

PROPAGATION

If the plants are increased by seed, rust disease will be less likely. They should be sown outdoors in summer, then overwintered in frames if the garden is situated in a cold area. Cuttings may be taken in late summer and rooted in a frame.

PLANTING

Winter	Spring	Summer	Autumn

The best planting time is in the middle of spring. The plants should be spaced out at a distance of 2-3ft (60-90cm) from each other.

PROTECTION

The young plants are rather fragile and need to be protected from severe weather conditions, which could kill them before they have established.

FEEDING

Feed the plants with a mulch of organic matter, just before flowering. This will encourage more vigorous blooming.

WATERING

Watering is not generally required, although if a long, hot, dry period occurs, make sure that the plants are kept well watered.

STAKING AND PRUNING

Any plants that are over 5ft (1.5m) should be staked. Restrict each plant to two or three spikes only, removing any unwanted stems while the plant is still small.

Above Hollyhocks were once grown as florist's flowers and exhibited at shows. The fungal disease, rust, can be a great problem and contributed to their decline in popularity at one time.

Below Slugs are also a nuisance, feeding on young growth and on leaves. Hand-pick these pests at dusk and put slug bait down at the base of plants, away from pets.

Anemone

There are three groups of anemones that are popular as garden plants: the wood anemones or windflowers *(A. nemorosa, A. apennina, A. blanda)* and their hybrids; those sold as cut flowers or florist's anemones (de Caen, St Brigid) and the Japanese anemones *(A. x hupehensis japonica)*, which is a tall-growing, herbaceous plant. The pasque or Easter flower used to be regarded as an anemone, but it is now classified as *Pulsatilla*, and is quite distinct with long silky-fluffy hairs on its leaves and petals. Japanese anemones will grow where nothing else can, but they spread so vigorously that strict control is essential to prevent them from completely overrunning a border.

The wood anemones flower in spring with white, blue and pink blooms on 5in (12cm) stems. The florist's anemones are red, blue, purple, white, pink or cream, 4-8in (10-20cm) tall, and flower from spring to autumn and even in winter, depending on when they were planted. Japanese anemones are summer-flowering in white or pink and grow to a height of 2-2½ft (60-75cm).

PESTS AND DISEASES

Plum rust This is likely to be the main problem on florist's anemones, infecting the leaves on the underside in spring and preventing flowering. The disease persists from year to year and is difficult to control, even with propiconazole. The best treatment may be to destroy affected plants and to spray nearby plum trees.

Three distinct kinds of anemones can be grown in gardens: florist's anemones, in vivid colours of scarlet, blue-mauve, pink and crimson; the delicately shaded windflowers, which do well in light woodland and flower in spring *(above)*; and the tall Japanese kind, which flowers in late summer *(right)*.

SOIL

The wood and Japanese anemones will grow in most conditions. The florist's anemones however, prefer a fertile and well-drained soil.

POSITION

Anemones are adaptable plants and can survive equally well in conditions of either sun or a little shade.

PROPAGATION

The wood anemones can be increased by seed sown in late winter or mid-summer. The florist's anemones can also be sown in mid- summer, or increased by tubers, when thinning out overcrowded sites. The Japanese anemones can be divided in autumn or spring.

PLANTING

Winter	Spring	Summer	Autumn

All groups can be planted in autumn or spring. The florist's anemones may also be planted in summer at a depth of 3in (7cm). and a distance of 6in (15cm). The wood anemones should be 4-6in (10-15cm) apart; the Japanese kinds 2ft (60cm) apart.

PROTECTION

Protection is not generally required for any variety, although the florist's anemones need protection from rain and should be provided with cloches.

FEEDING

Japanese anemones do not require any feeding. The florist kinds need a leaf- mould mulch after flowering, and the wood anemones need one in autumn.

WATERING

Watering will not be required, as anemones are able to survive without any added moisture.

STAKING AND PRUNING

Pruning and staking are not necessary, although the Japanese kind need to have excess rhizomes removed.

Aquilegia

The columbine is an old-fashioned, cottage garden plant whose multi-spurred flowers are purple, blue, pink and carmine red. Aquilegias are native of temperate climates and can be found growing wild in meadows and mountainous sites.

A. vulgaris grows about 1½ft (45cm) tall and hybridizes freely, so is able to self-sow and produce seedlings which may be double- as well as single-flowered. Advantage has been taken of this inclination to cross-pollinate to produce the McKana hybrids, a race 2½ft (75cm) tall, with fewer, but much longer, spurs, and bicoloured flowers in shades of pale yellow, light red, crimson, white, blue, pink and mauve. Columbines flower in early summer with the cultivated hybrids tending to open out in late summer. Even when not in bloom, aquilegias are decorative because they have leaves divided into rounded lobes, especially attractive as they unfold.

PESTS AND DISEASES

Leaf miners Leaves can be infested with this pest during the summer months, resulting in severe withering if the pest is allowed to get out of control. Hand-pick any badly damaged leaves; spraying may also be necessary.

Greenfly and **caterpillars** Greenfly can cover the flowers thickly in early summer; some species of caterpillar may also eat holes in the foliage. Hand-picking as soon as damage is noticed is usually all that is necessary.

Aquilegias, sometimes called columbines, grow naturally in mountainous districts, in pastures and beside paths. They cross-pollinate with great ease and will self-sow. The foliage is quite distinctive *(below)* as the leaves have a tripartite form. Their funnel-shaped flowers *(right)* are equally recognizable and handsome. They are relatively pest- and disease-free, although aphids and leaf miners can be troublesome.

Above Aquilegias come in many shades of purple, blue, crimson, magenta, pink and white. *A. alpina* is deep purple and can be found growing wild in mountainous areas of France.

SOIL

Soil requirements are not difficult to fulfil . They will grow in most soils, although a well-drained site is preferable.

POSITION

These plants can adapt their growth to suit sunny or shady sites, and thrive equally well in both.

PROPAGATION

There are two basic methods of propagation. Seed may be sown at the end of the summer, or division may be performed in spring or autumn.

PLANTING

Winter	Spring	Summer	Autumn

There are two suitable times of year to plant aquilegias: autumn or spring.

PROTECTION

The hardiness of the aquilegias, means that they do not require any form of protection throughout the year.

FEEDING

These plants are able to grow satisfactorily on their own, so that no feeding of fertilizer or manure is necessary.

WATERING

These attractive plants can survive without any additional watering, except in dry periods.

STAKING AND PRUNING

Deadhead the plants, unless seeds are required. The flower stems should be cut down just after flowering has occurred. No staking will be necessary.

Aster

The original Michaelmas daisy, *A. novi-belgii*, is a native of North America. It grows to a height of 4ft (1.2m) and has violet flowers in autumn. The other main species, which is used to produce the modern garden hybrids and strains, is *A. nova-angliae*. This blooms in pink or light violet-purple and reaches a height of 6ft (1.8m). However, the Michaelmas daisies that are grown today are about 3ft (90cm) tall, with flowers coloured magenta, purple, pink, maroon, crimson, light or dark blue, white and rose. A dwarf strain has been developed from these, between 9-12in (22-30cm) tall, which forms little bushes covered in flowers in similar colours.

PESTS AND DISEASES

Mildew Although asters are undoubtedly beautiful plants, flowering at their best when other plants are dying down, many are prone to this fungal disease. The disease can have the effect of turning the leaves and stems snow-white and will eventually cause the plant to wilt long before the flowering display has run its full course. Some varieties of aster are partially resistant, so it is worth taking the trouble to acquire these — visit local gardens at the end of summer and note the varieties which are free from the disease. Otherwise, space the plants out adequately, thin the clumps themselves, keep well watered in dry weather and use sparing quantities of a concentrated fertilizer rather than a large quantity of bulky manure. Spray with benomyl or thiophanate-methyl at three-weekly intervals, starting from mid-summer until flowering finishes.

Eelworms These pests mainly affect the dwarf varieties. As there is no means of effective control, it is important to obtain plants from good, reputable nurseries. Plants affected by eelworm will be stunted, with distorted, twisted leaves and a few, malformed flowers. If you suspect the presence of this pest, burn the plant, roots and all, and avoid replanting asters in the same place for at least two years.

Slugs Young shoots may be eaten by slugs in the spring.

Greenfly and **caterpillars** Occasional infestations of leaves and stems may occur in early or late summer.

Asters provide a beautiful display, varied not only in the form of their flowers, but also in colour: shades of pink, blue, red and white. *Aster novi-belgii* is a species that is native to North America. It is recognizable by its slender, pointed, deep green leaves. The flowers appear in early to mid-autumn. 'Freda Ballard' *(above)* is one variety, which grows up to 3ft (90cm) tall, with semi-double flowers in a shade of deep carmine. 'Marie Ballard' is another variety *(far left)*, which grows to the same height, with double flowers and is light blue in colour. Asters can, however, be affected by mildew in late summer and should not be planted too close together *(left)*.

SOIL

Most soils will suit the growing requirements of the aster, provided there is no excess moisture present and the soil contains reasonable amounts of nutrients.

POSITION

These plants need to be positioned in the light and preferably where they can receive direct sunlight.

PROPAGATION

Increase is usually performed by division, either in autumn or spring. It is also possible to take cuttings, but these should be made under frame in summer.

PLANTING

Winter	Spring	Summer	Autumn

Autumn and spring are the most suitable seasons in which to plant.

PROTECTION

These are hardy plants, which are able to withstand most weather conditions without any extra protection.

FEEDING

Feed the plants with a high-potash compound fertilizer in mid-summer, making sure that the manure is well watered in.

WATERING

A constant supply of water is essential during the hotter months, to ensure the healthy survival of these plants.

STAKING AND PRUNING

Remove the weak stems from tall plants, so that only five or six strong stems remain. Pruning should be carried out at the beginning of summer, together with any staking that is needed.

Buxus

Box is primarily used for hedges, for edgings and for topiary, as its thick and slow growth responds well to formal clipping. The small, round leaves are closely packed on the stems, and *B. sempervirens*, common box, can grow into a large shrub or small tree 20ft (6m) tall; *B.s.* 'Suffruticosa' is a dwarf form which grows to about 12in (30cm) tall. Native of the Mediterranean region, box is now extensively used for hedges in Europe and North America. The wood is close-grained and heavy, and highly suitable for carving objects such as chess pieces and musical instruments and for supplying rulers, yardsticks, planes and anything which needs a hard, reliable surface.

PESTS AND DISEASES

Box suckers These insects feed on the leaves at the tips of shoots, causing the leaves to curl inward so that the shoot appears to end in a globular leaf-cluster. Feeding starts in spring and sooty mould often appears on the leaf surfaces lower down. Spray in spring and early summer with dimethoate. In the winter following an attack, any shoots affected the previous summer should be cut off well back down the stem.
Box gall midges The

presence of this pest is revealed by pale yellow blotches on the leaves, which turn brown during the summer, as the larvae feed within the leaf tissue. Cut off the affected shoots; in heavy infestations, spray the shrub with dimethoate.
Die-back This is a fungal disease infecting shoots, causing them to die from the tip in the growing season — apparently for no reason. Affected shoots should be removed, cutting well back into the healthy growth, and burnt.

Box can be clipped into a good, formal, dense hedge. *(above).* The dwarf variety, *B. sempervirens* 'Suffruticosa' is ideal for edging beds and borders, especially when combined with bedding plants such as French and African marigolds. It can be kept trimmed to about 12in (30cm) tall and provides a neat foil to the brilliance of flower colours

SOIL

Soil is not a problem with this plant, as it can grow in   any reasonable garden site.

POSITION

This is an adaptable shrub, which will survive equally   well in sunlight or shade.

PROPAGATION

Cuttings, which are 3in (7cm) long, should be taken in a sheltered place outside at the end of summer. An   alternative method of increase is by layering in autumn.

PLANTING

Winter	Spring	Summer	Autumn

The time to plant is from autumn to spring, placing the hedging plants 12in   (30cm) apart and those wanted for edging, 6in (15cm) apart.

PROTECTION

As a hardy, barrier-type shrub, the box is capable of   withstanding most weather conditions.

FEEDING

An annual mulch is a basic requirement for this shrub, as this will encourage the   vigorous growth needed for hedging.

WATERING

Additional watering is not required, as this plant is able   to thrive without excess moisture.

STAKING AND PRUNING

The hedges will need control-type cutting back during the growing season, which will involve clipping   approximately three times from late spring to the end of summer. Staking is not necessary.

Callistephus

China asters are among the prettiest and most desirable of annual-flowering plants, with flowers in all shades of violet, purple, rose, crimson, red, pink, creamy yellow, white and blue-violet. The flowers are generally daisy-like, 3-4in (7-10cm) wide, although some are incurved, just like miniature chrysanthemums, some are like powder-puffs, others are feathery-petalled or reflexed and some are pompons, button-shaped flowers in single colours or bicoloured with a contrasting centre. They vary in height between 6-30in (15-75cm) depending on the type and flowering time is from late summer into autumn.

China asters flower late in the summer and continue flowering well into autumn. They grow particularly well in hot summers, and in sunny positions. As well as purple and pink varieties *(above* and *right)*, they are also available in crimson, white, lavender, blue-mauve, red, lilac and cream.

SOIL

Not all soil conditions are suitable for this plant and, to flourish, it will need a well-drained and fertile soil.

POSITION

An open, sunny situation will suit these plants best, and encourage healthy blooming.

PROPAGATION

Mid-spring is the best time to increase by seed. Thinly sow the seeds in seed trays, sited in a warm environment, and then prick them out when the seedlings are large enough to handle.

PLANTING

Winter		Spring		Summer		Autumn	

Plant out at a distance 6-12in (15-30cm) apart, at the end of spring. These plants need gentle handling at all stages, and care should be taken not to damage the roots.

PROTECTION

Protection should be provided at night if a frost is forecast, especially after the plants have first been bedded.

FEEDING

During the warmer months a liquid feed will need to be applied, as frequently as twice a week.

WATERING

This is a thirsty plant, so it is important to ensure that it is well supplied with water at all times.

STAKING AND PRUNING

No staking will be necessary, provided the roots are not damaged during planting. No pruning is required either.

PESTS AND DISEASES

Wilt One of the most common, yet mysterious, ailments affecting China asters is a disease which causes the plants to wilt suddenly, without warning, even in moist conditions. The disease is a soil-borne fungus which infects the roots, blocking absorption of moisture; the stems turn black from the base upward and will be brown inside. Affected plants cannot be cured and must be burnt. Asters should be planted in another place the following year or the soil sterilized — choose wilt-resistant strains.
Foot rot is another soil-borne disease and is widespread among bedding plants and herbaceous perennials. Soon after planting, the base of the young plant turns brown and the entire plant collapses; sometimes this is preceded by the leaves turning yellow. This disease should also be suspected if a plant is growing slowly and if its leaves are smaller than those of its companions. Treat the disease in the same way as wilt — but there are no resistant varieties.
Cucumber mosaic virus This disease results in small, malformed flowers, many more than usual, and yellow mottling on the leaves. There is no cure; affected plants should be destroyed.
Greenfly and **root aphids** Bad infestations can occur in hot, dry conditions.

Camellia

These beautiful flowering shrubs come from China where they can grow into trees up to 30ft (9m) tall. In colder regions, however, 10ft (3m) is more likely to be their maximum height. Spring is the flowering time for *C. japonica*, of which there are many hybrids in the colour range pink, rose, red, crimson, white, striped and variegated. Flowers can be 2-6in (5-15cm) wide, depending on whether they are single or double bloomers. *C. reticulata* hybrids have larger single or semi-double flowers in late winter, but need the protection of a conservatory.

Camellias are spectacular spring-flowering shrubs whose flowers vary in shape and form. Types of flower form include the formal double *(right)*; the anemone-centred *(below left)*; the peony *(far right)*; the fimbriated; and the single londs, which has a centre of prominent golden stamens forming a brush.

PESTS AND DISEASES	
Scale insects and **mealy bugs** Infestations by these pests can be heavy. **Vine weevils** The grubs of these pests feed on the roots. **Virus** The infection takes the form of yellowish or white variegation of the leaves and white variegation of flowers. The virus does not appear to adversely affect the plant's growth, and may be decorative. **Brown buds** Sun shining	onto frosted buds and blooms on early mornings can cause browned buds and petals with brown edges. The remedy is to position plants carefully so that they receive sun later. **Sun scald** Hot sun can produce large pale brown patches on young leaves; keep plants out of the midday sun. **Lime-induced chlorosis** This causes yellowed leaves.

Below Camellias are fairly hardy plants and can withstand quite severe frosts. Flower-buds can even be encased in ice and escape damage, as long as they do not receive early morning sun the following day. If this does happen, the petals of open flowers will turn brown and the flower-buds will go brown and will fail to open up.

SOIL

An acid to neutral soil will provide the best growing conditions, and the plants will flourish if they are also supplied with plenty of humus.

POSITION

Plant camellias in a site where they can receive some sun and some shelter. Dappled shade is most suitable.

PROPAGATION

Take cuttings in late summer, placing them in a peaty soil and warm environment. Increase by seed is also possible in early spring.

PLANTING

Winter	Spring	Summer	Autumn

Plant in autumn or spring, making sure that you choose a site where the roots will have enough space in which to spread.

PROTECTION

These trees need to be protected from cold winds, so should be grown in a sheltered place originally, or provided with artificial shelter.

FEEDING

A mulch should be applied in autumn and then a feed of high-potash compound fertilizer in the middle of summer.

WATERING

The camellia does not like excess moisture, so it is not necessary to provide any additional water.

STAKING AND PRUNING

Pruning is not a vital exercise, but may be performed after flowering to shape the plant attractively. Some staking will be needed to support the young plant.

Ceanothus

Californian lilac

Ceanothus used to be a relatively unknown shrub, but its flower spikes, which vary from powder-blue to deep blue, are now being seen more often in gardens. It can grow unsupported, provided it is sheltered from wind and is not in a frost-pocket, or it can be cultivated as a wall shrub, facing into the sun. There are spring-flowering kinds and summer-autumn hybrids, although there may be flowers intermittently throughout the season on both types. Their height varies and some are prostrate, although in general they are 6-12ft (1.8-3.6m) tall.

Californian lilacs may be deciduous or evergreen, and can be grown as wall shrubs or out in the open *(above)*. Their blue flower spikes appear from spring to autumn depending on the species *(right)*; they do best on chalky soil and with shelter from the cold wind.

SOIL

A good soil, which is well drained and fertile, will

encourage the healthiest growth from these shrubs.

POSITION

Sunlight is required for these plants, so it is

advisable to find them a light, open site.

PROPAGATION

Take cuttings that are 3in (7cm) long, at the beginning

of autumn, and keep them in a cool greenhouse initially.

PLANTING

Winter	Spring	Summer	Autumn

Agreeable conditions are needed for planting. In mild areas, autumn is a suitable time, but where winters are likely to be severe or where

drainage is doubtful, plant out in spring. Leave a distance of 6-8ft (1.8-2.4m) between each plant.

PROTECTION

A cover should be provided in the first winter after planting if it is very wet or

cold. The plants should always be protected in severe winters.

FEEDING

An annual mulch is necessary in autumn to

encourage vigorous growth and healthy blooms.

WATERING

These lilacs do not generally require additional water, but

during a dry period, some moisture will revive them.

STAKING AND PRUNING

The evergreen types of Californian lilac have two different pruning times. The autumn-flowering ones need to be cut back in spring, and those that flower in the spring should be given a

light pruning immediately after they have flowered. Deciduous types can be pruned at the same times as the evergreens, but harder, to remove half the previous season's growth.

Centaurea

This hardy perennial is rarely mentioned or seen, yet it is highly decorative, obliging and extremely hardy. The flowers are normally bright blue, although pink varieties are now in existence. They have a fruity fragrance. Blooming lasts until early summer, with a repeat flowering later and sometimes a third in mild autumns. The smoothly hairy, grey-green leaves last from spring to autumn and, grown in good soil and sun, the 15-18in (37-45cm) stems are strong enough not to need staking.

Cornflowers are among the easiest of herbaceous perennials to grow *(below and below left)*. Slugs and snails may eat leaves and flowers in wet seasons; later in the summer plants can be infected with mildew *(below right)*.

PESTS AND DISEASES

Slugs and **snails** These will eat the leaves and even the flowers in wet seasons.
Mildew Old growth will be infected in mid-summer if it has not been cut off to make way for the new stems already appearing.

SOIL

Soil requirements are not too demanding for this plant, as it tends to flourish in any average type.

POSITION

Cornflowers prefer to be positioned in sunlight, although they will grow in slight shade.

PROPAGATION

There are two suitable methods of increase. Either sow seed, or divide and replant, in autumn or spring.

PLANTING

Winter	Spring	Summer	Autumn

Planting should take place in autumn or spring, spacing the plants out at a distance of 12in (30cm) apart.

PROTECTION

The sturdiness of the cornflower means that it does not need to be protected from any type of weather.

FEEDING

These plants do not require any feeding, unless they are grown in light, sandy soils. In this case a feed should be applied in early spring and an annual mulch in mid-spring.

WATERING

These plants grow prolifically and do not need to be watered in normal weather conditions. However, during prolonged droughts some moisture should be provided.

STAKING AND PRUNING

If the old flowering stems are cut down completely as soon as flowering has finished, this will encourage repeat blooming. Supports will only be necessary where stems are weak or the plants have been damaged by wind or rain.

Chaenomeles

Japonica is a slow-growing shrub, familiar as an early spring-flowering plant, whose vermilion blooms sometimes even appear at the end of mild winters, or in sheltered gardens, and always before the leaves. Varieties are available with pink ('Apple Blossom'), deep red ('Rowallane'), white ('Nivalis') and salmon-pink, double flowers ('Falconet Charlot'). Sometimes called the ornamental quince, its hard, oval-shaped or round, green fruits whose colour changes to yellow as the fruit matures, will set after hot summers and can be used for flavouring apples or making jelly.

The width of the japonica is greater than its height, ranging from 3-8ft (90-240cm); the stems are sharply spined at the leaf joints. It responds well to training against a wall and is also a good shrub in the open.

Below Japonica is extremely hardy and moderately slow-growing. It mainly flowers in the spring, but there may be some flowers in mild winters. It can be trained to grow flat against a wall and some varieties will grow up to a height of more than 10ft (3m).

PESTS AND DISEASES

Fireblight Although japonica is one of the plants which can be infected by this bacterial disease, it seldom is.
Birds In winter, damage may be caused by birds pecking out flower-buds.

SOIL

This shrub does not require any particular soil and most average ones are suitable.

POSITION

The japonica is a useful garden shrub, as it is able to thrive in both sun and shade.

PROPAGATION

Layering is one form of propagation, which should be carried out in early autumn. Seed sown when it is ripe, is another method.

PLANTING

Winter	Spring	Summer	Autumn

Planting can occur anytime between autumn and spring. Space each plant out by a distance of 3-8ft (1-2.5m).

PROTECTION

The japonica is a sturdy shrub, which can survive in most weather conditions without any additional protection.

FEEDING

Feeding will encourage flowering, but it is not essential. A high-potash fertilizer may be applied in mid-summer.

WATERING

Watering is not a great concern, because the japonica can survive well enough without any extra moisture, unless a prolonged drought occurs. In this case, make sure the shrub is well watered.

STAKING AND PRUNING

Pruning is necessary to encourage flowering and will involve cutting back the new sideshoots by two-thirds in mid-summer, and any new growth on the ends of leading shoots by half. Staking is only necessary if the shrub is to be trained against a wall. In this case, tie the growth to horizontal wires as it extends.

Cheiranthus

Wallflowers are perennial plants if they are grown on light soils and in mild, sheltered gardens, but their bloom is not as good in their second and subsequent flowering years. The sweet and distinctive fragrance of their flowers is intensified by the warmth of the spring sun, and the range of colours — mahogany, gold, magenta, lemon-yellow, crimson and pink — is a relief from the yellows which seem to predominate during spring.

PESTS AND DISEASES

Wallflowers need careful handling and good growing conditions to thrive and can be infected by several pests and disease.

Wirestem A soil-borne fungal disease similar to damping-off, wirestem occurs at the seedling stage. The constricted stem results in a stunted plant with few flowers. Avoid putting in infected plants; the following year, sow seeds in a different site or in sterilized compost.

Flea beetles These insects are minute and black, or black and yellow-striped, and hop when disturbed. Appearing at the end of spring, they can invade the leaves of seedlings or young plants, eating tiny, round

holes in the leaves. Keeping the soil well watered and free of debris helps to avoid this pest, which can also be treated with derris dust.

Cabbage root fly Maggots may feed on the roots of young plants from spring to late autumn, causing plants to wilt and collapse suddenly. Transplants are particularly susceptible. If this pest has caused trouble before on wallflowers or brassicas, sprinkle diazinon on the soil around seedlings and in planting holes when transplanting.

Powdery mildew This fungal disease can occur in late summer to autumn, but usually only in dry summers. Spray benomyl or thiophanate-methyl to treat.

Above and **right** Wallflowers are members of the same plant family as cabbages and Brussels sprouts and tend to be attacked by the same pests and diseases. Well-drained soil, a sunny position and firm planting will help to produce strong, bushy plants, less susceptible to infections.

SOIL

A well-drained soil is essential, otherwise the plants will die during the winter. An alkaline soil is preferable to acid.

POSITION

Wallflowers should be positioned in a site that is open to sunlight, but sheltered from any winds or draughts.

PROPAGATION

Increase is by seed, sown at the end of spring. Set the seeds in rows and thin them out twice, leaving them finally at a distance of 6in (15cm) apart.

PLANTING

Winter	Spring	Summer	Autumn

Wallflowers should be planted in their flowering site in the middle of autumn, and spaced out at a distance of 9-12in (22-30cm) apart.

PROTECTION

Protection from wind is essential. Other precautions should involve ensuring that the plants are bedded firmly, otherwise they will be flattened by wind or snow.

FEEDING

Application of a potash compound fertilizer in spring will encourage healthier blooming during the season.

WATERING

No watering needs to be supplied to these plants, as they are able to survive without extra moisture, even in dry conditions.

STAKING AND PRUNING

Remove the tips of the main and subsequent shoots as this will encourage bushiness. No staking is required.

Chrysanthemum

There are so many different kinds of chrysanthemum that it is possible to see a continuous succession of flowers in bloom from the start of summer until mid-winter. The hardy annuals start to flower in early summer and go on through until autumn; the early greenhouse kinds will flower later in summer up to the end of autumn and the late cultivars in a greenhouse from late autumn to mid-winter; the Korean and pompon types bloom from autumn to winter outdoors. All are decorative garden plants and excellent as cut flowers. The hardy annuals have single flowers with petals coloured in concentric rings, and ferny leaves. They grow to a height of 1-2½ft (30-75cm). Greenhouse chrysanthemums have large double flowers, whose petals are reflexing or incurving, or large, single blooms, in colours such as bronze, pink, yellow, orange, magenta, red, cerise, white and cream, with a height between 2½-5ft (75-150cm). Koreans have large, daisy-like flowers or little button pompons with the same range of colours, although the singles have yellow centres and are 6-30in (15-75cm) tall.

Above and **right** The beautiful flowers of the chrysanthemum can be picked from mid-summer until late autumn, later if a greenhouse is available. The autumnal colours of red, orange, bronze, yellow and crimson are typical of the large-flowered varieties.

PESTS AND DISEASES

While the list of pests and diseases associated with the chrysanthemum looks formidable, many of its enemies are the routine ones and most, in any case, are confined to the greenhouse types.

Capsids These insects can do a great deal of damage to greenhouse plants when they are moved outdoors in the warmer weather. Feeding is concentrated on the youngest leaves and growing points of the stems, but damage is difficult to detect until long after it has occurred and the bugs have moved onto fresh pastures. One symptom is the appearance of pinprick holes which gradually enlarge so that leaves become tattered and one-sided. Crooked or dwarfed flowers are another symptom, but by this time it is too late to prevent damage from worsening. Capsids run rapidly about the plants and make for the soil when disturbed, so they are hardly ever seen. If trouble has occurred previously, spray plants with dimethoate at the end of spring and repeat three weeks later; spray the surrounding ground as well.

Chrysanthemum leaf miners If this pest is allowed to go unchecked, leaves can be so badly affected that they shrivel up and fall off. Remove the damaged leaves as soon as they are noticed and spray with dimethoate if the infestation continues.

Eelworms Infestation by eelworms is both common and serious, and mainly affects leaves and buds. Leaves show brown patches between the veins, then wilt and die, from the lowest ones upward. Buds can be killed and affected flowers malformed. Eelworms can survive on weeds and in plant debris for about 12 weeks. Immersing the crowns in hot water, maintained at exactly 115°F (46°C), will kill the eelworms. The crowns should be free of soil, the stems cut down and long roots trimmed back. After the crowns have been immersed in hot water for five minutes, plunge them into cold water and pot them ready for taking cuttings.

Verticillium wilt This is another serious problem; plants are infected through the roots, from the soil. Top leaves wilt in the daytime, lower leaves turn yellow and shrivel; the stem is stained brown internally, a symptom which can be seen if the stem is cut transversely about 6in (15cm) above the base. Destroy affected plants, including the roots, together with any fallen plant tissue. Remove compost or soil from the planting area and do not plant chysanthemums in the infected site until several years have elapsed.

Leafy gall This bacterial infection causes a proliferation of shoots at soil level, stunted growth and poor flowering. The infected plants should be completely destroyed and tools and hands scrupulously cleaned to prevent the infection spreading. Do not plant in the infected site for several years.

Virus Greenhouse chrysanthemums can be affected by a number of viruses. Tomato aspermy is a particularly common one, which causes small, malformed flowers and, occasionally, streaking of flower colour. Stunt is likely to appear on plants of American origin, and results in small plants with pale flowers. As with any virus disease, there is no effective means of control and infected plants must be completely destroyed.

Slugs and **snails** may eat new shoots and **earwigs** may attack the petals. **Greenfly** tend to infest the tips of stems, young leaves and flower-buds, and **whitefly** will infest the leaves in summer. **Mildew** may occur on greenhouse cultivars in late summer.

SOIL

Most soils will suit all types of chrysanthemums, provided they are relatively fertile and well drained.

POSITION

Chrysanthemums prefer sunny, sheltered positions. Koreans and Pompons can also grow in some shade.

PROPAGATION

Hardy annuals are increased by sowing seed in spring. Cuttings should be taken in late winter to reproduce greenhouse types. Pot on successively, until final potting, or a transfer outside if they are early-flowering plants. Koreans and pompons should be divided every three years in spring.

PLANTING

Winter	Spring	Summer	Autumn

Hardy annuals can be sown straight outdoors in mid-spring. Summer-flowering, greenhouse varieties may be planted out in late spring. Koreans and pompons should be planted in spring, 1½-2½ ft (45-75cm) apart.

PROTECTION

The best protection that can be provided for these plants is some shelter from cold winds and severe weather.

FEEDING

The greenhouse varieties in pots will need liquid feeding weekly until they flower. No other feeding is necessary.

WATERING

Watering is necessary for young plants, especially the greenhouse kinds, and during dry conditions.

STAKING AND PRUNING

Growing tips should be pinched out in mid-spring. On the greenhouse varieties, all except the top flower-buds should be removed. The late-flowering kinds must be taken back inside in autumn. Greenhouse varieties need some staking when put outside.

Chrysanthemums come in a wide range of colours. Flower forms also vary greatly, from the ball-like incurves to the turned-out petals of the reflexed type. The 'decorative' varieties *(left and bottom)* are numerous and equally diverse in their colour range. There is a spoon-shaped variety *(below)*, which has long tubular or spoon-shaped petals and is quite distinct from other varieties.

Clematis

Old man's beard or traveller's joy *(C. vitalba)* is a native of Europe, including Britain, and North Africa, which indicates that most cultivated varieties are easily grown in cool, temperate climates. Even the slightly tender species, such as *C. armandii* and *C. alpina*, will only be damaged by severe winters. Some hybrids will not display their best flower colour unless they are planted against a wall or fence, facing away from the sun, for example 'Barbara Dibley', 'Barbara Jackman', 'Nelly Moser' and 'Sealand Gem'. Others need to face the sun, such as 'Lady Northcliffe', 'The President', 'W.E. Gladstone', 'Huldine' and 'Lady Betty Balfour'. Flowering time depends on the variety, but will occur some time in spring through the summer into autumn; the large-flowered hybrids are at their best during summer. All colours are represented, and height (or length) can be 8-30ft (2.4-9m) and more.

PESTS AND DISEASES

Clematis wilt This affects newly planted and young plants in their first few years; shoots that had been growing vigorously, suddenly wilt completely in a matter of days, and do not recover. The cause of this condition has not been established, although a fungus may be associated with it. Removal of the affected shoots at ground level sometimes results in the appearance of healthy ones later in the season.
Earwigs Holes may be eaten in petals and leaves from mid-summer onward.
Weevils The edges of leaves may be eaten.

Climbing plants are always an advantage in a garden, covering walls with a carpet of colour. Clematis climb by twining their leaf petioles around the nearest support, such as a trellis on a wall or fence, the branches of a tree, or wires stretched between posts. The large-flowered clematis hybrids are spectacular *(above* and *far-right)*, flowering in early summer and mid-summer and growing 13½ft-15ft (3-4.5m) tall. The species clematis, such as *C. macropetala (right)*, are also attractive, with pointed petals and a centre of prominent stamens.

SOIL

This climber needs the right soil constituents. A well-drained, fertile soil, verging on alkalinity, is preferable.

POSITION

The ideal site for this plant is a place where it will receive maximum sunlight. and a cool root run.

PROPAGATION

Layer shoots when the plants are one and a half years old, between mid-autumn and mid-spring.

PLANTING

Winter	Spring	Summer	Autumn

Planting should occur anytime between autumn and spring, whenever the weather permits.

PROTECTION

No protection is generally necessary, although *C. armandii* needs some shelter in severe cold.

FEEDING

Application of a heavy mulch is required every spring, to provide the necessary food.

WATERING

Watering is not generally necessary, however, in droughts, the plants should be kept well watered.

STAKING AND PRUNING

Pruning depends on the flowering time. The large-flowered group that bloom from mid-summer onward, should be cut back hard in late winter, leaving just 3ft (90cm) of stem. The large-flowered kinds that bloom in early summer, however, should be only lightly pruned in late winter and any dead growth should also be removed. Spring-flowering plants should be similarly pruned, immediately after flowering and also one or two of the oldest shoots should be removed. As a climbing shrub, supports will have to be provided for the twining leaf stems.

Crataegus

Hawthorns are small trees, which makes them very suitable for the garden. They flower in late spring in white, pink or red, with single or double blooms, depending on the species and variety, and are followed by brilliant red or orange-yellow berries (haws). Birds are encouraged to make nests in hawthorn branches because they are so twiggy. For the same reason hawthorns are good, closely-knit hedges, made impenetrable by their extremely sharp spines. The average height of the hawthorn is 15ft (4.5cm), with a spread of almost equal size. The Glastonbury thorn *(C. monogyna 'Biflora')* sometimes flowers in winter before the main flowering.

PESTS AND DISEASES

Fireblight This is the most serious problem as it is a bacterial disease, rapidly spread and often fatal. Symptoms — including brown and black withered leaves and dead blossoms — first show up in late spring. The presence of the disease, which can affect other plants of the rose family, should be notified to the appropriate authorities who will advise on treatment.
Caterpillars Small, differently coloured species may feed on the leaves, making webbing as they do so, from spring to early summer. No treatment is necessary unless the infestation is bad. These caterpillars may also be found on cotoneaster, willow, euonymus and ornamental apple.
Birds The haws are relished by birds, with the exception of those of *C. carrerei.*
Mildew This occasionally occurs in late summer.

The thorns (may or hawthorn) are versatile plants, which can be grown as small flowering trees, formal hedges or as shrubs. *C. oxyacantha (above)* is a European species which flowers in late spring and has red haws; a variety with yellow berries is occasionally seen growing wild.

SOIL

There is no problem with the type of soil, and any average one will provide a suitable growing medium.

POSITION

The hawthorn is not a difficult tree to position, as it can grow equally well in sun or shade.

PROPAGATION

Increase is done by seed. The haws, however, must be left stratified in damp sand outside for a year, before sowing can take place.

PLANTING

Winter		Spring		Summer		Autumn	

Plant from autumn through to spring, leaving a distance of 4in (10cm) between each of the hedging plants.

PROTECTION

The hardiness of the hawthorn means that protection is generally unnecessary, even in severe conditions.

FEEDING

It is not necessary to feed or manure these trees, as they will grow very satisfactorily without any fertilizers.

WATERING

Hawthorns can survive without extra watering, unless a prolonged drought occurs, when they will need some added moisture.

STAKING AND PRUNING

The trees will need staking when they are young, to ensure correct growth. Formal hedges should then be clipped twice, in early and late summer.

Crocus

Crocuses come from the Mediterranean region where they are baked by long, hot summer droughts. Purple, yellow and white are the most common colours, but there are species and varieties in blue, violet-blue, lavender, lilac, rosy lilac, purple streaked on yellow, orange and feathered purple or lilac on white. Flowering is in spring but there are also autumn crocuses, such as *C. speciosus*. Besides the garden varieties, *C. chrysanthus* and *C. tomasinianus* are particularly decorative and are early flowering.

PESTS AND DISEASES

Crocuses have few pest and disease problems. Although they can be afflicted by a wide range of fungal diseases, in practice they very rarely are. The most common fungal problems are those which affect other bulbs such as gladioli, narcissi and tulips.

Birds and **small mammals** Sparrows, in particular, will attack the yellow-flowered varieties. Squirrels and, occasionally, mice dig up and eat the bulbs. Black cotton, netting or repellants will help.

Crocuses come in many delicate shades of purple and blue, together with yellow, orange, cream and white *(above and right)*. The most common type of crocus flowers in early spring, but some flower in autumn among the fallen leaves, others in late winter.

SOIL

To encourage maximum flowering, the bulbs should be provided with a well-drained and fertile soil.

POSITION

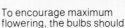

Crocuses need plenty of sunlight and should be planted right out in the open.

PROPAGATION

Increase can be carried out by seed, but the plants will also self-seed. Separating offsets is another useful method of propagation.

PLANTING

	Winter	Spring	Summer	Autumn

Bulbs should be planted in mid-autumn if they are the early-flowering type. Autumn-flowering kinds must be planted in late summer and the remainder can be bedded in mid-autumn. Place the bulbs at a distance of 3in (7cm) apart and at a similar depth below the soil surface.

PROTECTION

Protection is not necessary, but it is advisable to find a spot that is sheltered from wind, to encourage early flowering.

FEEDING

After these bulbs have flowered, a light feed will benefit them. Apply some hoof and horn or potash fertilizer.

WATERING

Watering is not generally required, as these plants can thrive in even the driest conditions.

STAKING AND PRUNING

As these are only small plants, no staking is necessary. It is also unnecessary to prune crocuses.

Dahlia

Dahlias always make an impressive show in the garden. Planted in a mass, their brilliant colours dazzle the eye and make all other autumnal flowers look sombre and faded. Among the range of flower shapes are giant decoratives with multi-petalled blooms, formal show flowers, pompons, singles, cacti, anemones and double-tiered, bi-coloured collarettes. Heights vary from 2-5ft (60-150cm). The bedding dahlias, with small, single or double flowers, grow 6-12in (15-30cm) tall and can start flowering in mid-summer. The dahlias in Mexico grow wild in hedges and along roadsides, up to a height of 10-12ft (3-3.6m), but they are not hardy in cool, temperate climates.

There are varieties of dahlia to suit every type of garden site, from flowerbeds to borders and greenhouses. Among the most useful are those in the decorative group *(above* and *far right)*. The small, single-flowered kinds *(right)*, which grow to 12in (30cm) tall, can be massed to provide colour for bedding from mid-summer.

SOIL

A moist soil is one necessary requirement, but it must also be well drained and fertile.

POSITION

These plants need a sunny position in the garden to encourage healthy blooming.

PROPAGATION

To increase this plant cuttings may be taken, or the tuber divided, or seed may be sown in spring.

PLANTING

Winter	Spring	Summer	Autumn

Plant unsprouted tubers outside in mid-spring, 3in (7cm) deep and 1½-6ft (45-180cm) apart. This will depend on the variety, but the average planting distance is 3ft (90cm) apart.

An alternative method of planting involves starting off single tubers, each with an eye, in a temperature of 55°F (13°C), planting in a pot and replanting outside in late spring.

PROTECTION

Dahlias must be kept free of frost throughout their winter storage time.

FEEDING

A liquid feed is an important measure, applied once a week from mid-summer through into autumn.

WATERING

Dahlias are thirsty plants and need to be supplied with plenty of water throughout their life.

STAKING AND PRUNING

Supply strong stakes for these plants, as many as three or four for each plant. The tubers must be dug up in autumn, labelled, the stems cut down to 6in (15cm), any soil cleaned off and the tubers left upside down in a dry place for a few days. Once they have dried out, store them in soil or moist peat.

PESTS AND DISEASES

Earwigs Probably the best-known dahlia pest, earwigs feed on the petals, reducing them to rags, and eat holes in the leaves. The traditional way of control is still a good method. Since earwigs hide during the day, providing hiding places enables them to be trapped easily. Flower pots, stuffed with straw or newspaper, and turned upside down on top of garden canes, will successfully trap a good number. Otherwise, spray with trichlorphon.

Tuber rot To prevent rot in stored tubers, select those which are free from injury, unbruised and not diseased already. Keep them free from frost. If any do rot, cut the diseased part away, well into healthy tissue, and dust with sulphur or benomyl. Remove the storage material immediately surrounding the rotten tuber and plant it in fresh material.

Slugs and **snails** eat emerging shoots and **caterpillars** will devour leaves and flowers. **Capsids** can cause severe damage and **thrips, greenfly** and **red spider mites** may also occur. Greenfly spread a serious disease called **mosaic virus**, causing yellow mottling of the leaves or distortion, and stunted plants.

Grey mould (*Botrytis cinerea*) This sometimes infects the buds and petals in damp, warm weather or in enclosed, crowded conditions. Remove the affected parts and spray the plants with benomyl or thiophanate-methyl.

Frost damage This blackens all top growth and kills the plant. The first frost in autumn is the signal for lifting the tubers. In spring, young top growth should be protected by cloches.

Caterpillars can bite large holes in dahlia leaves *(above)* and will also eat the flowers. These pests can be removed by hand; chemical controls are usually not necessary. Capsid bugs feed on the tips of shoots and on young leaves at the top of stems, leaving pinprick holes which enlarge to produce tattered leaves *(below right)*. Capsid damage on flowers may result in lopsided buds that fail to open. Spray with an insecticide such as malathion to control. Leaf miners tunnel and feed inside leaves *(bottom right)*. Winding pale lines or pale brown blisters show up on the leaf's upper surface. Hand-pick and destroy affected leaves as soon as they are seen and spray if the attack continues or is particularly severe.

Delphinium

Regal is the only adjective to describe the delphinium. It is the queen of the herbaceous border, the rounded spikes of vivid blue, purple, white or cream dominating all the other perennials in summer. Together with roses, delphiniums are synonymous with the English garden. Even the individual florets are delightful, sometimes as much as 3in (7cm) wide, with furry stamens forming a golden or black eye, and a spur or two at the back of the petals. The height of the modern hybrids can range between 3-7ft (90-120cm), the Pacific hybrids being particularly good. These all need strong stakes, but the race known as the Belladonna hybrids, with slightly smaller flowers, grow to 3-4ft (90-120cm), and can do without support unless the garden or site is open to regular wind. They are better as cut flowers, too, lasting well in water without any preparation. Red, pink and orange-red are the alternative colours, but the plants are only 1½-3ft (45-90cm) tall and with smaller, loosely clustered flowers. 'Pink Sensation' is one and *D. nudicaule* is another.

Traditionally blue, delphiniums are also available in shades of purple *(above right* and *right)*, as well as cream and white. Each flower can be as wide as 1½in (3cm), often wider, and has five petals and a centre of prominent, usually black, stamens. Delphiniums will self-sow, and since they cross-pollinate easily, there is a fair chance that any seedling that results will be a good enough hybrid to warrant naming *(above)*.

Left Delphiniums dominate the herbaceous border, their flower columns towering above other plants. They usually need staking to prevent their beautiful flower spikes being broken by wind or rain.

PESTS AND DISEASES

Slugs These pests can be a nuisance in spring, eating the shoots right down as they come through the soil. Precautions need to be taken in advance.

Caterpillars Green, velvety caterpillars, in particular, may feed on the leaves during the summer, but hand-picking is usually sufficient to control them.

Greenfly and **earwigs** are occasionally troublesome.

Black blotch This fungal disease appears in summer on stems, buds and leaf stalks as well as leaves. The disease spreads rapidly in wet weather and can destroy all the leaves. As there is no effective cure, plants should be destroyed. If the disease is noticed at an early stage, remove the affected stems to check further trouble.

Cucumber mosaic This disease can be a serious problem. Symptoms include yellow mottling on the leaves, poor flowering and slow growth. Affected plants should be dug up and destroyed, including the roots. New delphiniums should be planted in a different place.

Fasciation This is a condition which affects delphiniums, among other plants, occasionally. The central stem becomes flattened and enlarged and the number of flowers in the spike considerably increased. The cause is not known — it may be bacteria, weather or insect damage — but the plant is not seriously harmed.

SOIL

Soil constituency must be correct and should be deep, moist, slightly heavy and fertile.

POSITION

Choose a sunny, open position for this plant, and preferably one that is sheltered from any strong winds.

PROPAGATION

Increase may be performed by sowing seeds outdoors in spring; by division in autumn and spring; or by taking cuttings, 3in (7cm) long, from the young shoots in spring. These cuttings must start off in a sandy soil under cover.

PLANTING

Winter		Spring		Summer		Autumn	

Planting can occur at anytime between autumn and spring. The plants should be spaced out at a distance of 2-3ft (60-90cm).

PROTECTION

Some protection from prevailing winds is important, as these are such tall plants that they are prone to this type of weather damage.

FEEDING

An annual mulch is required in early spring, then, throughout the summer months a liquid feed is necessary.

WATERING

These plants will produce their magnificent blooms without additional watering. However, it is always advisable to make sure that they are kept moist during dry weather.

STAKING AND PRUNING

Like dahlias, these plants need to be supported by three or four stakes. Pruning is not necessary.

Dianthus

Carnations both smell and look impressive with their colouring of pink, red, white, magenta, crimson and yellow and their spiky, silvery grey leaves. The border carnations are slightly taller than the pinks at 12in (30cm) and flower in summer; pinks are about 9in (22cm) tall and flower in early summer. The 'gillyflower' of Elizabethan times, border carnations became florist's flowers in the eighteenth century, by which time there were hundreds of varieties, and almost as many competitive exhibitions. Sweet williams could possibly be an even older introduction to Europe, brought in by the Carthusian monks during the twelfth century. Like the pinks and carnations, there were once many more varieties than there are today, and well over 100 were available in early Victorian days. Colours are similar and the height of their stiff-flowering stems is about 1½ft (45cm), but they lack the strong fragrance and grey leaves of their relations. Nevertheless, they are easily grown, colourful plants for massing and will self-seed.

PESTS AND DISEASES

Unlike greenhouse carnations, pinks and border carnations have few problems.

Rust fungus This disease frequently attacks sweet williams. Symptoms include rust-coloured bumps on the underside of leaves and pale green spots on the upper side. The dark red cultivars and those with red-green leaves are resistant; the disease is less likely to occur if the plants are grown in the best conditions — in a sunny place with well-drained, rather poor soil.

Leaf spot Varieties of this fungal disease sometimes infect leaves and can be controlled by hand-picking and spraying regularly with thiram.

Thrips These may cause damage in summer, producing a silvery speckling on buds, flowers and leaves.

Red spider mites This pest may be a problem in hot, dry summers.

Tortrix moth caterpillars This caterpillar feeds on the leaves, spinning webs which weave the leaves together.

Greenfly can occasionally be a problem, and **leaf miners** may cause trouble from autumn onward.

Sweet williams, *D. barbatus*, are old-fashioned flowers traditionally associated with cottage gardens. Their cultivation dates back to the twelfth century in Britain; during the reign of Henry VIII (1509-1547), they were sometimes called 'velvet williams'. These plants self-sow very readily in warm sites and sandy soils, to give great variation in colour and markings *(left* and *far left above)*. Light or dark red with spots or stripes are the typical colours of the wild forms *(above)*, but pink, white, rose, black-red, purple, bicoloured, white-eyed and fimbriated flowers all occur. Massed together they are a spectacular sight *(above left)*, flowering throughout the summer.

Carnations *(right)*, a species of dianthus, are very popular plants and are available in many vivid shades of red, pink and yellow, as well as white. Some are strongly scented, and all do well in sunny beds and borders.

SOIL

A light and well-drained soil, with a good alkaline content, is the most suitable type of soil.

POSITION

Border carnations, pinks and sweet williams prefer to be situated in light, open, sunny places.

PROPAGATION

Border carnations and pinks can be increased by layering in mid-summer or by sowing seed in cold frames in spring. Cuttings may be taken after flowering. Sweet williams should be sown outside at the beginning of summer, then thinned alternately as soon as they are large enough to handle and again to a distance of 3in (7cm) apart.

PLANTING

Winter	Spring	Summer	Autumn

Border carnations and pinks should be planted in autumn or spring. Space the plants out by 1½ft (45cm), and plant firmly at a shallow depth. Transplant sweet williams to their flowering position in mid-summer, 9-12in (22-30cm) apart.

PROTECTION

The only essential protection necessary for this plant, is during severe winter weather.

FEEDING

A liquid feed of high-potash fertilizer is most beneficial at the end of spring and beginning of summer.

WATERING

Carnation roots can find enough moisture in the soil, although some water is necessary in dry weather.

STAKING AND PRUNING

Flowering stems will need supporting, preferably using split canes. If the new shoots are thinned out, bigger flowers will be encouraged.

Border carnations and pinks, both species of dianthus, are often strongly perfumed *(top)*. *D. caryophyllus* is the wild forerunner of the modern kinds; very fragrant, it was once used as a herb. *D.*

deltoides is the maiden pink *(above)*, flowering all summer and growing wild in Europe on sandy soils. It varies in colour from deep red to pale pink or white and does well in sunny rockeries.

Erica

The true heathers belong to the genus *Erica*, but plants also regarded as heather, although more suitably called heath or ling, are the callunas (*Calluna* spp) and daboecias. Natives of lower mountain slopes and moorlands of cool, temperate climates, heathers are extremely hardy, tough, dwarf shrubs, 6-12in (15-30cm) tall, flowering profusely in late summer, autumn and winter. Their colour range includes pink, white, purple and red in varying shades; *E. carnea* cultivars flower in winter, *E. cinerea* in late summer and autumn. *Calluna vulgaris* and daboecia cultivars flower from summer to early winter. Callunas have the bonus of variously coloured foliages, notably gold, orange, red, grey, grey-green and bronze.

Excellent low-growing shrubs for groundcover or for labour-saving gardens, ericas mainly flower from late summer to early winter *(below* and *bottom).* They are most effective when planted in broad clumps to show off their foliage.

PESTS AND DISEASES

The main problems are likely to occur with cultivation, but young shoots can also be severely decimated by **rabbits** and **hares**.
Phytophthora root rot This fungal disease is fatal. Affected plants will be stunted, with small, yellowing leaves; growth will be slow and eventually all, or part, of the plant will die. Waterlogged soil, too much organic matter, wind-rocking and prolonged wet weather all encourage the disease to develop. Affected plants should be destroyed and, since the disease can affect many ornamental trees and shrubs, replanting should be avoided for as long as possible.

SOIL

A peaty soil with an acid content, which is also well drained and light, will suit these shrubs. *E. carnea*, however, is one species that can tolerate a little alkalinity.

POSITION

Heathers do need sun, but also require some shade. It is preferable to plant them in an open site, where there is also some relief from hot sun.

PROPAGATION

These plants can be increased by two methods. Layering should be performed in spring and division in mid-autumn.

PLANTING

Winter	Spring	Summer	Autumn

The best time to plant is between autumn and spring. Make sure the plants are spaced at a distance of 1½ft (45cm) from each other.

PROTECTION

These low-growing shrubs can survive in any type of weather condition and do not need any protection.

FEEDING

Heathers are hardy shrubs, which are able to survive in bleak conditions with no attention, so it is not necessary to feed them.

WATERING

Watering will not normally be required, unless a prolonged dry period occurs, when some moisture should be supplied.

STAKING AND PRUNING

The only pruning necessary is to clip the plants, using shears, after flowering. This should be done in alternate springs. Staking is not necessary as they are hardy, low-growing shrubs.

Euonymus

The spindle tree *(E. europaeus)* is a familiar small tree seen in hedgerows in temperature areas, especially Europe, with its eye-catching, colour-clashing fruits in pink and orange. These follow inconspicuous, greenish white flowers in summer, on a deciduous plant up to 25ft (7.5m) tall. There are improved forms of it which are especially suitable for the garden. Another commonly seen species is *E. japonicus*, an evergreen, with bright, shiny leaves, which is very popular for formal hedges. A third species has come into its own recently as groundcover, *E. fortunei radicans*, and *E.f.* 'Variegatus', which are both evergreen; 'Variegatus' has white, pink-tinted leaf edges.

For trouble-free groundcover which is not invasive, *E. fortunei* 'Variegatus' *(top)* is hard to better. It roots along its stems, forming a carpet, and will grow over walls or rocks in sun or in shade. Blackfly can infest *E. europaeus* in summer *(above)*, feeding on the leaves so that they curl up; shoot tips become distorted and die.

PESTS AND DISEASES

Blackfly and **small caterpillars** These insects may occur but are unlikely to be serious. The hedging species, *E. japonicus* and its cultivars, may also suffer from these predators.
Scale insects These insects, which resemble mussels in shape, can also be serious.
Mildew This is the main problem on *E. japonicus* and can be serious. Dry soil, lack of nutrients and a stuffy atmosphere are all conducive to its spread. The right cultivation is important; seaside conditions are most suitable. In a formal hedge, removal of the affected shoots can spoil the overall appearance. If the disease does occur, spraying should be carried out immediately using a mildew fungicide.

SOIL

Most soils are suitable for these plants, but they grow especially well if the soil content is slightly chalky.

POSITION

Most of these shrubs can grow in sun or limited shade, although the variegated-leaved kinds require sunlight. An open site is preferable for all types.

PROPAGATION

Take hardwood cuttings in mid-autumn for most of these plants. The groundcover kinds, however, should be increased by division.

PLANTING

Winter	Spring	Summer	Autumn

The deciduous kinds can be planted anytime between autumn and spring, whereas the evergreens should only be bedded in either autumn or spring. Hedging plants must be spaced out by 15-18in (37-45cm).

PROTECTION

This shrub is hardy enough to withstand most weather conditions, and does not need protecting.

FEEDING

It is not essential to feed these shrubs, unless they have been positioned in a poor soil, which is lacking nutrient content. In this case apply a fertilizer dressing in early spring and mulch in late spring. This will be necessary every year.

WATERING

The spindle tree does not need any watering unless the weather is dry for any length of time.

STAKING AND PRUNING

The trees will have to be staked when they are young, to ensure good, sturdy growth. Pruning is needed to shape and space the plants, although formal hedges need clipping in late summer or early spring.

Ferns

These foliage plants were popular in Victorian times. There are many hardy ferns which can transform a dank, sunless patch of soil into a graceful and decorative bed or border, even into a feature of the garden. Some ferns die down in autumn, some are evergreen. All have beautiful foliage or fronds, although these are not necessarily the shape that is typically attributed to ferns. The hartstongue, for instance, has a long unbroken tongue-like frond; the hardy maidenhair has delicate, rounded leaflets on wiry stems, and the rustyback *(Ceterach officinarum)* has long, narrow fronds, leathery and more like leaves than a feathery fern.

PESTS AND DISEASES

Problems are largely caused by pests rather than diseases, but seldom occur on outdoor plants.
Slugs, snails, woodlice and **millipedes** These feed on young roots and new fronds just uncurling through the soil. To keep these pests permanently at bay, make sure that there are no rubbish heaps nearby.
Greenfly These sometimes feed on the tips of fronds. Hand-pick as soon as they are seen.
Leaf miners Black patches on the upper stems of the ferns indicate the presence of these insects. Control is a matter of hand-picking as soon as they are seen.
Scale insects and **vine weevils** If plants are grown in warm, temperate climates, these insects can also prove a hazard. Spraying with malathion will help, but some ferns are sensitive: follow the manufacturer's directions.

Ferns are deservedly enjoying a revival of popularity, both as houseplants and in the garden, were they are ideal for shady, damp areas otherwise difficult to plant effectively *(above)*. Ferns have few problems but can be severely attacked by scale insects, which show up as small, brown, raised spots on the underside of fronds and on stems *(right)*. These pests are more likely to appear in dry conditions.

SOIL

A moist soil, which is preferably acid and contains some peat, is the ideal growing medium for ferns and will encourage the maximum foliage.

POSITION

These plants, unlike the majority of plants, thrive in shady conditions, preferring the dark to sunlight. Avoid putting them out into light, sunny positions.

PROPAGATION

The best method of increase is by division in spring. The spores will self-sow in the right conditions.

PLANTING

Winter	Spring	Summer	Autumn

Planting can take place in either autumn or spring, spacing the plants out as required.

PROTECTION

These plants can be left to grow freely and do not need any form of protection.

FEEDING

It will be necessary to feed with a mulch of peat if the plants seem to be lacking vigorous growth or have dulled in colour.

WATERING

Ferns like to have plenty of moisture so ensure that they are kept well supplied with water at all times and especially during dry weather.

STAKING AND PRUNING

It is not necessary to stake or prune these plants, as they grow prolifically on their own.

Forsythia

The yellow blossoms of this deciduous shrub light up the whole garden in early spring, when it is one of the first and most welcome of the flowering shrubs, after the long winter weeks. It grows vigorously and will need plenty of space, especially in heavy soil, as an average *F. x intermedia* will grow to 8x8ft (2.1x2.1m) in size. One with large, copiously produced flowers is the cultivar 'Lynwood'; *F. ovata* is a smaller species, growing slowly to about 4ft (1.2m) high and wide.

PESTS AND DISEASES

Birds Unfortunately, forsythia is prone to pecking, particularly if the garden is one where birds are regularly fed. If repellants sprayed onto stems and buds do not help, try dabbing with tree grease or using foil strips as scarers. Preventative treatment should be started early in the winter.

Capsids These may feed on the young leaves.

Galls Galls, which appear as small swellings on the stems, sometimes with embryo roots, often develop on the forsythia. No treatment is necessary except to remove affected stems if they have become too disfigured.

Honey fungus This fungal disease attacks through the roots and may kill the shrub, which must be removed completely.

The brilliant yellow showers of forsythia blooms are among the first flowers to appear in spring, brightening up the garden after dull winter days *(far right)*. These bushes are vigorous, and quickly become large and rather tangled if they are not carefully pruned *(above)*. Do not cut off all the flowered shoots immediately after flowering, just remove one or two of the oldest completely — right down to soil level or back to strong, new shoots — and thin out some of the remaining flowered growth. This will encourage healthy, well-developed shoots *(right)*.

SOIL

The soil requirements of forsythias are minimal, too, as they will flourish in any soil type.

POSITION

Forsythias are easy plants to grow and can survive equally well in either sunshine or shade.

PROPAGATION

Take hardwood cuttings in autumn, or increase by layering, which may also be carried out in autumn.

PLANTING

Winter	Spring	Summer	Autumn

The shrubs should be planted between autumn and spring. If they are required to form a hedge, the plants must be placed at a distance of 1½-2ft (45-60cm) apart.

PROTECTION

No protection is required, as forsythias are strong enough to stand up to most conditions.

FEEDING

These plants do not need much attention, and can grow well without the addition of any feeds or fertilizers.

WATERING

Water application is not necessary in normal conditions, however, if there is a prolonged drought, some water will revive the plants.

STAKING AND PRUNING

Staking is not generally necessary, but if *F. suspensa sieboldii* is to be grown, a wall or fence will be needed as a support. Pruning is not required every year, but, when it is, pick out one or two of the oldest shoots which have already flowered, and cut them off as low down in the bush as possible. This may be needed every other year and should take place immediately after flowering.

Fuchsia

Leonard Fuchs (1501-66) was a German botanist and the fuchsia, named in his memory, is an intensely coloured, flowering shrub native to South America. Bright carmine red and deep purple form an unlikely colour combination which is, in fact, a most effective feature. Bright red and purple are characteristic colours of the outer tube and the inner petals, but much intensive work on hybridization has produced plants whose flowers are coloured pink, white, lilac, lavender, blue-purple and red. There are also species, less often grown, with orange or orange-red blooms.

Fuchsias are pollinated in the wild by hummingbirds, whose long, spike-like beaks are ideal for acquiring the nectar at the bottom of the long, tubular calyx. The modern fuchsia hybrids, which are mostly double-flowered and not very hardy, are commonly about 2ft (60cm) tall, festooned with flowers from mid-summer until autumn and, if kept in a cool greenhouse, for most of the winter as well. The single species such as *F. magellanica* and its associate 'Riccartonii', used for hedging, are hardy except in the severest winters. Fuchsias are deciduous shrubs.

Below Fuchsia flowers are quite distinctive in form, and this is emphasized by the fact that the outer petals are often different in colour from the central ones. The 'Ricartonii' variety *(left)*, much used for hedges, has single flowers with long, narrow tubes.

PESTS AND DISEASES

Capsids, greenfly and **leaf-cutter bees** attack outdoor plants. **Whitefly, red spider mites, scale insects** and **mealy bugs** may occur on greenhouse plants.

Fuchsia flowers are usually red on the outside, with a bright purple cluster of central petals, but hybridization has resulted in many variations. Pink and purple, pink and white, purple and white and red and white are just some of the combinations. Flowers all in one colour are also available *(right)*, and there are double varieties, the doubling largely being of the central petals. A charming flowering shrub, the fuchsia looks particularly attractive planted slightly above eye-level, so that the underside of the pendulous flowers can be seen *(above)*. Flowering can continue for many weeks in cool climates.

SOIL

Rich and well-drained soils will encourage the healthiest growth from these plants.

POSITION

These plants need to have sunlight, although they can grow if they are given a little shade. It is preferable, however, to put them in a position where they are facing the sun.

PROPAGATION

Increase must be done in warm conditions. Either take cuttings of the shoot tips in spring and early summer, or sow seed in the spring.

PLANTING

	Winter		Spring		Summer		Autumn	

There are two suitable times to plant: early autumn and mid-spring. Leave spaces that are 2ft (60cm) wide between each plant. This should be decreased if you are dealing with hedging plants, to 15-18in (38-45cm).

PROTECTION

The autumn mulch not only acts as a feed, but will also protect the plants during the winter if it is piled high over the crowns.

FEEDING

An annual mulch should be applied in autumn, after flowering, to help the plants through the winter.

WATERING

It is not necessary to water these plants for most of the year, except when long, dry periods occur.

STAKING AND PRUNING

The middle of spring is the best time to prune. All the dead shoots have to be removed, and then the remaining stems should be cut down to a few inches. Hedges, on the other hand, should only be lightly trimmed. No staking will be required.

Gladiolus

These summer-flowering corms are among the most elegant and beautiful of garden plants, and are superb as cut flowers. The magnificent spikes of the large- and small-flowered hybrids start to appear in mid-summer, with the Nanus group appearing in early summer. There are many named hybrids in all colours and shades, which are so popular that societies exist devoted solely to these plants and their cultivation. Gladioli are natives of South Africa and the Mediterranean region; they grow to about 2-4ft (60-120cm) tall.

PESTS AND DISEASES

Thrips These pests cause disfiguration of flowers and leaves in the summer.
Greenfly, slugs, snails and **caterpillars** can all be troublesome.
Virus Mottling and light streaks on the leaves and broken flower colour indicate this type of infection.
Fungal disease Corms are prone to several types of fungal disease, notably **dry rot, corm rot, hard rot** and **core rot**. Dry rot makes leaves turn brown and rot at soil level. The corms will have dark brown or black spots on the outside. Corm rot shows up on stored corms as dark brown or black spots and blotches, mostly on the lower side. The corm becomes mummified. Reddish brown spots on the outside of the corm indicate hard rot. Leaves will have brown spots as well; the corm will eventually shrivel. The disease develops in wet seasons. Corm rot is soft and extends outward, the leaves turn light brown and yellow and the plant dies. Cold, wet seasons encourage it.
Scab This bacterial disease is also serious. Symptoms include yellow depressions on the corms and brown spots on the leaves. Any corms that show blue mould, spotting, rotten patches or any evidence of shrivelling must be destroyed. If disease has occurred, do not replant gladioli in the same site for as long as possible. Dip corms in benomyl or thiophanate-methyl solution before planting the following year.

Right Gladioli flower after the bearded irises, continuing flowering through the summer into early autumn if planted in succession in the spring. Their glowing colours and consistently well-formed petals make them an ideal exhibition plant. They are easy to grow provided the soil is well drained and the site is sunny.

A variety of garden pests may eat the leaves *(right)* and flower heads *(above)* of the gladioli. These include slugs and snails, caterpillars and earwigs, all of which are capable of climbing a considerable height up the plant. They may also feed on the corms of growing plants. Slugs and snails are a particular nuisance, feeding at night and thriving in mild, moist conditions. Well-fertilized soils, with plenty of organic matter, also encourage them. Hand-pick any that are visible. Otherwise, spray the plants with metaldehyde, which may only stun the pests, but will make hand-picking easier.

SOIL

A deep, fertile soil, which has good drainage, is a particularly important requirement. It is essential to supply the right growing conditions.

POSITION

Sunlight is a crucial growing requirement to encourage healthy growth and flowering in summer.

PROPAGATION

Propagation involves planting cormlets in spring. Plant to a depth of 2in (5cm), but do not expect flowers until the second year. Seeds may also be sown outdoors in spring, but flowers will not appear until the third year.

PLANTING

Winter	Spring	Summer	Autumn

Plant in spring and space the corms out, so that they are 6in (15cm) apart and 4in (10cm) deep.

PROTECTION

Protection is not necessary during growth, but in early autumn, after flowering has finished, make sure you dig up the corms, avoiding injury. Keep the largest corms, cut off the leaves and store over winter in a frost-free, dry, cool place. Remove the old shrivelled corms from the base of the new ones.

FEEDING

Dig manure into the soil in the autumn before planting the corms, and then work in a compound fertilizer just a week before planting.

WATERING

Make sure that the plants are kept well watered in dry conditions. Otherwise no extra moisture is needed.

STAKING AND PRUNING

As soon as the flower-buds appear, the plants will need staking. Use a cane, attached to the opposite side of the stem to the buds, to support the plant.

Hebe

These evergreen, flowering shrubs are not very tall plants, averaging a height of 2-4ft (60-120cm), although some can grow to 5-6ft (1.5-1.8m). The varieties that come from New Zealand have pretty spikes of flowers in the middle of summer, but again there are exceptions such as 'Midsummer Beauty', with blue-lilac and white flowers earlier in the summer, and 'Autumn Glory', which is purple-coloured and flowers continuously from late summer to early winter. Colours are in the crimson, violet, lavender, pink, white range, and the *speciosa* hybrids are especially attractive, flourishing in sea air. The white-flowered *H. pinguifolia* 'Pagei' has grey leaves forming mats of foliage, which are excellent as groundcover.

Hebe is a trouble-free evergreen shrub, whose flower spikes appear from mid-summer onward. Typical shades are purple, blue and lavender *(below)*, but crimson, pink and white also occur *(bottom)*.

PESTS AND DISEASES

Leaf spot This takes the form of black spots surrounded by yellowing areas on the leaves. Considerable premature defoliation and weakening of the plant will result. Thorough removal of affected leaves and collection of fallen ones, every two weeks or so, will help in control. It may also be necessary to cut the plant back severely to encourage fresh uncontaminated growth. Repeated spraying with benomyl will help if other measures fail.
Mildew Yellow or light brown spots occur on the leaves of young plants; these subsequently fall. Spray with mancozeb after removing affected leaves.

SOIL

Most soils will suit these shrubs, although it is preferable to find a site that is well drained and a slightly chalk-based soil.

POSITION

These plants prefer to be grown in sunny conditions, but can survive in a little shade.

PROPAGATION

The best method of propagation is by taking soft cuttings. This should be carried out in summer.

PLANTING

Winter	Spring	Summer	Autumn

There are two suitable planting times: either in mid-autumn or in spring. Make sure the site is in a sheltered part of the garden.

PROTECTION

Not all of these plants are hardy and some protection will be needed in severe weather. This particularly applies to the *speciosa* hybrids.

FEEDING

Mulch annually in spring and also apply a potash fertilizer in early spring.

WATERING

Hebes should be kept well watered during any prolonged drought, but otherwise watering is not generally required.

STAKING AND PRUNING

A light pruning will be required in the middle of spring, to shape and tidy up the plants. Staking is not necessary.

Helianthemum

These low-growing, evergreen shrubs are natives of Europe, including Britain. They can be cultivated to trail down over rocks in any sunny niche, and will provide a mass of bloom throughout the summer. The colours of the saucer-shaped flowers, 2in (5cm) wide, vary, depending on the cultivar and include pink, deep red, orange, yellow, white, salmon, brick-red and rose pink. Each flower only lasts a day, but there are so many that blooming is constant. Sun roses need little care but it must be the right care, and they must be planted in a suitable site. They will then flower profusely and grow vigorously, as pest and disease problems do not occur.

Helianthemums, or rock roses, are ideal for both rocky sites and stony soils *(above)*. They are natives of Mediterranean climates, where they grow wild on steep hillsides. Some helianthemums are trailing in habit, others upright and low-growing, but all flower well.

SOIL

Put into well-drained soils where there are also rocks present, over which the stems can trail.

POSITION

Sun roses must be situated in the full glare of the sun. Flowering will then be as impressive as it should be.

PROPAGATION

Propagation may be carried out in spring by division, or in summer by taking cuttings, 2in (5cm) long, and cultivating them in a sandy soil, under a frame.

PLANTING

Winter	Spring	Summer	Autumn

Plant in mid-autumn or mid-spring, leaving a space of 1½ft (45cm) between each plant.

PROTECTION

The best protection for these plants is to site them in a sheltered place. This will ensure that they grow vigorously and flower profusely. Extra protection is necessary in severe winters.

FEEDING

Sun roses do not need any fertilizer application. They will bloom prolifically enough without feeding.

WATERING

Water is not generally necessary, although will obviously be beneficial in prolonged droughts.

STAKING AND PRUNING

Hard cutting back will be required directly after flowering has finished. Dead flower-heads should be removed with shears, as well as part of the stem, 2in (5cm) long. There may be dead growth beneath the mass of flowering shoots, which must also be removed.

Helleborus

The hellebores were regarded in ancient times as powerfully medicinal plants, of particular use for hysteria, nervous complaints and as a purgative, and were used for these purposes by the Greeks and Romans. In fact, the plants are poisonous if more than the prescribed quantities are eaten. They are handsome perennials, flowering through winter and in early spring. The Christmas rose *(H. niger)* is white, the Lenten rose *(H. orientalis)* is pink or maroon and *H. lividus corsicus* is a light green species, flowering in spring. All are about 1-2ft (30-60cm) tall.

PESTS AND DISEASES

Slugs and **snails** These pests eat leaves and young shoots in the spring and the flowers in winter as they unfold.
Fungal disease A fungal infection results in dark brown or black blotches on leaves. Leaves then wither and the plant eventually dies. Remove and destroy affected leaves and treat occasionally with a copper-containing spray. The disease can spread rapidly in autumn or spring.

Hellebores provide attractive blooms in winter, suitable for a mixed border. They are also excellent as cut flowers, as they are very long-lasting, and their foliage is another asset. *H. lividus corsicus (above)* has three-lobed, evergreen leaves with cup-shaped, yellow-green flowers. *H. Orientalis (right)* produces cream-coloured blooms and is purple-speckled inside.

SOIL

A moist, fairly heavy soil is the most suitable site, provided the soil is also well drained.

POSITION

These winter-flowering plants need to be placed in partial or dappled shade, but preferably not full sunlight.

PROPAGATION

Increase can be carried out by seed, which should be sown outdoors as soon as it is ripe. Division is another method and should be performed immediately after flowering. This is important as these plants do not like to be disturbed once they are established.

PLANTING

Winter	Spring	Summer	Autumn

Plant at the end of autumn or at the beginning of spring. The plants should be spaced out, 1-1½ft (30-45cm) apart.

PROTECTION

It is advisable to protect the plants in winter by covering them with cloches. This will ensure that the flowers are kept clean.

FEEDING

Apply a leaf-mould mulch in spring to all plants, and those bedded in light soils will also require an application in early autumn.

WATERING

Additional watering will be necessary in dry weather, but is otherwise not required.

STAKING AND PRUNING

There is no need to assist these plants with any staking or pruning and it is best if they can be left undisturbed.

Hibiscus

The tree hibiscus *(H. syriacus)* is closely related to the exotic South Sea island kind and has the same shaped flower, with the long central column of stamens. Flowers start appearing in late summer and undeveloped buds may still be present in early winter as the leaves fall. They flower profusely in red, purple, blue, magenta or white, and grow slowly to about 8-9ft (2.4-2.7m) tall and almost to that width.

PESTS AND DISEASES

Problems are few aside from routine pests such as **greenfly, caterpillars, capsids** and **leafhoppers.**

Lichen may occur on the branches of the hibiscus *(right)*, where conditions are too moist. *H. syriacus* is a shrubby species *(below)*, whose flowers appear in late summer to early autumn. There are many varieties with colours varying from white pink and red to purple.

Aphids may attack the buds and opened flowers *(below)*, of tropical species. Remove by hand or spray with insecticide.

SOIL

These plants are able to grow in any moderate to poor soil, provided it is relatively well drained.

POSITION

If this shrub is placed in direct sunlight, it will produce fuller and more luxuriant blooms.

PROPAGATION

Take half-ripe cuttings of short sideshoots, with their heel attached, in mid-summer. Put these cuttings into a frame and make sure the atmosphere is kept humid. Layering is another method of increase and is also carried out in mid-summer.

PLANTING

Winter	Spring	Summer	Autumn

Plant in spring, but do not be surprised if the shrubby hibiscus does not sprout at once. It takes a long time to establish and may not show any signs of growth until summer. Even when established, this type of hibiscus is one of the last to come into leaf.

PROTECTION

Protection from strong, cold winds is advisable, and it is often better to plant in a sheltered spot in the first place.

FEEDING

The only feeding that is needed is to apply a light mulch in spring to maintain good soil conditions.

WATERING

These shrubs can generally survive without any additional water, except when a prolonged dry period occurs. In this case, it is advisable to make sure that some moisture is supplied.

STAKING AND PRUNING

The hibiscus is a sturdy shrub that does not need any staking. Pruning is not required either.

Hydrangea

Hydrangeas flourish in seaside gardens. They grow into mounds of bushes, 5ft (1.5m) high and wide, and are topped with large, round balls of pink, blue, purple or white flowers in summer, which last into autumn. In inland gardens they need to be sheltered from strong or cold winds and draughts. Hydrangeas with round flower heads are called Hortensias, those with flat heads are the Lacecaps. There are also climbing species and some taller, more tree-like kinds.

PESTS AND DISEASES

Capsids These insects are very partial to hydrangeas, feeding lavishly on the young leaves, tips of shoots and flower-buds during the first half of the summer.
Grey mould, mildew and **leaf spot** These diseases sometimes infect the leaves and stems.
Slugs New stems may be attacked as they come up through the soil.

Lime-induced chlorosis Yellow leaves at the tips of the shoots, spreading to leaves lower down the stems, are caused by this disease, which is in turn brought on by a soil that is too alkaline. Alkalinity is sometimes required to maintain a particular flower colour, but if conditions are too extreme, chlorosis will occur.

H. macrophylla is the common hydrangea *(far right)*, which has many varieties. Flower colouring depends on the acidity/alkalinity of the soil. In acid soils, flowers are naturally blue, and if pink or red plants are required, plants should be watered with ground lime. In alkaline soils, pink or red flowers can be changed to blue or purple by mixing iron sulphate with rainwater. This may only be done to established shrubs. Where a soil is too alkaline, the flower colouring will be affected *(right)*. If the leaves begin to turn brown and curl at the edges *(below)*, sufficient moisture is lacking.

Soil conditions that are too alkaline will adversely affect leaf colouring. Chlorosis will occur, causing yellowing between the veins of the leaves *(left)*. H. paniculata is distinguished from the common hydrangea by its arching flower heads, which appear in the second half of summer. They are white, turning pink with age *(right)*.

SOIL

These plants are fairly particular about their site and do require a fertile, well-drained soil.

POSITION

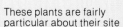

Hydrangeas can survive in either sun or some shade, but preferably not total shelter from sunlight.

PROPAGATION

Take cuttings from the tips of new, ripe shoots in late summer and keep them protected under a closed frame. Otherwise, take rooted suckers in late winter or spring.

PLANTING

Winter	Spring	Summer	Autumn

Plant in autumn or spring and make sure you leave a distance of 3-5ft (90-150cm) between each plant.

STAKING AND PRUNING

If the old flower-heads are left on the plants through the winter, they will protect the new buds beneath. This old growth should be cut back in mid-spring, leaving a pair of good, healthy buds. Cut out the dead shoots and one or two of the oldest shoots as well. Thin out any new shoots that sprout at ground level, although you may find that the slugs have already done this.

FEEDING

An annual mulch will encourage growth, and should be applied in late spring. Sequestrated iron and colourants should be supplied, if they are required, to offset any degree of soil alkalinity.

WATERING

When dry weather occurs, make sure that the plants receive plenty of water or they will wilt and die.

PROTECTION

These plants need to be sheltered from strong winds and draughts, as well as from severe frosts.

Ilex

The glossy, prickly, evergreen leaves and bright red berries of holly are a winter display, but the plant itself is an all-year-round decoration in the garden, especially if cultivars with yellow- or cream-coloured leaf margins are grown. There is an even pricklier version of *I. aquifolium* called 'Ferox', whose small leaves are covered in prickles on the upper surface. Only the female plants will carry berries and another male plant is necessary to be certain of fruits. Holly hedges tend to be slow-growing, but they are handsome shrubs and most effective barriers.

PESTS AND DISEASES

Leaf miners These pests can be a serious problem, disfiguring the shiny leaves and causing them to fall early. Symptoms of infestation include pale or brown blotches and tunnels on the leaves. Hand-pick any affected leaves and destroy them. Spray with dimethoate in bad attacks.

The evergreen, slow-growing holly makes a superb hedge. Dense and prickly, it can withstand yearly clipping. Holly with variegated leaves and red or yellow berries makes a good ornamental tree *(above)*. Leaf-spot fungal diseases may occur if the plant is short of food or water *(right)*. The main problem, however, is leaf miner.

SOIL

A moist soil is preferable, but avoid choosing a site where the soil is waterlogged.

POSITION

Sun or shade are suitable, but too much shade will make variegated-leaved kinds plain green in colour.

PROPAGATION

Increase can be carried out by seed, which must be stratified in autumn and then sown outside a year later.

Heeled cuttings can also be taken from sideshoots in summer, provided with a little extra warmth.

PLANTING

Winter	Spring	Summer	Autumn

Plant in early autumn or late spring. Space out the hedging plants at a distance of 15-30in (37-75cm) apart.

PROTECTION

Only the specimen trees require any protection from cold winds in winter.

FEEDING

These shrubs can survive without any fertilizer application, although those grown in poor soils will require some feeding.

WATERING

The holly tree tends to need attention in its early years, until it has become established. This means that water should be applied copiously after planting, especially if dry weather occurs. Overhead spraying will also be required daily.

STAKING AND PRUNING

Young trees will need staking to give them initial support. It is not necessary to provide regular pruning. However, if you want to shape specimen trees, this should be done in late spring. Formal hedges need an annual clipping at the end of summer.

Iris

The elegant iris is ideally suited to waterside planting. The severe and formal silhouette of its leaves perfectly complements the precise, glass-like smoothness of the water.

Irises have been cultivated for at least 3,500 years, firstly by the ancient Egyptians and then by gardeners of other civilizations ever since. The bearded iris hybrids of *I. germanica* and the Dutch and English iris, which flower in summer, are the best known, but *I. reticulata*, a scented mixture, 6in (15cm) tall, is equally desirable, flowering in mid-winter. The Japanese irises, *I. kaempferi* and *I. laevigata*, are exquisite, with large flowers, 5-6in (12-15cm) wide, flowering in mid-summer. All colours are represented, often in subtle shades such as mahogany, bronze-yellow, black-purple, velvety blue and salmon peach. As well as the normal flower fragrances, aromas of fruit and chocolate float on the warm air of a summer day. *I. florentina* is the plant that supplies Orris root, which smells of violets and is used in pot-pourri.

Left Infestations of greenfly, which can attack any plant, result in mottled flower and leaf colour, distortion of buds and stunting. Hand-picking will help to eliminate the problem. The bearded iris *(below left)* flowers in early summer and is available in a range of colours and scents. The upright petals are called 'standards', the lower, turned-down petals are the 'falls' and the ridge of hairs on the upper side of the lower petals, the 'beards'.

PESTS AND DISEASES

Slugs and **snails** These pests can be a nuisance on the leaves.

Caterpillars A variety of caterpillars may feed on the foliage, in particular the larvae of the iris sawfly.

Bacterial soft rot This is a common problem of the rhizomatous type of iris, such as the bearded iris, and can also affect bulbous irises, especially if they are grown in badly drained soil.

Leaf spot Symptoms include grey or brown spots, with yellow to reddish margins, on leaves. This condition is worst in wet weather or if the soil has limited drainage. Hand-pick badly affected leaves and spray with mancozeb every few weeks for the rest of the season. Remove and destroy dead leaves in the autumn.

Ink disease This is characterized by black blotches and streaks on the bulbs and black markings on leaves, preceded by yellowing in those areas. Bulbs are ruined if they are infected and should be burnt. Bulbous irises such as *I. reticulata* should be planted in a different place the following year.

SOIL

The bearded and bulbous irises require a well-drained soil, preferably lime based. The Japanese irises, however, do not like lime: *I. kaempferi* needs a wet soil, and *I. laevigata* actually requires shallow water.

POSITION

Irises will thrive in open, sunny positions. They require sunlight to produce their colourful blooms.

PROPAGATION

Sow seeds, as soon as they are ripe, in sandy compost under frame. Division of rhizomes is another method of increase. Offsets can be separated in autumn.

PLANTING

Winter	Spring	Summer	Autumn

Plant the bearded kinds in mid-summer, autumn or the start of spring. Space them 1-1½ft (30-45cm) apart, with half the rhizome above the soil. The Japanese irises can be planted in mid-autumn or early spring, 2ft (60cm) apart; the bulbous type from late summer to early autumn, 3in (7cm) deep and 6in (15cm) apart.

PROTECTION

Protection will not be required, as these plants can withstand most adverse conditions.

FEEDING

The bearded irises will need a phosphatic fertilizer dressing straight after flowering. The Japanese kinds require liquid feeding during the summer.

WATERING

Watering is not generally necessary, although it is important to make sure that *I. kaempferi* are kept well watered during droughts.

STAKING AND PRUNING

Staking and pruning are not necessary, as these hardy plants are able to support themselves.

Although the majority of irises are summer-flowering, there is a dwarf species called *I. reticulata* that flowers in winter *(far left)*. Only 6in (15cm) tall, it is ideal for rock gardens or containers. The Japanese irises look like large brightly coloured butterflies perched at the top of stems *(above)*. They need wet conditions in which to grow for most of the year, unlike the rest of the irises. *I. kaempferi (lower left)* and *I. laevigata (left)* are particularly suitable for moist soils. Leaf spot sometimes infects the leaves of irises *(centre left)*. This is usually the result of a fungal disease and will be found on those species that require dry conditions, but are actually growing in badly drained soils.

Kniphofia

Sometimes called torch lilies, kniphofias are indigenous to South and East Africa, from which places they were first introduced to Europe in 1707. In general, flowering is in late summer, but can extend from early summer into autumn with the right choice of species and varieties. Plants with orange, red or white pokers can be obtained as well as the usual orange-red and yellow, bicoloured kind, with heights varying from 2-5ft (60-150cm).

The right cultural conditions are very important. If these are not supplied, the plants will languish from year to year and never really display themselves at their best.

PESTS AND DISEASES

Earwigs The tubular flowers are ideally suited to infestations by these pests.

Red hot pokers or torch lilies, as the kniphofias are commonly called, are natives of southern Africa and are at their most magnificent in fertile, sandy soil and situated in plenty of sunlight. Their unusual shape, with their long stems and tubular or spike-shaped flower heads *(left)*, make them stand out in any border. They generally grow to a height of about 3ft (90cm) but they can grow to 6-8ft (1.8-2.7m) tall. Colours are an orange-red and yellow *(below)* for the typical forms, but also orange, cream and various shades of red.

Planted in clumps *(above)*, kniphofias provide a splendid and dramatic display. This is mostly due to their striking shape, but also to their mass of rush-like foliage. They are a useful plant to grow as they do not require a great deal of attention and can be left in the same site for several years, provided the soil is well drained. It is advisable, however, to remove the flower spikes, after they have faded *(left)*. Breaking the heads off close to the basal shoot will encourage future flowering. Each of the tubular flowers have open ends that point downward and provide an ideal place for earwigs *(right)*. These insects will then feed on the petals during the night, making them ragged and torn. This, in turn, means the flowers fade and the plant may become diseased.

SOIL

A deep, sandy soil, which is also well drained and fertile, containing plenty of rotted organic matter, is ideal for these plants.

POSITION

As natives of Africa, these summer-flowering plants can ony be expected to flourish if they are positioned in full sunlight.

PROPAGATION

Increase can take place by division, provided replanting occurs as quickly as possible. The brittle roots must also be handled with great care and must not be allowed to dry out. Flowering is unlikely to occur until the second summer.

PLANTING

Winter	Spring	Summer	Autumn

The roots of this plant are wide-spreading, so sufficient space must be provided. A distance of 2-3ft (60-90cm) should be left between each plant. Planting time is in spring, and it is advisable not to disturb the plants for several years after this.

PROTECTION

In autumn, tie the leaves together above the crown to protect the plant from winter wet and subsequent rotting.

FEEDING

A mulch should be applied in spring, to ensure healthy flowering and vigorous growth.

WATERING

The roots must not be allowed to dry out while they are establishing. Water in prolonged droughts.

STAKING AND PRUNING

It is not necessary to stake the plants, because they grow upright naturally. No pruning is required.

Lathyrus

The sweetpea is fragrant and beautifully coloured in pastel shades of mauve, blue, pink, cream, red and rose-pink. Some hybrids have picotee edges to the petals and there are now strains which only grow 2-3ft (60-90cm) tall, which do not need supports and are a mass of flowers all summer.

Right and **below** Sweetpeas flower from mid-summer right through until the middle of autumn. They are typical 'pea' flowers of the Leguminosae plant family, to which they belong, and are usually found in delicate pastel shades. They are mostly climbing plants, but there are also short-growing kinds for massing and bedding. These are called 'Knee-high' and only need sticks for support.

PESTS AND DISEASES

Thrips Sweetpeas can be badly disfigured by thrips feeding on flowers and leaves in summer.
Viral diseases Greenfly, infesting the leaves and leaf tips, can spread viral diseases such as **streak** (bean yellow mosaic), which causes brown or pale yellow stripes on stems, and **pea mosaic**, which causes flecks and streaks on the flowers. Plants will be stunted and cease to grow.
Black root rot and **foot rot** These are the most common causes of a plant withering and dying.
Slugs and **snails** will eat young plants as soon as they are set out, and **birds** tend to peck off flower-buds.
Mildew may occur toward the end of summer.

The climbing plants attach themselves to their supports by means of leaf tendrils. The plants need to be supplied with stakes and may also need tying in *(above)*. Cordon-trained sweetpeas should be supplied with canes, 5-7ft (1.5-2.1m) tall, with one stem attached to each cane by string. The flowers *(left)* should consist of an upright rounded petal, two side-petals and two more petals at the base, folded together forming the keel.

SOIL

A well-drained, rich soil, which was well manured and deeply dug in the autumn before planting, is preferable.

POSITION

Sweetpeas thrive if they are positioned in the full rays of the sun and in a spot that is sheltered from the wind.

PROPAGATION

The best method of propagating the climbing sweetpea is by sowing seed outdoors in spring.

PLANTING

Winter	Spring	Summer	Autumn

Plant in spring, leaving a distance of 6in (15cm) between each plant, and at a depth of 2in (5cm).

PROTECTION

Protection is not an essential requirement for most sweetpea climbers, but young plants sown in autumn need shelter in a cold frame for the winter.

FEEDING

Fertilizer application is not generally required, although it sometimes benefits the plant to have an occasional liquid feed. The cordon-trained sweetpea needs a weekly liquid feed throughout the summer.

WATERING

Watering is not a necessity with these climbers, unless a long dry period occurs, and then they should be well watered.

STAKING AND PRUNING

Supply netting, twiggy sticks or a trellis on walls or fences for support. Growth may be allowed to proceed unchecked, although if flowers are picked frequently, blooming will be more prolific.

Lavandula

The smell of lavender has a sweet pungency with an aromatic undertone. Its fragrance and also its moth-deterring qualities first encouraged the Elizabethans to put lavender sachets among their clothing and bed-linen. As a perfume it is refreshing, and it was probably added to water for washing by the Romans, as the name is derived from the Latin, *lavandus*, 'to be washed'.

PESTS AND DISEASES

Leaf spot and **shab disease** Both of these occur in the wrong cultural conditions or under mono-cropping. Leaf spot shows as small, round, brown spots on stems and leaves and causes the leaves to fall. It is associated with shab, in which entire shoots wilt suddenly from the beginning of summer, and die. Spraying with thiram sometimes helps, but it is advisable to take tip cuttings at once and start new plants well away from the diseased bush.

The fragrant flowers of this much-loved, evergrey shrub *(above)* have inspired the name for the colour purple-grey. The plant has been used to supply perfume for hundreds of years from the time of the Romans and even earlier. A great number of butterflies, including the cabbage white butterfly *(right)*, bees and other pollinating insects are likely to be attracted by their powerful scent.

SOIL

A well-drained sandy soil is the most suitable site for these shrubs. They even prefer a medium to poor quality soil.

POSITION

Lavender flourishes if it is placed in direct sunlight, where it will emit sweeter-smelling scents.

PROPAGATION

Cuttings may be taken from the tips of the plants in summer. However, the rooted cuttings must be protected in the winter in a cold frame.

PLANTING

	Winter	Spring	Summer	Autumn

There are two planting times: the beginning of autumn or mid-spring. Space the plants at a distance of 2-3ft (60-90cm) from each other.

PROTECTION

Protection will only be required in severe winters, but it is advisable to find the plants a sheltered position in the first place.

FEEDING

These plants grow prolifically, without the help of any mulches or fertilizer dressings.

WATERING

Watering is not necessary, even in very dry weather. In fact, these plants seem to thrive in drier conditions.

STAKING AND PRUNING

Cut away flower-heads in dry weather as soon as they have faded. A spring pruning will also be required, just as the new growth is starting, to remove the previous year's growth by half its length. This will prevent the bush becoming leggy. Staking is not necessary, because lavender is a low-growing bush.

Ligustrum

Hedge and privet are almost synonymous in the English language and, although privet is easily grown, tough and virtually indestructible, this does not offer any explanation for its common name. It has been suggested, by a famous Victorian gardening writer, that its name is derived from the fact that it was often planted in gardens to conceal outdoor lavatories (privies). Alternatively, it may be an adaptation of the word 'private', where hedges or privets were planted to make an otherwise open garden private and impenetrable to prying eyes.

Ligustrum ovalifolium is a bush densely covered with evergreen leaves, which makes it a very useful barrier. However, it is worth first considering it as a specimen shrub, as it has long clusters of white flowers in summer with an aroma which some people like, but others detest. Black berries follow the flowers and it grows 15ft (4.5m) tall.

PESTS AND DISEASES
Caterpillars The larvae of the privet hawk feed on the leaves during summer, but as these insects are fast becoming an endangered species and do no real harm to plants, they are best left alone. **Leaf miners** mark the leaves with pale brown blotches, and **leafcutter bees, thrips** and **scale insects** occasionally occur in large numbers. **Honey fungus** This can be a serious problem. **White root rot** This is another serious problem. As soon as leaves start to turn yellow and fall in summer, this rot should be suspected. However, by this stage it is already too late to save the plant. The roots will probably be covered in white fungal threads, which darken with age. Like honey fungus, the disease spreads to plants on either side — privet hedges may die in sections. Infected plants should be dug up completely and destroyed, and the soil replaced or sterilized.

Privets are usually only considered useful as hedging plants, with their thick, evergreen foliage. *L. ovalifolium* 'Aureum' *(above)*, however, has bright yellow leaves, which provide a very vibrant focal point. It needs sun, becoming poorly coloured in shady sites.

SOIL

Soil is not a problem. The plants will be happy in any soil, which makes them suitable as hedges in any area.

POSITION

These shrubs do not have to be situated in any particular spot. They can thrive in either sun or shade.

PROPAGATION

The method of propagating this shrub is by taking hardwood cuttings in the middle of autumn. They are quite hardy and can be rooted outside in the normal way.

PLANTING

Winter	Spring	Summer	Autumn

Plant between autumn and spring, spacing the hedging plants at a distance of 8-18in (20-45cm) apart, depending on their age and size of roots at the time of planting.

PROTECTION

These shrubs are so hardy that any protection would be wasted. They can survive in almost any adverse conditions.

FEEDING

Some feeding will be beneficial. A spring mulch will encourage healthy growth, especially where the shrub has been planted in particularly poor soil.

WATERING

It is rarely necessary to apply any extra water, although some water will revive growth in prolonged droughts.

STAKING AND PRUNING

The privet grows prolifically, so that formal hedges will need clipping two or three times each growing season, but with not less than a month between each cutting. No staking is required.

Lilium

As the rose is the queen of shrubby plants, so the lily is the queen of the bulbous kingdom. Tall and graceful, its distinction and fragrance ensure it a place in every garden. Some lilies are rare and costly, but the regal lily *(L. regale)* and the madonna lily *(L. candidum)*, are among the least expensive, both heavily fragrant and pure white with golden anthers.

Depending on the species or varieties, lilies can flower throughout the summer. They grow to a height of between 2-6ft (60-180cm), and are coloured white, gold, orange, purple, green, pink or deep red, spotted and striped.

The lily genus is a widespread one, found in temperate climates throughout the world, and is among the most beautiful of flowering plants. It is divided into several groups whose growing needs vary. Flower shapes also vary, from the superb trumpet hybrids *(right)* to the reflexed kinds *(far right)* or wide-spreading, open varieties *(above)*.

SOIL

Different soils suit different types of liles. *L. auratum* for instance, requires a well-drained, acid soil, and *L. candidum* prefers an alkaline soil.

POSITION

Most lilies need to grow in sunny conditions, although some kinds prefer partial shade.

PROPAGATION

Divide bulblets and offsets, and plant in autumn. Scales can be taken from bulbs just after flowering and planted out a year later. In autumn or spring, seed can be sown in boxes of sandy soil and then planted out two years later.

PLANTING

Winter	Spring	Summer	Autumn

Plant lilies in late autumn, except for *L. candidum*, which must be planted in late summer. Place the stem-rooting kinds 6in (15cm) deep, although *L. candidum* should only be just covered with soil. The non-stem-rooting types only need to be 4in (10cm) deep. Plant each bulb on a handful of silver sand.

PROTECTION

Protection is needed against winter rain. Young shoots should be covered with cloches in spring as protection against frost.

FEEDING

An annual mulch of leaf-mould should be applied in spring to maintain the right soil structure.

WATERING

Water freely during the growing season and whenever a prolonged dry period occurs.

STAKING AND PRUNING

The taller varieties of lilies will need some support, against bad weather. No pruning is necessary.

The lily flower usually consists of six petals, often with protruding stamens *(left)*. Varieties can be found in most colours, except blue, looking particularly magnificent in oranges, reds and yellows. Some varieties are easier to grow than others and it is worthwhile investigating which are the least troublesome.

PESTS AND DISEASES

Lily beetles These tiny, bright red beetles and their dark yellow grubs feed on leaves and stems from late spring through the summer. Spray with resmethrin, if hand-picking does not provide sufficient control.
Greenfly can be troublesome, and **slugs, snails** and **rabbits** will eat new shoots. **Squirrels** dig up bulbs and eat them.
Virus Lily viruses can be a serious problem, so care should be taken to acquire bulbs from reputable sources, preferably specialist bulb suppliers. Symptoms include yellow mottling of leaves and distorted flowers.
Lily disease This fungus produces round or oval brown spots on leaves, which then wither starting at the bottom of the plant; flower-buds die. The disease spreads rapidly in wet weather; *L. candidum* is particularly susceptible. Destroy all infected vegetation and badly affected plants and spray the remainder with benomyl or dichlofluanid, repeating every two weeks. Other possible diseases include **rust** and **leaf spot. Foot rot** and **blue mould rot** may affect stored bulbs, in which case the bulbs should be destroyed. **Grey bulb rot** is a tulip disease, which can also affect lily bulbs. The plants should be dug up and destroyed and the surrounding soil removed.

147

Lonicera

Honeysuckle grows wild in hedgerows and light woodland; it scrambles over other plants, twining around them to reach the light. Its heavily scented, creamy yellow and pink flowers first appear at the start of the summer. There are improved garden forms of *L. periclymenum*: the early Dutch *(belgica)* and the late Dutch *(serotina)*. Other species have red or orange trumpets, but do not necessarily have a fragrance, and *L. japonica aureoreticulata* has leaves veined in a mosaic of yellow. Some are shrubby; the tiny, dark green-leaved *L. nitida* can be used to provide a closely knit, evergreen hedge.

A sweeter scent than that of the honeysuckle would be difficult to find, especially after dark, and no scented garden should be without it. *L. periclymenum* is the typical species and is a native of Europe. It has pink and cream or white flowers followed by round red berries *(above)*. Other species have orange or deep yellow flowers *(top)*, although they are not necessarily fragrant. The climbing kinds will twine up their supports to 20ft (6m) tall *(right)*.

PESTS AND DISEASES

Problems are few: if honeysuckle is grown in a hot, dry position, bad infestations of **greenfly** may occur; **leaf miners** are another possible pest.

SOIL

A fertile and well-drained soil will encourage the most vigorous growth and the healthiest plants.

POSITION

Honeysuckle likes the sun, but not all day, so partial shade is advisable. The roots also need shade to provide a cool root run.

PROPAGATION

Layering is generally the accepted method of increasing the honeysuckle. This must be carried out in autumn.

PLANTING

Winter	Spring	Summer	Autumn

Either plant in autumn or spring. The hedging variety of *L. nitida* should be planted with a distance of 1½ft (45cm) between each plant.

PROTECTION

The shrubby plants are not as hardy as the other kinds, and will require some frost protection in spring.

FEEDING

Mulch the plants with an annual application of leaf-mould in spring, enough to maintain the plants.

WATERING

These plants can survive well without water, except in prolonged dry weather, when they will welcome some moisture.

STAKING AND PRUNING

For climbing plants, supports should be supplied, such as walls or fences with wires, or trellises, pergolas, archways or stout posts. The plants will need pruning back to ensure they remain in the space provided for them. It will occasionally be necessary to remove old shoots after flowering. Hedge clipping should occur once a month, from late spring to early autumn.

Lupinus

The first lupins grown in Europe were annuals; the yellow tree lupin was discovered in California in 1792, and the ancestor of the perennial that is so familiar today, *L. polyphyllus*, was first introduced from British Columbia in 1826. The flower colours were originally only blue, purple, red or yellow, but crossed with the tree lupin, hybrids in many colours and bicolours have been produced, known as the Russell lupins after their hybridizer. Flowering time is in summer, with an average height of 3ft (90cm). The tree lupin grows quickly to about 5ft (1.5m) and flowers in its second year from seed in white, yellow or blue. It is, unfortunately, only a short-lived shrub.

Lupins are herbaceous perennials and are well suited to any border. For good, clear colour and long, regular flower spikes, the Russell hybrids are unbeatable *(left)*. However, slugs and snails will eat the shoots as they come through the soil in spring, later infesting the leaves *(below)*, and sometimes the stems.

PESTS AND DISEASES

Slugs and **caterpillars** Slugs attack the young shoots in spring; caterpillars the leaves in summer.
Leaf spot This often infects plants, producing dark-coloured spots surrounded by a lighter zone. Leaves wither and fall from the base of the stem progressively upward. In time, affected plants become stunted and poorly flowered. Remove affected leaves as soon as the disease is seen and treat with a spray containing copper. Improve the fertility of the soil.
Virus A viral infection will cause yellowing between the veins and brown streaking on the stems.
Foot rot and **mildew** may also infect the plants.

SOIL

These are acid-loving plants. They also like a deep and well-drained soil to allow maximum root expansion.

POSITION

The best position for lupins is in sunlight. However, they will survive if they are placed in dappled shade.

PROPAGATION

Increase can be carried out by sowing seed in spring, or cuttings may be taken from the new growth in mid-spring. The cuttings must be nurtured in cold frames.

PLANTING

Winter	Spring	Summer	Autumn

There are two suitable planting times, either in autumn or spring. Make sure that there is a gap, 2½ft (75cm) wide, between each plant.

PROTECTION

Both the young and fully grown plants can withstand most weather conditions, so it is not usually necessary to supply them with any protection.

FEEDING

Avoid over-feeding these plants, but if you apply a small mulch of rotted garden compost in spring, flowering will be more prolific in summer.

WATERING

Too much water will drown these plants, but they cannot survive long without any moisture. It is advisable to supply them with some water in prolonged droughts.

STAKING AND PRUNING

These plants are sturdy enough not to need supports, even though they are so tall. No organized pruning is essential, but a tidying-up exercise can be done after flowering.

Magnolia

Magnolias are one of the most beautiful of the flowering shrubs and trees. Magnolia has also become the recognized name for a particular shade of white, a thick, opulent, creamy colour, which is a fitting partner to the equally luxurious perfume of the flowers of some species.

The shape of the large flowers as they unfold has given magnolias the alternative common name of tulip-tree, although the true tulip-tree is *Liriodendron tulipifera*, a forest tree with green and orange flowers. In spring, magnolia trees look as though they have been lit up, with candles on their bare branches. Some species have pink-purple flowers. *M. stellata* has flowers with strap-shaped petals and is a shrubby plant, slowly growing to about 10ft (3m) tall. *M. x soulangiana* is a spring-flowering shrub and is one of the easiest to grow; *M. grandiflora* is evergreen and flowers in summer after its eighth year.

The magnolia was originally a native of the north American states and the Himalayan region. They are very popular flowers with their large, creamy white petals, which are sometimes tinged with a shade of pink *(below)*. Some species, such as *M. virginiana*, also have a strong, distinctive fragrance. Although they are generally pest-free, snails may be attracted to the foliage of the magnolia, and will eat holes in the leaves *(left)*. These pests are encouraged by moist conditions, especially in spring or autumn, and after mulching. They will feed at night leaving a slimy trail. As soon as this is noticed, the snails should be hand-picked.

SOIL

A

If possible, choose a deep, well-drained soil, which is moist and fertile. All varieties prefer acid soil, and *M. x soulangiana* should avoid lime-based soils completely.

POSITION

This shrub prefers to be sited in a sunny, sheltered spot. However, it will also grow in dappled shade.

PROPAGATION

Layering is one form of propagation and should be performed in the spring. The layers will take two years to root. Seeds may be sown in a cold frame, as soon as they are ripe. Germination takes between 12-18 months.

PLANTING

Winter			Spring			Summer			Autumn		

Spring is the most suitable planting time and late spring for the evergreen types. When planting, take care not to injure the roots.

PROTECTION

It is preferable to take measures to protect these shrubs before planting. Make sure, for instance, that they are sheltered from any wind or draught. Do not try planting them in a cold garden. Flower-buds will need frost protection.

FEEDING

A spring feed is important especially in the early years. Apply leaf-mould or a leafy compost dressing.

WATERING

The only watering that the trees will require is during an excessively dry period. Otherwise the roots will take up whatever moisture is in the soil.

STAKING AND PRUNING

Staking may be necessary in the early years. No pruning is required.

PESTS AND DISEASES

Magnolias are relatively free from pests and diseases: the main problems occur with cultivation. **Capsid bugs** and **scale insects** are both likely to occur, with the latter occasionally causing a serious problem. **Birds** may damage the flowers by pecking; **grey mould** may infect the flowers and buds in cold weather, especially after frost damage; and **leaf spot** and **die-back** sometimes show up.

Magnolias are prone to cold damage. Either frost or cold wind will damage the buds and petals *(top)*, causing them to die-back. The affected areas will be infected with grey mould, which will make the leaves turn brown and wither, eventually causing further die-back to occur *(above)*. Acid to neutral soils with good drainage are preferable, otherwise chlorosis, yellowing leaves *(left)*, will appear where the soil is alkaline. This discolouring will also occur where roots are not functioning as they should.

Malus

These are excellent trees for small gardens. The group consists of varieties derived from the crab apple *(M. pumila)*, a white-flowered tree, 20-30ft (6-9m) tall, with yellow fruit, 1-1½in (2-3cm) wide. 'Golden Hornet' usually has a glut of yellow, pear-shaped apples; 'John Downie' has larger fruits, flushed red; 'Montreal Beauty' has orange-scarlet apples, and *M. x purpurea* has crimson flowers, purple-green leaves and purple fruit.

Although the ornamental apple potentially has a formidable list of pests and diseases, in practice few occur. They are useful shrubs as they will grow in most soils and sites. *M.* 'Lemoinei' *(above)* is one of the outstanding hybrids with dark purple leaves, which become bronze-coloured at the end of summer and during autumn. The flowers are followed by dark purple-bronze fruits.

PESTS AND DISEASES

Crab apples are prone to many of the pests and diseases that affect the apple family as a whole, including common problems such as **greenfly, capsid bugs, caterpillars, red spider mites, leafhoppers, leaf suckers, mildew, chlorosis, birds, rodents, wasps, frost, woolly aphids, canker, fireblight** and **honey fungus.**
Scab This common fungal disease of apples shows up as black or brown spots on fruit; the fruit later cracks. Severe defoliation can occur in summer, and shoots will be blistered. Fallen leaves should be collected in autumn and burnt, and the affected parts of shoots pruned in winter. Spray captan four times: just before the buds burst in spring; at the 'pink bud' stage; when most of the petals have fallen and then three weeks later.

SOIL

Most soils are suitable for this tree, although a well-drained soil will ensure the best results.

POSITION

The crab apple prefers to be positioned in direct sunlight, where its fruit will flourish. However, it can survive in partial shade.

PROPAGATION

Seed may be stratified and sown in spring, but is unlikely to be true to the variety. Layering or hardwood cuttings may also be tried.

PLANTING

Winter	Spring	Summer	Autumn

Once a suitable site has been established, choosing the right planting time becomes important. This will fall between autumn and spring.

PROTECTION

The crab apple is a hardy tree. which can stand up to most weather conditions. Protection is not necessary.

FEEDING

These trees benefit greatly from feeding at the end of spring. A mulch of rotted organic matter is all that is needed, and may also be applied in autumn.

WATERING

No extra water is generally necessary, although the trees are not able to survive without water during very long, dry periods.

STAKING AND PRUNING

The trees will need to be trained when they are young, to ensure upright growth. This means supplying the young trees with supports, until they are established. Pruning is only necessary as a tidying-up exercise after flowering.

Narcissus

N. pseudonarcissus is a daffodil native to Britain, but many species come from Mediterranean countries, especially Spain and Portugal, as well as North Africa and parts of Asia. These bulbous plants with their spendid yellow, white, pink and orange blooms signify the end of winter and the beginning of the milder spring weather. There are many different species and varieties, including jonquils, the little hoop petticoats, the cyclamen-flowered narcissi, the familiar trumpet daffodils and all the dwarf varieties.

The flowers may be completely yellow, or white and yellow *(left)*, such as *N.* 'Tudor Minstrel', or white and orange *(right)*, for instance *N.* 'Fermoy', or orange, pink and cream or various combinations of these colours. The daffodils have long, central trumpets on their flower heads, whereas those of the narcissi are reduced considerably to not much

Easily grown bulbs, the daffodils and narcissi are at home anywhere in the garden. They can be planted in mixed borders or as part of a formal spring bedding scheme in neat rows. Alternatively, they can be scattered at random on a grassy site and planted where they fall, then left to naturalize over the years *(above)*. They will grow in most sites, fitting between plants, and may be planted below creepers, against a wall, where they will bloom and die down before the creeper flowers *(left)*. The leaves should not be cut when the grass is mown, but allowed to die down naturally.

more than a frill. The shape and size of the flower heads can vary dramatically, depending on their situation: whether they are growing in the garden or in the wild. The climate will be responsible for the flowering times, which can occur from the middle of winter in some parts, to the very end of spring in other places.

SOIL

Most of the narcissi will thrive in ordinary, but well-drained soils. The daffodil prefers a fairly deep soil.

POSITION

These bulbous plants are able to grow equally well in either sunny or shady situations. They are particularly prolific bloomers.

PROPAGATION

Separation of offsets or sowing seed in autumn are the usual methods of propagation. The seed will flower between three to eight years later.

PLANTING

Winter	Spring	Summer	Autumn

Early autumn is the usual planting time. Plant daffodils and other large bulbs at a distance of 4-6in (10-15cm) apart. If you are planting in heavy soil, place the bulbs 4in (10cm) below the surface, and 6in (15cm) deep in light soils. The dwarf varieties can be spaced out at the same distance as the large bulbs, but should be set 2-3in (5-7cm) deep into the ground.

PROTECTION

It is not necessary to supply protection of any kind as these are particularly hardy plants.

FEEDING

It is often advisable to apply a little compound fertilizer just after flowering.

WATERING

There is no need to water as the plants actually thrive with a good baking in summer.

STAKING AND PRUNING

No staking or pruning is necessary, but 'grassiness' arises if the plants are left to grow for many years without being dug up. 'Grassiness' is the state where the parent bulb has produced so many offsets that the top growth consists mostly of narrow leaves. This clump must be dug up and the bigger bulbs retained for replanting, while the offsets are discarded.

PESTS AND DISEASES

Narcissus fly grubs These insects, light grey in colour, feed inside the bulbs during summer and can destroy them completely. Symptoms include yellowing leaves, stunted growth and small flowers, or none at all. Infested bulbs should be burnt and the soil around the remaining bulbs dusted with HCH (BHC). The chemical should be raked in and holes and cracks in the soil filled, so that the top growth of the plants is surrounded by soil. Repeat the raking in summer and avoid planting any bulbs that feel soft.
Eelworms Bulbs infested with this pest have pale, twisted leaves with yellow patches. Growth is stunted and there will often be no flowers. Cutting the bulbs crosswise will reveal light brown concentric rings. Destroy infected bulbs, together with all other vegetation in the area, and avoid replanting narcissi or any other bulbs in the same site for three years.
Virus Typical symptoms of viral diseases are twisted leaves with yellow streaking, twisted flower stems and flecked flower colour. Narcissi that are small and poorly flowered may also be infected. These viruses are carried by greenfly and eelworm. All infected plants should be destroyed. Take care to obtain healthy bulbs from specialist nurseries.

Nymphaea

Plants which grow in water usually need little encouragement: few pests and diseases trouble them and the constant moisture and abundant food provided by rotting vegetation and animal remains are guaranteed to make any plant flourish. Water-lilies are no exception, and *N. alba*, growing wild throughout Europe, takes over any stretch of water in which it settles. Cultivated water-lilies have yellow, red or orange blooms and some of the tender kinds can also have blue flowers.

Water-lilies add charm and colour to any pool, with their large, cup-shaped flowers and floating, plate-like leaves *(above)*. There are species to fit most depths of water from 6-48in (15-120cm) and deeper. The white-flowered kinds are hardy and natives of temperate climates, but there are yellow-flowered kinds *(right)*, which belong to a different genus, *Nuphar lutea*. These aquatic plants, with their smaller and cup-shaped flowers, are suitable for shady sites, where the nymphaeas are not able to grow.

SOIL

These plants can be planted straight into water. They require a rich, fertile soil, which has been saturated before planting if it is not at the base of the pond.

POSITION

Choose a sunny, open position for these water- loving plants and avoid planting in the shade.

PROPAGATION

Division in spring is the best method of increase. The tender kinds, however, should be propagated by seed, also sown in mid-spring.

PLANTING

Winter		Spring		Summer		Autumn	

There are two methods of planting, and both should take place in late spring. Either plant the lilies in the base of a pool, or in potting compost in baskets weighed down with stones. Planting depth should be between 9-24in (22-60cm), depending on the vigour and variety of the plant concerned.

PROTECTION

The tender kinds require a minimum water temperature of 55°F (13°C), and an air temperature of 50°F (10°C).

FEEDING

It is not advisable to feed water-lilies, as manure can actually be harmful to them. The rich soil should be sufficient to feed them.

WATERING

Watering is obviously not a concern, as the lilies are constantly surrounded by water. However, they will do better if the water is kept clean during early growth.

STAKING AND PRUNING

The plants will adapt their growth to suit their environment and do not need any external support. Pruning is only required to control growth in summer.

PESTS AND DISEASES

Water-lily greenfly These pests are green or brown in colour. They cluster on the undersurface of the leaves, around the buds and on the open flowers, causing discolouration, curling and weakening. Treat by hosing the insects off the lilies into the pool.

Water-lily beetles Both adults and larvae are brown; both feed on the upper surface of the leaves in summer. Treat by hosing the beetles off the lilies into the pool.

Leaf spot Black spots and blotches on leaves indicate a fungal disease. Leaves may die completely. Pick off and destroy infected leaves.

There are hardy and tropical species of water-lilies. Both are easy to grow, although the hardy species are more suited to temperate climates, as they can thrive in most water and atmospheric temperatures. The tropical kinds, however, will not flourish in cold conditions. There are variously coloured, hardy water-lilies, which include the Marliacea hybrids, with yellow *(above)*, pink, bronze and red shades among their colouring. The flowers of water-lilies tend to open out with the light of day and close when the rays of the sun begin to fade. The leaves vary in size and offer shade to fish and also prevent algae from accumulating in the water. The leaves, however, are prone to leaf spot, which results from a fungal disease. These appear as circular, pale brown spots, which turn yellow with time.

Paeonia

The border peony is *P. lactiflora*, whose cultivars and hybrids are commonly grown. *P. officinalis* also plays a large part in the production of these delightful flowers. Single and double flowers occur, coloured pink, white, red, crimson, rose and carmine; some have differently coloured central petals, and some have central clusters of deep golden stamens. The tree peonies are quite different in habit and are rather gaunt shrubs, but the flowers of the Moutan peony *(P. suffruticosa)* and its hybrids are very beautiful.

The crimson peony, *P. officinalis (below)*, is an ancient and much-loved plant, which once had herbal uses. It flowers in late spring, and there are now many hybrids in shades of red, pink and white.

SOIL

There are some soil requirements. These consist of a moist and fertile site, which is also deep and well drained.

POSITION

These plants tend to prefer the sun, although some shade is useful as a relief from excessive sunlight.

PROPAGATION

Divide the plants in spring, or sow seed at the beginning of autumn. The seed must be kept in a cold frame.

PLANTING

Winter	Spring	Summer	Autumn

Plant in autumn or spring, leaving 2in (5cm) of soil above the brittle, fleshy roots. Space each plant out, at a distance of 2ft (60cm) apart. Choose the plant site carefully, as peonies dislike disturbance.

PROTECTION

Peonies will thrive without any form of protection. The plants are hardy and prefer to be left undisturbed.

FEEDING

Apply a mulch in early spring, and feed weekly with a high-potash fertilizer in the month before flowering.

WATERING

It is important to water copiously in dry weather, as these plants cannot survive without some moisture.

STAKING AND PRUNING

The taller varieties will require some support, especially if they are in exposed positions. No pruning is necessary.

PESTS AND DISEASES

Peony blotch Border peonies are often afflicted with this fungal disease, which produces large brown patches on the leaves. Although these look unattractive, the disease is not serious. Removing affected leaves and spraying with mancozeb if the symptoms persist is all that is needed.

Peony blight This is caused by a strain of grey mould specific to peonies. Dark-coloured patches develop on stems at soil level, on leaf stems and at the base of leaves and on the leaves themselves. Leaves wilt and infected flower-buds do not develop. Cut the plants right down to soil level in autumn; remove and replace soil around the stems. When new growth appears in spring, spray it with benomyl three times, at two-weekly intervals.

Bud disease Symptoms are poor flowering or non-flowering. Buds turn brown and do not unfold; the stalk of the bud hangs down and discolours. Insufficient potassium, water shortage, heavy watering following drought, or low night temperatures preceding hot, sunny days can all cause the trouble.

Phlox

Phlox is the Greek word for 'flame'; the Greek verb *phlego* means 'to burn' and the name is probably an allusion to the brightness of the flower colours. Phlox illuminate any border in summer, whether they are varieties of *P. paniculata* or the annual *P. drummondii*; the little *subulata* species, 6in (15cm) tall, are equally brilliant in the rock garden in the spring and early summer. Border phlox grow to 1½-4ft (45-120cm) tall and their flowers, which are 1in (2.5cm) wide, grow in clusters in many shades of purple, blue, crimson, salmon, lilac, pink and white. Seldom seen in numbers or good growing conditions, the potential of phlox for garden ornament is largely unfulfilled.

The tall border phlox is the best-known form of the genus, but the dwarf kinds, such as *P. drummondii* (*above*), make excellent bedding plants for summer. They provide a remarkable display of colour.

PESTS AND DISEASES

Leaf spot Dark brown spots appear on the leaves. Pick off the affected leaves and spray the plants with benomyl.

SOIL

Generally, a deep, well-drained soil, which is fertile and fairly heavy, is the most suitable type for these plants. Annuals, however, prefer a lighter soil.

POSITION

Areas which receive sun make the most suitable sites for these plants. They will also accept a little shade.

PROPAGATION

Take root cuttings just at the end of winter. Other propagation methods include division or seed sowing in autumn or spring.

PLANTING

Winter	Spring	Summer	Autumn

Planting times vary. The perennials should be put in during autumn or spring; the alpines and annuals in spring. Space the plants out by 9-24in (22-60cm) apart, depending on the type.

PROTECTION

These plants are not normally affected by external factors, and can withstand most weather conditions without any protection.

FEEDING

Apply a mulch in spring. From the end of spring to the beginning of autumn, a liquid feed may be applied every week.

WATERING

Watering is not necessary during the majority of the year. However, should there be an excessively dry period, make sure that the plants are well watered, or they will start to droop.

STAKING AND PRUNING

The only pruning that will be required is to remove the weakest stems from the perennials. No staking is necessary.

159

Polygonatum

The derivation of the common name for this plant, 'Solomon's seal', has several explanations. They all refer to the scars left on the rootstocks by the leaves, which are thought to look like the impression of a seal.

The dangling, white, tubular flowers of this woodland plant appear in early summer, along stems about 2ft (60cm) high; there is a pink-flowered species, but it is rare and difficult to obtain. Solomon's seal spreads quickly, so its planting site needs to be chosen carefully, unless it is to be put in dry soil.

PESTS AND DISEASES

Caterpillars A sawfly caterpillar is the only real enemy of this plant. Grey, with black spots and a black head, this caterpillar feeds on the leaves, stripping them down to the midrib during the early part of summer. Hand-picking is the best control.

Lily beetles This pest, a tiny, bright red beetle, may also invade. Spray with resmethrin, if hand-picking does not provide sufficient control.

Solomon's seal grows naturally in woodland. Its flowers, which appear in late spring, dangle down below the stem *(above)*, while the leaves grow on the upper side of the stem *(below)*.

SOIL

A moist soil is the most suitable place to plant, although the ground must also have good drainage.

POSITION

Solomon's seal is a useful garden plant as it is happy to grow in shady sites. It is important to ensure that it is provided with a cool root run, although the flowers may be situated in sunlight.

PROPAGATION

Division is the most popular method of propagation for Solomon's seal. This should be carried out in spring or autumn.

PLANTING

Winter	Spring	Summer	Autumn

The planting time for Solomon's seal extends from the beginning of autumn to the end of spring. Make sure a gap of 12in (30cm) is left between each plant.

PROTECTION

No protection is generally necessary, so long as the roots are kept shaded from direct sunlight.

FEEDING

A spring mulch will encourage vigorous growth and revive the plant after harsh winter weather.

WATERING

These plants do like moisture, but extra watering is not required, unless there has been an excessively dry period.

STAKING AND PRUNING

Staking and pruning are not necessary, as these plants are hardy and vigorous.

Primula

These plants are ideal for heavy soils and moist situations, as well as being extremely hardy and resistant to cold weather. The primula group is also highly decorative, and can flower from spring until summer, with the right choice of species and varieties. Auriculas have the additional attraction of fragrance; *P. beesiana, bulleyana, denticulata* and *florindae* are all handsome species, 2ft (60cm) tall. They flower in orange, rose, lilac or yellow, and do well beside streams.

Primroses, polyanthus, cowslips and auriculas form part of the primula genus and there are many other species providing delightful flowers in many colours from spring into summer *(right* and *below right)*. Some primula flowers grow in whorls up stems, which can be 2ft (60cm) tall *(below)*. All colours except black and brown can be found.

PESTS AND DISEASES

Slugs and **snails** These pests will attack plants in spring, and are particularly attracted to auriculas.
Leaf spot A dark variety with a yellow halo can be troublesome on the blue-flowered primroses or polyanthus. Pick affected leaves and remove fallen leaves. Spray the plants thoroughly with benomyl or mancozeb, repeating three weeks later.
Birds The flowers may be stripped as they unfold.
Red spider mites Infestations may occur in hot, dry conditions.

Froghoppers or cuckoo-spit insects are sucking pests that feed on plants, but seldom do great damage *(above)*. They are easily washed off with a strong jet of water.

Primula denticulata (above) is an easily grown border primula, which does well beside water or in a rock garden and grows up to 12in (30cm) tall. It flowers during the spring. *P. beesiana (upper right)* is another beautiful primula, which flowers in early summer. It will hybridize freely when planted beside *P. bulleyana,* to produce seedlings that will grow in a variety of colours around the parent plants. The primrose, *P. vulgaris,* is a dwarf species, found growing naturally in woodlands in temperate climates. Single or double forms occur, and colour range is considerable *(right),* although yellow is the most commonly found. Polyanthus are thought to have originated from crosses between the primrose and the cowslip.

SOIL

A moist and well-drained soil is essential. If possible, choose a site near water, and soil that contains organic matter.

POSITION

These plants actually seem to prefer shady sites. There are also varieties that need some sunlight.

PROPAGATION

Increase can be carried out after flowering, by process of division. An alternative method is to take seed and sow it as soon as it is ripe.

PLANTING

Winter	Spring	Summer	Autumn

The most suitable times to plant primulas are during the spring and autumn months.

PROTECTION

Primulas are very hardy plants, which can endure almost any weather conditions. For this reason, it is not necessary to protect them.

FEEDING

A mulch, applied at the beginning of spring, will do much to revitalize the plants after a hard winter.

WATERING

As these plants like moist conditions, it is important to ensure that they are kept well watered during dry periods.

STAKING AND PRUNING

There is no necessity to provide any supports for young or older plants, as they are sturdy enough to support themselves. Pruning is not required either.

Primula vialii (left) is among the most distinctive of the primula species. It is a native of China and was first cultivated in 1907. The heights of the flowering stems vary between 1-2ft (30-60cm), with the flower spikes up to 8in (20cm) long *(above)*. The beginning to middle of summer is the usual flowering time for these spectacular poker-like flower spikes, with the tubular flowers changing colour as they mature. The leaves are long and lanceolate-shaped, pale green in colouring, and grow at the base of the stem. Damp soil, containing some leaf-mould, will encourage the healthiest growth.

Prunus

The ornamental cherries are among the prettiest of the small flowering trees, growing to an average height of 20ft (6m), with an even wider spread, and there are some that are vase-shaped. The Japanese varieties are the most attractive, such as 'Shimidsu Sakura' with double white, fimbriated flowers, 'Pink Perfection', 'Ukon' with creamy yellow, double flowers and vase-shaped habit, and 'Amanogawa', with double, pink flowers and upright growth. A beautiful weeping cherry is 'Kikushidare Sakura', with double, pink flowers, and a winter-flowering kind is *P. subhirtella* 'Autumnalis', with single, white flowers appearing intermittently throughout the winter. The genus also includes laurel, *(P. laurocerasus)*, used for evergreen hedging, capable of growing to 20ft (6m) high, and thus providing good screens as well as dense, formal hedges.

PESTS AND DISEASES

Caterpillars and **blackfly** may attack the cherries and birds will peck the buds.
Gumming This is a condition in which sticky, amber-coloured gum oozes from the bark. It may be caused by injury to the branch or trunk, and is often a sign of bacterial canker. Good feeding and watering is helpful if it is not bacterial. Remove any dead wood underneath the gum and cover the wound with a wound-sealing compound.
Lime-induced chlorosis Cherries suffer from this disease if grown in the wrong type of soil.

The prunus genus contains the Japanese flowering cherries and also ornamental plums and peaches *(above) P. persica (left)* is an ornamental and can be grown in a double-flowered form. Formal hedges can be made from the flowering plums *(below)*, mixing the green- and purple-leaved forms.

Bacterial canker is a serious disease on ornamental cherries *(right)*, and can kill off shoots, branches and even the whole tree, if the canker is allowed to encircle the affected limb. Cracked and splitting bark should be pared away back to the healthy tissue, and the wound should be treated with a sealing compound.

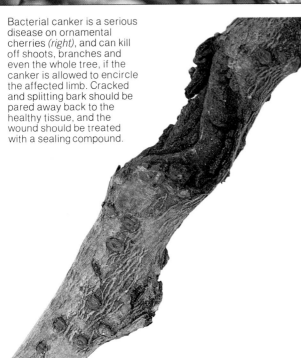

SOIL

Avoid shallow, chalky soils, which will encourage yellow leaves. A deep, fertile soil is preferable.

POSITION

The cherry and laurel prefer to grow in open, sunny positions. However, they can also be situated where there is partial shade, but the sun will encourage healthier blooming.

PROPAGATION

Grafting is an effective way to propagate fruit trees. Otherwise, taking hardwood cuttings in autumn is the best method of increasing the laurel, but these are slower to take root. Seed sowing is useful for cherry species.

PLANTING

Winter	Spring	Summer	Autumn

Most varieties can be planted from autumn through winter into spring, except for the laurel, which should be bedded in either autumn or spring and spaced out by 1-3ft (30-90cm) apart.

PROTECTION

The young trees may need some protection from small animals, which are liable to chew the bark. Wire-netting should be placed around the base of the tree. No other protection is necessary.

FEEDING

Some feeding is required, in the form of a spring mulch. No other fertilizer dressing is necessary.

WATERING

These are not very thirsty shrubs, and even during dry periods, they can survive without additional watering.

STAKING AND PRUNING

Staking is necessary where the trees are in an exposed position. Shape the trees at the end of summer. The laurel hedge will need clipping in spring or late summer.

Rhododendron

The rhododendron's only serious rival, as the most beautiful and varied of flowering shrubs, is the rose. It is, however, without doubt, the largest genus, having over 500 species and uncountable varieties, hybrids, strains and cultivars, which include the azaleas. Most of the rhododendrons come from the Himlayan regions of India, China, Burma and Tibet, but many azaleas are inhabitants of Japan, and it is from there that the famous 'Fifty' Kurume azaleas were chosen by a plant hunter called E.H. Wilson in the nineteenth century.

The size of the rhodendendron plants can vary from alpine dwarfs to large trees 60ft (18m) high, although most garden species are about 5-10ft (1.5-3m) tall. All colours can be found and flowers are funnel-shaped, tubular, bell-like or saucer-shaped, in clusters or ones and twos.

Rhododendron flowers are produced in clusters *(right)*, with the main flowering time in late spring. Azaleas are part of the rhododendron group, and can be deciduous or evergreen. They provide a range of brilliantly coloured flowers, which cover the whole bush and planted *en masse (below)* are an unbeatable sight.

SOIL

    A

A well-drained, preferably acid soil is conducive to the healthy growth of this plant.

If possible, it should contain some leaf-mould.

POSITION

This flowering shrub does not like direct sunlight. Dappled shade is

preferable, or at least some shade from the sun during the course of the day.

PROPAGATION

Seed may be sown in winter, provided some warmth is supplied. Heel cuttings, 3in (7cm) long, may be taken in summer, but these do not always root successfully.

Layering may be carried out in late spring, but this also has rooting drawbacks, often taking up to two years for rooting to occur.

PLANTING

Winter	Spring	Summer	Autumn

Plant in autumn or spring, remembering that these shrubs take up a large

amount of space and grow to a significant height.

PROTECTION

The only serious climatic hazard is a severe frost.

Some protection must be supplied if this is likely.

FEEDING

The roots will require a good leaf-mould mulch in spring

to maintain the nutrient soil content and structure.

WATERING

Otherwise the plants can be left to their own devices.

Watering is only necessary in severe droughts.

STAKING AND PRUNING

These are sturdy shrubs, which do not require any staking. Pruning is needed to shape the plant.

Deadheading is important after flowering has occurred.

Rhododendrons *(top)* vary in size with the smaller ones making suitable rock-garden plants. One of the most difficult pests to control is the vine weevil, which will attack both the rhododendron and azalea. The adults bite segments out of the edges of the leaves at night *(left)*. This is only half of the problem, however, as their dull white grubs live in the soil and feed on the roots. Another common complaint occurs when the plants are grown in alkaline soil, and is known as chlorosis. The leaves will gradually turn yellow *(above)* from the tips of the shoots downward, the plants will then cease to grow and will eventually die.

The colour range of the azaleas is enormous, including unusual blends of pinks, oranges and reds. Although they require moist conditions to produce these exotic shades, in damp climates where there is either too much atmospheric humidity or frequent rain, there is a tendency for lichen to grow on the shoots and branches *(above)*. This growth can be removed by hand to a large extent. However, if this does not stem the problem, spray the affected areas with tar-oil winter wash. This will destroy the alien growth, but should only be applied to the deciduous kinds of azaleas. Lichen is not actually very harmful to the plants, but is generally considered unsightly.

PESTS AND DISEASES

Provided rhododendrons are grown in the right type of soil they suffer from few problems. Pests and diseases which may occur include **whitefly, leafhoppers, azalea leaf miners, rust, scale insects, leafcutter bees, vine weevils** (adults and larvae), and **lime-induced chlorosis.**

Phytophthora root rot This causes slow growth and stunted plants with yellow leaves. All or part of the plant may eventually die. Excess moisture will encourage the disease. Affected plants should be destroyed and replanting in the same site avoided.

Bud blast On evergreen species, buds turn brown and are covered in black bristles, often following attacks by rhododendron

leafhoppers. Remove affected buds and destroy them. Spray the plants with mancozeb or captan the following year before flowering; then repeat monthly. Leafhoppers should also be controlled. If buds turn brown, but are not covered with black bristles, the cause is **frost.**

Rhododendron bugs These sucking insect pests can cause serious damage. They feed on the underside of leaves; leaves droop, turn rust-coloured underneath and mottled yellow and green on top. The bugs are tiny and black and mostly found during the summer, spreading rapidly in sunny, dry places. Small infestations can be dealt with by hand-picking; more serious cases should be controlled by spraying with

derris, resmethrin or malathion at intervals starting at the beginning of summer. As a further precaution, remove infested shoots early in the following spring to prevent the eggs laid on them from hatching.

Azalea gall This disease is most often found on azaleas, especially those grown in containers and in warm, enclosed, humid conditions. It can also infect rhododendron leaves. Symptoms are thickening of leaves, stems and flowers, which also turn a whitish grey. Affected parts, which are mainly the leaves, should be removed and burnt, and the plant sprayed with Bordeaux mixture or captan to protect it.

Rosa

The roses that are most commonly grown are not suitable garden plants for any gardener who wants to be carefree. They need a good deal of attention and are the target of many pests and diseases. The group known as the old-fashioned shrub roses, however, are a useful alternative as they take up much less time and are just as floriferous.

Both the cluster-flowered (floribunda) and the large-flowered (hybrid tea) bush roses have superbly shaped flowers, which lend themselves ideally to floral decoration and exhibition work — the cluster-flowered hybrids, in particular, are good for garden decoration. Many flower continuously from summer to autumn, and many of the new ones are fragrant. Colours and shading become more beautiful each year, and now include brown, green, silvery grey, blue-violet, amber and a fluorescent shade of orange-red.

Rosa rugosa (top), sometimes known as the Ramanas rose, is a vigorous and extremely hardy plant. It is also easily grown and disease-resistant and so is often used for hedges. The single flowers can measure 4in (10cm) wide, and appear throughout the summer. They are fragrant and coloured purple-pink in the species itself, but in shades of this colour and white in the hybrids. The flowers are usually followed by hips, which are large, handsome and tomato-shaped *(above)* R. glauca, until recently known as *R. rubrifolia,* is grown mostly for its foliage colouring, which is most intense if grown in a little shade *(left).* The height and spread are between 5-7ft (1.5-2.1m), and the pink flowers, which appear at the beginning of summer, are followed by many red hips.

SOIL

    N

Roses are adaptable shrubs and will grow in most soils.

However, a clay-type, fertile soil is preferable.

POSITION

A light, sunny spot is the ideal site for roses, although

they can grow in dappled shade.

PROPAGATION

Budding can be carried out in mid-summer; hardwood cuttings should be made in mid-autumn; or seeds can

be taken from the hips and stratified in sand for up to 18 months, before sowing outside in spring.

PLANTING

Winter	Spring	Summer	Autumn

Plant in autumn, winter or spring, making sure that the roots are well spread out. Space the plants 1-3ft

(30-90cm) apart. Shrubs and climbers should be 5-10ft (1.5-3m) apart.

PROTECTION

Any slightly tender species or young plant will need to

be protected, particularly when frost is likely.

FEEDING

Supply fertilizer dressing in early spring and early

summer. A mulch is also required in late spring.

WATERING

Watering is not generally necessary, except when a

long spell of dry weather occurs.

STAKING AND PRUNING

Staking will be required for standard roses, especially climbers. Pruning should be carried out in early spring, with two exceptions. Ramblers need pruning in early autumn, and old-fashioned shrub roses need shaping in summer. Suckers

must be pulled off as soon as they are seen, or they will take over the plant at the expense of the variety. Deadheading is necessary for flowering. However, if you want hips for decoration or seed, do not deadhead.

Roses are the most popular of the flowering shrubs. Their beautiful and often fragrant flowers continue to appear all summer and autumn. However, these blooms are often infested with aphids *(above)* and may need to be sprayed with insecticides at intervals during the summer. Water shoots *(left)* appear on bush roses during the growing season. These are strong growing shoots which flower late and may, therefore, be caught by frost. As they are rather soft, this can be damaging and protection may be necessary.

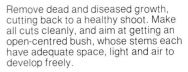

Remove dead and diseased growth, cutting back to a healthy shoot. Make all cuts cleanly, and aim at getting an open-centred bush, whose stems each have adequate space, light and air to develop freely.

Remove weak growths completely, making the cut level with the parent stem. This will concentrate the plant's strength on the good shoots and encourage these to grow more vigorously.

Cut out any stems that cross over other stems, removing the weaker growth. This will discourage overcrowding, which would hinder healthy growth. Also cut out any stems that grow into the centre of the bush.

Sucker growth on roses *(left)* consists of shoots produced from the rootstock. They can be distinguished from the stock or variety by the greater number of leaflets on each leaf, and by the darker colour of the foliage and stem. Such growths should be removed as soon as possible. They should be pulled off the root or parent stem, so that the 'eye' is completely removed to prevent further sprouting *(right)*. Alternatively, they should be cut as close to the point of origin as possible.

Bedeguars or Robin's pincushions are occasionally seen on roses *(right)*. They result from the activities of a gall wasp, which lays eggs in unopened buds, which then react by producing a ball of green, followed by bright red, filaments. The larvae overwinter in these balls and emerge as adults in late spring. Leaf galls *(upper far right)* also occur on roses, which may be due to midges, sawflies or gall wasps. Slugworms are the larvae of sawfly and resemble tiny slugs. Leaf tissue is eaten *(lower far right)* to leave the skeleton of the vein network, and bad attacks will slow down the growth of the plant. Black spot on roses *(below* and *bottom)* cannot be mistaken as the margins of the rounded spots are fringed. These will coalesce on the leaf surface so that large patches are affected.

Common pests which attack floribunda, hybrid tea and the climbing and rambling roses include **greenfly, capsids, leafhoppers, leaf suckers, red spider mites, cuckoo spit insects, caterpillars** and **thrips.** Common diseases include **mildew, rust, crown gall, lime-induced chlorosis, grey mould,** and, occasionally, **viruses.**
Leaf-rolling sawfly maggots These larvae feed inside leaves and cause them to roll from their edges down and inward, in which state they remain for the rest of the season. Feeding starts at the end of spring and, although little damage is done, the amount of leaf surface available for photosynthesis is considerably diminished, thereby slowing down the plant's development. Hand-pick affected leaves and hoe the soil in early spring, since the maggots overwinter in the ground. Spray with dimethoate early in summer to aid control.
Rose slugworm larvae These feed on the surface tissues until only a network of leaf veins remains. The larvae are black or yellow, similar to miniature slugs in appearance, and feed any time between late spring and early autumn. Again, the photosynthetic area of the leaf is reduced. Spraying is effective — bioresmethrin will have good results applied to both surfaces after the larvae have been hand-picked. Soil cultivation is also helpful.
Leafcutter bees These insects clip semi-circular pieces off the edges of the leaves, using the clippings to line their nests. The bees can be found in woodwork or holes in the soil. They are solitary bees, like the mining bees on lawns, and act as pollinators. Control is not necessary. Other plants invaded by these insects include laburnum, privet and lilac.
Tortrix moths These draw leaves together with threads and feed in small, unopened buds.
Lackey moths The larvae of these insects make tents of webbing on the plants, and feed inside the webbing. Removal of the tents and

A variety of caterpillars will feed on rose leaves *(left)*, biting large holes in them, and often attacking the buds and petals. The tortrix caterpillar will even spin the leaves together with its web. Caterpillars vary in colour and may be green (angle shades moth), yellow, red and black (grey dagger moth) yellow and black (buff tip moth) or hairy (vapourer moth), and can be very damaging. It is preferable to hand-pick them, where possible, and move them onto wild plants. Be careful with the hairy kind as they can cause extreme irritation to the skin. Otherwise, spray the plants with derris or trichlorphon.

PESTS AND DISEASES

hand-picking the insects is often all that is needed.

Chafer beetles The variety that attack roses are a metallic green colour and feed on the buds. This causes lopsided buds or means that the buds do not unfold at all. They also feed on the flower petals and stamens and make holes in the leaves. The large, white, brown-headed larvae, up to 1½ in (3.5cm) long, live in the soil and feed on the plant roots. Control of the adult is difficult, but the grubs can be treated by working HCH (BHC) into the soil. They are most likely to be found when digging land that has been uncultivated for some time.

Black spot This is probably the most well-known rose disease in both country and suburban gardens, although it is much less of a problem in cities and towns. The fringed black spots start to appear on leaves in spring and increase to such an extent that a bush may be defoliated by mid-summer. Affected leaves turn yellow before they fall. The trouble is accelerated in warm, wet summers, and in gardens with mild climates and a high annual rainfall. Some varieties are more prone to the disease and some are partially resistant. Yellow or orange colouring on the petals indicates a more susceptible variety. *R. foetida*, which is a species much used for breeding, is particularly sensitive to the disease. Some cultural control can be obtained by removing the affected leaves as soon as they appear in spring, then collecting up fallen leaves in autumn, as these can still spread the disease. Hard pruning in early spring is also required, as the disease can survive through winter on the shoots. Ensuring good soil drainage and growing the plants in the sun will help plants to grow strongly and ripen their growth. Use sulphur-containing fungicides for chemical control, or captan or thiophanate-methyl every two weeks from early spring onward.

Leaf spot Various dark-coloured spots may appear on the leaves. These are usually a result of unsuitable soil conditions, or the bushes have been planted badly.

Canker This problem occurs on stems, especially at soil level. Sunken spots and patches appear and start to crack at the edges. If this cracking encircles the stem, the part of the plant above the cracking will die. Improvement of soil drainage is important. Any snags and stumps should be removed when pruning, as well as dead and broken stems. Cankered stems must be cut away below the canker and the remaining section sprayed with thiophanate-methyl. Try to avoid injuring the lower part of the stem. Badly cankered bushes should be dug up and burnt.

Bud disease This only occurs occasionally. Buds will droop without opening, because the stem just behind the bud has flattened and shrivelled so that it can no longer pass food and moisture to and from the bud. Insufficient potassium, water shortage, heavy watering after drought, low night temperatures followed by hot, sunny days or susceptible varieties can all contribute to the disease.

Balling This is a physiological disorder, affecting buds. The buds will grow to full size, but will not open, turning brown on the outside instead. This is a varietal problem, which often occurs in wet weather. A bad attack of greenfly can increase the problem.

Galls These are also known as 'Bedeguars' or 'Robin's pincushion' and can be found on stems. They grow from buds and change from green to bright red as they mature. They look like a ball of thread ends and are caused by gall-wasps. It is not necessary to take evading action, except to remove any parts that look unsightly.

Frost damage This can be harmful to young leaves and unfolding buds in early spring. Buds may be burnt brown, leaves crinkled and puckered with brown margins. However, little real harm is done.

Syringa

Lilac fragrance is one of the sweetest of flower perfumes, and a lilac in flower is sensed long before it is seen, especially after rain. The particular shade of pale purple, which has given lilac its common name, comes from the Arabic, *lilak; S. x persica* was one of the first to be cultivated in Europe and is a native of Iran.

Besides the garden hybrids, in white, mauve, crimson, blue-purple and rose-pink, there are also some elegant species that are very satisfying plants to grow, such as *S. x persica* itself, and *S. velutina* with lilac-pink flowers in drooping clusters, 6in (15cm) long, and velvety, dark green leaves. *S. microphylla*, is also attractive and is a small plant, only 3-4ft (90-120cm) tall, with rose-lilac flowers appearing twice a year at the beginning and end of summer. The height of the garden hybrids is eventually about 15ft (4.5m) and flowering time is in early summer.

The lilacs contribute colour and fragrance to the garden in late spring and early summer, although they are not particularly outstanding for the rest of the year. They are easily grown, provided the soil is not badly drained, and can occur in single and double varieties. The colour range includes purple, mauve, lilac, blue-mauve, crimson, pink, white and roses. *S. vulgaris* is a popular species, whose varieties also vary considerably in colour *(right and far right).* It is important to deadhead the plants after flowering has finished *(above right),* otherwise seed production will be encouraged and greatly decrease flower production for the following year. At this stage the plant can also be thinned out by removing weak and crossing branches.

Damage caused by leaf miner consists of pale biscuit-coloured blisters. The affected leaves should be hand-picked and the plant sprayed with HCH, if necessary.

SOIL

Most soils will satisfy lilacs, although a chalky loam is preferable. As long as the soil is not waterlogged, the plants should thrive.

POSITION

Choose a site that is positioned in the sun or in slight shade, but not in a heavily shaded area.

PROPAGATION

Propagate by layering in the spring, or take half-ripe cuttings in late summer. Try to avoid lilacs that have been grafted, as they tend to sucker badly.

PLANTING

Winter	Spring	Summer	Autumn

Planting can occur at any stage from autumn through to spring, whenever weather conditions permit.

PROTECTION

Once the plants are established and well rooted, there is no need for any protection.

FEEDING

If the plants are growing in a light soil, a mulch will be needed in spring. Bonemeal should also be mixed into the soil at this time of year, if the soil is not chalky.

WATERING

These plants can survive without additional watering. However, if a drought should occur, make sure that they are provided with some moisture.

STAKING AND PRUNING

As soon as any growth is seen in the first spring after planting, cut the stems back to a pair of good buds to encourage strong growth. Deadhead to prevent seed formation and, at the same time, thin out weak and crowded shoots. As the plant grows older, cut back hard one or two of the oldest shoots.

Tropaeolum

Nasturtiums have dramatically changed in appearance over the years. There was a time when the only varieties were the climbing kind, whose brilliant orange and yellow flowers were hidden by their large, round leaves. However, since the breeders have adapted them, nasturtiums have become low-growing, clumpy plants with masses of flowers above the leaves, spotted and blotched in all shades of orange, yellow, cream, red, salmon and mahogany. One strain, 'Alaska', has leaves marbled in cream. All varieties of nasturtiums are easy to grow.

PESTS AND DISEASES

Nasturtiums are easy to grow, although they are prone to **blackfly** in large numbers, and **cabbage white butterfly caterpillars** eat the leaves in some seasons. **Frost** will blacken the stems and leaves in autumn, and seed should not be sown in spring until such risk has passed.

Nasturtiums provide a jungle of colour in poor soil and sunny places. There are now short, bushy strains, such as this 'Tom Thumb' collection (*far right*). The 'Alaska' mixed collection of nasturtiums (*right*) flower well even in a little shade.

The caterpillars of the cabbage white butterly will feed voraciously on the leaves at any time from early to late summer and autumn (*above*). They will even damage the flowers by biting holes in the petals and stamens in the central tube (*right*). Hand-pick as soon as seen.

SOIL

A poor soil is actually preferable to a very fertile one for this plant, as this will encourage greater flowering and less foliage. The ideal soil is a well-drained, light, medium-quality soil.

POSITION

Choose a sunny site for the nasturtiums, although some varieties will flower in shady positions.

PROPAGATION

The only method of propagation for the annual species of nasturtium is by seed, sown in spring.

PLANTING

Winter		Spring	Summer	Autumn

Set the plants out at the end of spring. Leave a space of 6in (15cm) between each of the plants.

PROTECTION

No protection will be necessary, provided that planting is postponed until there is no danger of frost appearing.

FEEDING

These are very hardy plants, which seem to flourish without the aid of any feeding or fertilizers.

WATERING

There are no watering requirements for nasturtiums. Even during dry weather, they are able to thrive.

STAKING AND PRUNING

Supports are not necessary for the low-growing, bushy plants, but the trailing kinds will need to be supplied with some type of trellis work. No pruning is required.

Tulipa

The tulip is a very good spring to early summer-flowering bulb, and it is often neglected, taking second place to narcissi, daffodils and the small spring bulbs. The tulip species flower in early spring — *T. fosteriana* and *T. kaufmanniana* — then single and double garden varieties come in during mid-spring — the double varieties can last in flower for a month. Together with these, come the remainder: the Triumphs; the Darwins, which are the most well-known and popular, flowering in late spring; the lily-flowered variety; the Parrots with fringed petals;and the broken Darwins and Bizarres, carrying the flowering succession into summer.

Tulips can form an attractive part of a spring planting scheme, mixed with grape hyacinths and alyssum spilling over into a paved edging to the lawn *(above)*. The water-lily type of tulip *(upper right)* flowers early in spring, and is an excellent plant for the rock garden as it is only 6in (15cm) tall. The charming flowers come in shades of yellow, white, cream, pink and red, and combinations of these colours. In bad seasons, snow may cover the open blooms and leaves *(lower right)*, but the plants will be unharmed by the cold. However, the weight of the snow, if it covers them, can break off flower heads and stems.

SOIL

Soil requirements are fairly specialized, as these plants need a fertile soil with good drainage to grow well.

POSITION

Sunlight will encourage the most beautiful blooms on these plants. They do not respond well if they are situated in a shady spot.

PROPAGATION

Division of offsets is one method of increase. These should be planted at the beginning of winter, and they will flower in their third or fourth year. Seeds can be sown in cold frames in the second half of autumn, and will flower between four and six years later. Tulip bulbs can be left in their planting position after flowering and, either, dug up every three years, or every year in mid-summer. In both cases the bulbs should then be cleaned, graded and dried before storing and replanting.

PLANTING

Winter	Spring	Summer	Autumn
▓			

Plant the bulbs at the beginning of winter, leaving a distance of 6in (15cm) between each one.

PROTECTION

Tulips are able to survive without any protection so long as they are not in badly drained soil.

FEEDING

After the bulbs have been planted, it is advisable to apply a mulch to encourage healthy growth.

WATERING

Watering is not required, even in very dry periods, as these plants like a good baking from a hot sun.

STAKING AND PRUNING

It is not necessary to stake these plants, but it is better to plant them in a sheltered spot, to ensure that they grow upright. No pruning is needed.

Above and *right* Tulips are usually seen growing formally as bedding plants, and then lifted and stored until planting the following autumn. They may also be planted in small groups among perennial border plants and left there . Tulip colours are clear and brilliant. Some are feathered and streaked with a different colour, which means they are virus-infected, although this does not harm them. Others have fringed or pointed petals, and some are double flowered.

PESTS AND DISEASES

It is possible for many problems to occur, but in practice not many do. **Mice** will eat the bulbs in the ground or in storage, and **squirrels** will dig them up. Planting holly leaves with the bulbs is said to be a preventative. **Slugs** will eat the leaves in spring. **Eelworms** and **greenfly** may also infest the plants.

Tulip fire This is a type of grey mould which is specific to tulips. It is a common problem and very damaging, spreading rapidly when present. Symptoms include brown patches and spots on the leaves, especially along the margins; brown spots on flowers; mouldy buds and stems and badly withered shoots and leaves, occurring soon after they appear. The bulbs often have small, black growths on the outside and act as the spore cases of the disease. Affected plants and bulbs should be destroyed as soon as the disease is seen, to prevent infecting healthy plants. Plant tulips in a new site for three years. Unaffected plants should be sprayed thoroughly with benomyl, and when they are dug up, they should be dipped in a solution of this chemical, with a repeat dip before planting in winter.

Grey bulb rot This is another serious disease, where bulbs do not sprout in spring. These bulbs may have white threads on the outside or in the soil around them, as well as patches of rot starting at the top of the bulb. Roots will not be present. Destroy the bulbs and remove the soil if tulips are to be grown in the same place, or do not plant there for several years.

Shanking Sometimes buds remain small, turn yellow and wither without developing flowers. This is called shanking, and can be due to a fungal disease or roots damaged in the early stages of growth. It is not a serious problem and the bulbs should be left to grow, as they usually recover by the next season.

Viola

The velvety petals of the modern pansy hybrids can provide a continuous array of colour throughout spring and summer. Violets will scent the air in spring and autumn as there is also an autumn-flowering variety and the viola, a smaller version of the pansy, will flower even more profusely from late spring to summer.

One of the worst enemies of the viola tribe, and particularly pansies, is the slug or snail. They can easily eat entire plants, especially in wet springs and autumns, feeding on leaves and petals until they are completely decimated *(below)*.

PESTS AND DISEASES

Greenfly, slugs and **snails** are generally a problem, decimating the leaves of young plants. **Leatherjackets** and **cutworms** attack the roots. **Red spider mites** infest the plants in hot, dry weather, and **rust, foot rot, leaf spot** and **mildew** are also problems. Violets may be infested by **eelworms** and **midges**, whose larvae cause **leaf gall**. Tiny white or orange maggots feed within the young leaves, which become thick and roll inward. Several generations of maggots can occur within one growing season, so the damage can be serious. Affected leaves should be hand-picked as soon as they are seen, and the plants sprayed with dimethoate from late spring every three weeks until the attack subsides.
Stem rot produces decay at the base of the stems and yellowing leaves. This is a soil-borne disease and is worst in warm seasons and climates. If overwintering pansies become covered with leaves in autumn, rake them gently off, otherwise the pansies will be completely eaten away by **slugs** and other predators beneath.

The wild pansy *(V. tricolor)* is also called heart's ease *(right)*. The flower head is only 1in (2.5cm) wide. Its colouring can vary considerably between purple, yellow and white, and shades and combinations of these colours. The flowers appear throughout the summer. The garden pansy has much larger flowers, up to 2in (5cm) wide *(far right)* and sometimes more. *V. tricolor* is a parent of the garden variety.

Violet and viola   Pansy

SOIL

A moist, fertile soil that is well drained is the most   suitable site in which to position these plants.

POSITION

Violets like to be positioned in a little shade and not direct sunlight. Violas,   however, prefer to be situated in the sun.

PROPAGATION

Violets can be increased by their runners. Violas, however, do not have runners and are perennial   plants. They can be increased by seed, or cuttings, taken from their non-flowering shoots.

PLANTING

Winter	Spring	Summer	Autumn

Planting time occurs in spring. Leave a distance of   9in (22cm) between each of the plants.

PROTECTION

Protection is required when the weather is extreme in   any way. This may be wind, snow or rain.

FEEDING

A light mulch is required in spring. This will encourage   vigorous growth and healthy flowering.

WATERING

The plants should be well watered straight after they have been put into the   ground and during dry weather.

It is not necessary to stake these plants, especially the violas, as they tend to have prostrate, trailing stems.   Violets will need to have their runners removed as they appear. Violas do not have runners.

SOIL

A moist and fertile soil, that is also well drained, is most suitable. It is advisable to   add compost to the site, some months before planting.

POSITION

Place these plants in a shady spot, where they will   receive some sunlight for part of the day.

PROPAGATION

Take cuttings 2½in (6cm) long from the basal shoots in summer. Place them in a sandy soil in a cold frame. These cuttings will flower the following spring. Pansies can also be treated as biennials and sown in a nursery bed in summer   They may also be considered as half-hardy annuals and sown in late winter/early spring, as long as they are provided with some heat. These will flower in the summer of the same year.

PLANTING

Winter	Spring	Summer	Autumn

The best times to plant are in early autumn or spring. Make sure the plants are   spaced out at a distance of 6-9in (15-22cm) apart.

PROTECTION

These plants can survive most adverse conditions,   but they need protection against severe cold.

FEEDING

A mulch will be needed in late spring and a liquid feed   should be applied weekly throughout the summer.

WATERING

Watering is not generally required, provided the plants are situated in a soil   that is fairly moist. Extra water should be liberally applied in dry periods.

STAKING AND PRUNING

Pansies are low-growing plants that do not require   any staking or pruning.

Wistaria

The Chinese kidney bean, the alternative common name given to wisteria, climbs to a height of 100ft (30m) in the wild, and can have a trunk 5ft (1.5m) in diameter. It lives to a very great age and was introduced from China early in the nineteenth century. It is outstanding as a decorative climber, with its hanging clusters, 12in (30cm) long, and mauve flowers, in such profusion that they resemble a light purple waterfall in early summer. *W. sinensis* is the most common type, but there is also *W. floribunda*, which has a less vigorous growth to about 30ft (9m) high. It has purplish blue flowers, whose clusters are 3-4ft (90-120cm) long in the variety *macrobotrys*, and it has another variety, *rosea*, with rose-pink flowers.

Good specimens of wisteria will produce flowers in such abundance that a purple waterfall appears to be clothing the wall or fence on which they are growing *(below)*. It is a climbing shrub that needs plenty of room as it naturally climbs to more than 100ft (30m). Careful spur-pruning will keep it within bounds and, at the same time, ensure the maximum amount of flowering.

PESTS AND DISEASES

Problems are few, although flowering may be affected by **birds** pecking off buds and flowers as they open. Lack of sun and nutrients, particularly potassium, or immature plants may be other reasons for poor flowering. Pruning will encourage blooms. Occasionally **leaf spot** appears, but is not serious.

SOIL

A poor soil will not satisfy this plant. It needs a deep, moist and fertile site.

POSITION

Position these climbing plants in the sun. This will encourage vigorous and healthy blooming.

PROPAGATION

The best method of propagation is by layering, which can be performed between spring and summer.

PLANTING

Winter	Spring	Summer	Autumn

Spring is the most suitable planting time. Make sure that plenty of root room is provided.

WATERING

These plants need plenty of water, especially if they are growing against a fence or wall.

FEEDING

Provide a good mulch in the middle of spring to ensure good soil structure and encourage flowering.

PROTECTION

Protection is not required, as the plant is a native of cool, temperate climates where frost may occur.

STAKING AND PRUNING

Supply supports for the branches to twine around, such as a wall, fence with wires, trellis, pergola or tree. Pruning is required, unless the plant is climbing up a tree. Cut the sub-sideshoots back by half their length in mid-summer, with a further cutting in mid-winter, leaving just two or three buds. Cutting the sub-sideshoots is not essential, but it does help restrict growth and encourage flowering. When the plant is young, build a framework of sideshoots to fit into the space available, then cut these and the leader shoot to the length required.

Zinnia

Zinnia flower colours look as though they have come straight out of a child's paint-box, slightly unreal and artificial, but bright and glowing, unlike any other summer bedding plants. From Mexico, they are least likely to have problems if grown in a hot, dry environment, when they will last in flower for a long time. The garden hybrids of *Z. elegans* come in such rich colours as gold, crimson, orange, purple, salmon and rose-pink; the cultivar 'Envy' is chartreuse-green. They reach a height of 1-2½ft (30-75cm) and flower throughout the summer.

As natives of Mexico, zinnias revel in hot sunshine. Their gaily coloured flowers start to appear in the middle of summer and continue for many weeks. Heavy rain will damage the large flower heads, and, generally, damp conditions will affect growth. The Ruffles mixture *(above)* grows to about 2ft (60cm) tall, and is good for floral arrangements as well as providing stunning garden decoration.

PESTS AND DISEASES

Zinnias can be affected by a variety of problems which may damage other bedding and half-hardy annuals. Soil-inhabiting **caterpillars** and **grubs** will feed on roots of young and newly planted zinnias. **Slugs** and **snails** also feed on the leaves of young plants. **Greenfly, capsids, leafhoppers, thrips, mildew, grey mould, root** and **stem rots** are other possible problems.

SOIL

These plants are not difficult to grow and will survive in most reasonably fertile soils.

POSITION

Sunlight will encourage these plants to flower brightly. Shade will make the blooms less vibrant.

PROPAGATION

Propagation is best carried out by seed. Sow in a little warmth under glass in mid-spring, pricking the seedlings out as they grow and hardening them off ready for planting outside. Alternatively, in late spring, the seeds can be sown outdoors straight away into a well-prepared seed bed. Leave a gap of 8-12in (20-30cm) between each site, making sure several seeds are put into each of the sites. These should then be thinned out when the seedlings appear, so that only one plant remains in each place.

PLANTING

Winter	Spring	Summer	Autumn

Plant in early summer as the weather begins to get warmer. Space the plants 8-12in (20-30cm) apart.

PROTECTION

These plants can survive most bad weather, but need protection from severe frosts when first planted.

FEEDING

Once the plants have been bedded, mulch with garden compost or manure. When flowering starts, apply a liquid feed once a week.

WATERING

These plants are not happy in dry conditions, so water should be supplied copiously in drought.

STAKING AND PRUNING

Zinnias are relatively easy plants to grow, as they do not require any pruning or staking.

Glossary

Aeration The process of airing the soil — by spiking a lawn with a fork, for example.

Algae Primitive organisms, found growing in damp places as green powder or strands.

Alkaline A soil, or a substance containing chalk such as lime; some plants will not grow in alkaline soils.

Annual A plant whose life cycle is completed in a year or less, usually from spring to autumn, but also from autumn to late summer.

Bedding A system of planting that uses tender herbaceous plants, grown with protection while young and then planted out in summer.

Biennial A plant that takes two growing seasons to complete its life cycle, from germination to death after flowering.

Botrytis A common fungal disease also called grey mould; its scientific name is *Botrytis cinerea*.

Bud An embryonic shoot or flower, often with protective outer scales; potential fruit or flower-buds are round and fat; vegetative buds are long, thin and pointed.

Bulb A plant organ in which the leaf bases have been modified and swollen with food; it is, in effect, a bud.

Calcifuge A plant that will not grow in soil containing any form of chalk, rhododendron, for example.

Callus The tissue formed by a plant at a wound, which covers and protects it; in trees it is overlaid with bark.

Chlorophyll The green colouring matter found in the leaves and other parts of plants; iron is an integral part of it.

Chlorosis Yellowing of leaves. If lime-induced, this discolouration appears in the younger leaves first, at the shoot tips, and means that the iron needed to produce chlorophyll is not being absorbed by the plant roots because the plant is a lime-hater.

Compost heap A mixture of vegetative materials formed into a pile and left to rot into a dark-coloured, moist, crumbly substance.

Corm An underground plant organ, in which the modified and compressed stem becomes thickened and acts as a food store.

Cutting A portion of a plant, usually the stem, which is induced to form roots and, hence, a new plant.

Cutting, hardwood or ripe A length of stem about 10in (25cm) long, cut from the end of a current season's shoot in autumn, when it is brown or mature for most of its length.

Cutting, root A piece of root, 2-4in (5-10cm) long, used to increase herbaceous perennials. These cuttings are taken in winter.

Cutting, semi-hardwood or half-ripe The end 3-6in (7-15cm) of a young shoot, cut off when it is turning brown at its base, but is still green at the tip; it is taken from mid- to late summer.

Cutting, soft or tip The tip or soft, green end of a new shoot which is cut off, 3-4in (7-10cm) long, from spring to mid-summer.

Deadheading The removal of flower heads immediately after they have died, to prevent the plant wasting its energy on seed formation.

Deciduous A shrub or tree that loses its leaves in autumn.

Dormant The state in which a plant is not actively growing, although it is still alive. Dormancy usually occurs in winter, as a way of surviving cold or drought.

Evergreen A shrub or tree that retains its leaves all year, although not every leaf is everlasting — some leaves are shed all year.

Fallow Ground which has been dug and is left unplanted, partly to revitalize it, and partly to allow weed seeds to germinate so that the seedlings can be destroyed before planting or sowing cultivated plants.

Fertilizer A plant food in concentrated form, either powder or granular, containing one or more mineral nutrients such as calcium or iron.

Fimbriate Fringed, used to describe flower-petal margins.

Foliar Leafy, used to describe sprays containing nutrients, which are applied to leaves as a method of 'instant' feeding.

Frame A 'box' placed on the ground with sides made of brick or wood, and the lid of glass with a wooden framework. A frame is used for protecting tender plants in cold weather, bringing on rooted cuttings and seedlings, and for growing tropical plants, especially fruit, in temperate climates.

Fungus An organism separate from a plant or animal, which does not contain chlorophyll and needs organic matter to supply its food; yeast is a fungus.

Fungicide A substance that is used to control or eradicate fungal diseases infecting plants, usually a chemical.

Humus A brown-black substance, which can absorb a lot of moisture; it is formed from the rotting remains of organic matter, whether animal or vegetable; its presence is essential for the maintenance of a good soil structure.

Insecticide A substance used for killing insects, usually a chemical.

Layer A method of plant increase in which a slanting cut is made partially through a low-growing, one-year-old stem on the underside, opposite a leaf joint. The stem is pinned down onto the soil and the cut is covered with more soil. This is performed in spring or summer, when roots will form at the injury.

Lichen A plant form consisting of an alga and a fungus intermingled, the alga manufacturing food of use to both.

Light The 'lid' of a frame, consisting of panes of glass mounted in a framework; sometimes there is only a single large sheet of glass about 5x1ft (150x30cm) — this is called a Dutch light.

Lime A word describing several forms of calcium, such as calcium carbonate (chalk), but strictly calcium oxide (quicklime). It is used to decrease the acidity of the soil.

Manure Animal excreta mixed with bed-litter such as straw, sawdust, or wood shavings.

Mulch A layer of material, usually organic matter such as rotted manure or garden compost, placed on the soil surface around plants.

Offset A young plant produced from, and next to, a parent plant; bulbs are typical examples.

Perennial, herbaceous A plant with soft tissues, not bark or woody stems. It lives from year to year, and often dies down in autumn to ground level, although this does not apply to all species. The term generally refers to the flowering plants used in beds and borders.

Pesticide A substance used for controlling or eradicating organisms that prey upon plants, such as insects, fungal diseases, bacteria, snails and slugs, or small mammals.

pH A scale from 1.0-14.0 for measuring the acidity or alkalinity of the soil. Neutral is 7.0; anything below this point is acid and above is alkaline. Each figure needs to be multiplied by 10 to give the actual increase of acid or alkaline content in the soil.

Photosynthesis The process in plants whereby the green parts manufacture oxygen and carbohydrates in the presence of sunlight, from the water and carbon dioxide of the atmosphere.

Pruning The removal of shoots or branches from a plant in order to maintain its healthy growth, encourage flowering/fruiting, and keep its size under control without stunting it.

Rhizome A stem which grows underground and extends horizontally, sending up shoots. It is often fleshy and serves as a storage organ; pieces that break off will root and produce new plants.

Sequestrene A metal compound of such a type that the metal behaves in a different way to normal, and becomes available in chalky soils to plant roots, where it would otherwise be 'locked up .

Shrub A plant with many woody stems radiating from one point on the plant at soil level.

Sucker A shoot produced from the rootstock of a plant, as in roses; many suckers will take over the top part of the plant, but can be useful and form a method of increase, as in the stag's-horn sumach.

Topdressing An application of material to the soil or compost surface close to plants; it may be fertilizer or the replacement of the top few inches of compost in a container.

Tuber A storage organ, either stem or root, swollen with plant food and carrying the plant through its dormant period.

Index

Acknowledgements

The pictures on these pages were reproduced by courtesy of the following:
8, 9(l) The Harry Smith Horticultural Photographic Collection; (a,r) A-Z Collection; **10** (bl) Smith Collection, (tl) Ann Bonar, (r) A-Z Collection, (b) Richard Stone; **11, 12** (a) Smith Collection, **11** (b), **13** Spectrum Colour Library; **14** A-Z Collection; **20, 22-23** Spectrum Colour Library; **25** (l) Alex Arthur, (r) Spectrum Colour Library; **27** Smith Collection; **32** (a) Spectrum Colour Library; **34** (b) Edward Kinsey; **36** (tl) Alastair Campbell; **39** A-Z Collection; **41** (br) Edward Kinsey; **42** (r) Smith Collection, (l) Birmid Qualcast Ltd; **46** Spectrum Colour Library; **47** Smith Collection; **49** (t) Murphy Chemical Ltd; **50** (t) Alastair Campbell; **52** (r,c), **54** (b), **55** (c,b), **58** (l), **59** (l), **60, 65** (l) Murphy Chemical Ltd; **66-67** A-Z Collection; **68, 69** (t) Alastair Campbell; **70, 71** (t,l) Spectrum Colour Library; **73** (l) A-Z Collection, (r,b) Smith Collection; **74, 80** (t,cr), **81** (t) Ann Bonar; **84** (t) A-Z Collection, (b) Smith Collection; **85** Spectrum Colour Library; **88** Smith Collection; **92** (a) Ann Bonar; **97** (t) Royston Henry Osborne; **98** (l,t), **100** (a) Smith Collection; **102** (l,a,t), **103** (t) Ann Bonar; **106** Spectrum Colour Library; **112** Smith Collection; **119** (b) Spectrum Colour Library; **122** (a) Smith Collection; **125** Spectrum Colour Library; **132** Smith Collection; **140** (l) Edward Kinsey; **145, 153** Smith Collection; **155** (b) Ann Bonar; **159** Suttons Seeds Ltd, Torquay; **162** (ac,r) Royston Henry Osborne; **164** (l) Smith Collection; **176** (al) Alastair Campbell; **176** (ar), **177** Suttons Seeds Ltd, Torquay; **178** (t,c) Ann Bonar; (b) Alastair Campbell; **179** (t) Royston Henry Osborne; **182** Spectrum Colour Library; **183** Suttons Seeds Ltd, Torquay.

All other photographs property of Quill Publishing Limited

Key: (a) above; (b) below; (l) left; (r) right; (t) top; (c) centre

While every effort has been made to acknowledge all copyright holders, we apologize if any omissions have been made.